Random Variables

LORD ROTHSCHILD

COLLINS
8 Grafton Street, London W1
1984

William Collins Sons & Co Ltd
London · Glasgow · Sydney · Auckland
Toronto · Johannesburg

BRITISH LIBRARY CATALOGUING IN PUBLICATION DATA

Rothschild, Nathaniel Mayer Victor Rothschild, *Lord*
Random variables.
I. Title
082   PR6068.o/

ISBN 0 00 217334 4

First published 1984
© Lord Rothschild, 1984

Photoset in Baskerville
Made and printed in Great Britain by
T. J. Press (Padstow) Ltd

TO JOHN, PETER, THOMAS
AND SO FORTH

CONTENTS

Preface

1. First Words   *page* 13
2. The Professor   14
3. Duff Cooper in Paris, 1944   16
4. Bertrand Russell, 1955   18
5. The Agricultural Research Council, 1951   20
6. *Directions to Servants*   21
7. *Caveat Emptor*   22
8. A Good Investment?   53
9. An Unexpected Gift from an Unexpected Quarter   58
10. Fish Junior   60
11. Are I.Q. Tests Useless?   63
12. Standard of Living, 1980   64
13. Eminent Scientists   66
14. London Airport, 1980   67
15. A Holiday after Hard Work, with Kissinger and Charlie Schultz thrown in, 1974   69
16. Preparations for an Operation, 1980   71
17. In and Out of the Think Tank   73
18. One that Got Away   80
19. Death of the Tank   81
20. Royal Commissions   85
21. Annual Dinner of H.M. Customs and Excise, 10th May 1978   92
22. A Child's Guide to Biotechnology   97
23. Gutle, 1753–1849   101
24. The Shadow of a Great Man   105
25. 'You have it, Madam'   154
26. The Father of the Yishuv   199
27. The File is never Closed   203
28. Commonplace   206

7

Contents

Annex 1 – Bills of Exchange   215

Annex 2 – 3 per cent Consols 1817   216

Annex 3 – *The Romance of the Rothschilds*, by
    Ignatius Balla   217

Annex 4 – 3 per cent Consols 1815   218

Annex 5 – Calendar of Events, 1875   219

Annex 6 – Calendar of Events, 1875, through
    French eyes   220

Annex 7 – A Hydrodynamic Model of Gambling in
    Great Britain   221

Notes and References   222

Index   229

ILLUSTRATIONS

Morpho cypris   *Frontispiece*

Ornithoptera paradisea and gynandromorph
  orange tip   *opposite page 13*

Page from the sale catalogue of the Jerome Kern
  Library   *page 51*

Fuse of an underwater sabotage bomb   *page 59*

Cell for examining bracken spermatozoa in a
  known gas mixture, under the microscope   *page 61*

Hydrodynamic model of gambling in
  Great Britain, 1976   *opposite page 85*

Gutle Rothschild, 1753–1849   *opposite page 101*

The Shadow of a Great Man   *page 104*

Anti-semitic pamphlet, 1846   *page 129*

Baron Lionel de Rothschild, 1808–1879   *opposite page 154*

Baron Edmond de Rothschild, 1845–1934   *opposite page 199*

PREFACE

AFTER *Meditations of a Broomstick*[1] was published in 1977, a number of my friends said that the first chapter, which was wholly autobiographical, was good; but what a pity the autobiography stopped there. As a matter of fact, much more than the first chapter was autobiographical, but in the form of lectures and articles on subjects in which I was interested.

The same applies to this volume; but in addition, and partially to counter the comments mentioned above, I have included some accounts of a few episodes in my life. The fact that some of them are very short is not, I believe, a disadvantage. So here and there you will find glimpses of my relationships with such people as Bertrand Russell, Duff Cooper and a few others.

Again, however, there are several reprints of lectures and articles that should shed some light on their author's life, one of the purposes, I imagine, of an autobiography.

The reader will, I believe, understand why I have called this book *Random Variables*. Its chapters are variable in length, subject-matter and, no doubt, quality. It has no continuity – there is no thread running through it – which explains the adjective 'random'. There is, however, a remote chance that a mathematician might be taken in by the title. The phrase *random variable* refers to an abstract concept in mathematics, to do with the uncertain outcomes of actual or conceptual experiments – not a subject for discussion here, even if the common reader were interested.

This book, unlike that of my cousin Baron Guy de Rothschild, contains little or nothing about the *signes extérieures de la richesse*; nor anything about the wild animals, from fleas to gorillas, which adorn so many pages of my sister Miriam's recent book*.

Many people have helped me, particularly with the accounts of N. M. Rothschild and his son Lionel; they have been acknowledged elsewhere. Here, therefore, I only record my special thanks to Dick David, Richard Ollard and Kenneth Rose who read some

* See next page.

or all of my typescript and who made invaluable suggestions for improvement, almost all of which have been adopted.

Disraeli's letters to Queen Victoria of 24 November 1875 and to the Prince of Wales of 11 December 1875 are reproduced by gracious permission of Her Majesty the Queen.

I am also indebted to Her Majesty's Stationery Office for permission to reproduce the Hydrodynamic Model of Gambling in Great Britain, 1976, which was the frontispiece of the final Report of the Royal Commission on Gambling, 1978.

---

* Rothschild, Baron Guy de, 1983, *Contre bonne fortune*. Pierre Belfond, Paris.
——, Miriam, 1983, *Dear Lord Rothschild*. Hutchinson & Co., London; Balaban Publishers, Philadelphia.

FIGURE 2
Ornithoptera paradisea and gynandromorph orange tip

I

FIRST WORDS

I HAVE EXPLAINED in another place[1] that I was born into a family in which lepidopterology was a ruling passion and that, in consequence, one of the first words I learned, when about four I suppose, was *Morpho*, soon followed by gynandromorph and *Ornithoptera*. How many of the few who read these words will know what *Morpho* is? Fewer, I fancy, than the number who have seen and admired one, a reproduction of which is the frontispiece of this book.

THE PROFESSOR

PROFESSOR STANLEY GARDINER, FRS, was Professor of Zoology when I became an undergraduate at Cambridge. The first remark he made to me was: 'Rothschild, you will know all the first-year course already, so if you attend the lectures, you can keep your hands in your pockets.' This was quite enough to keep me away from the lecture theatre. I did attend once or twice and on one occasion an undergraduate (not me) let out a dove from a paper bag. It flew across the lecture theatre but Professor Gardiner paid no attention.

About a year later, Professor Gardiner accosted me in a passage in the Department of Zoology and said, 'Rothschild, I want to have a word with you,' so I went to his room where he said, 'How good is your German?' I replied, 'I did German at school, Professor, but not for long. I think I know enough to read a German scientific paper but I would need a dictionary by my side.' Professor Gardiner terminated the meeting by saying, 'I think you ought to improve your German, but don't do so by taking a German mistress.' I took the second part of his advice, more by accident than design.

Some years later, when I was researching in the Department of Zoology, Professor Gardiner put his head, and only his head, round the door of my room and said, with a look of great embarrassment, 'Dr Gray (later Professor Sir James Gray) says your research is rather good.' He precipitately withdrew his head. I was tremendously cheered up by Professor Gardiner's embarrassed praise and have always remembered since then that people appreciate to an unexpected and, perhaps, unwarranted extent a few words of praise.

The next and last time I had any contact with Professor Gardiner was of a somewhat different nature. I worked in the basement of the Department of Zoology and, during a certain phase of my work, I had to work late at night. One morning I got a message that the Professor wished me to see Inspector Davis of the Cambridge Police. Naturally I agreed. Inspector Davis wanted to know what time I had left the laboratory the evening before and how long it took me to get from the laboratory to my digs in Jesus Lane. I said I had left at about 10.00 p.m. that night and arrived at my digs at about 10.20 p.m. 'Curious,' the Inspector said, 'your landlady said you arrived back just before 11 p.m.; what were you doing in between?' I said I could not remember – perhaps I had got the times wrong but I did know I went straight back to my digs on leaving the Department. The Inspector became a good deal more aggressive and at last I asked him why I was being questioned in that way. He replied that some time between 8 and 10 on the evening before, someone had tried to break into the Department's safe, which was next door to my room, with a hammer and an oxyacetylene blow lamp. 'Clearly,' the Inspector said, 'he was after the morphia. You told me earlier you had heard nothing while you were in your room. Are you seriously suggesting that you would not have heard an intruder hammering away at a safe when there was just a thin partition between you and the intruder?' The penny having then dropped, I decided to make an appointment with the Professor to whom I said 'Professor, would you care to look carefully at the pupils of my eyes?' which he seemed unusually reluctant to do, so I went on, 'I wanted you to satisfy yourself that I am not a drug fiend.' The Professor said he agreed with me. In retrospect, I do not know whether the eyes of drug fiends are as revelatory as all that. From then on the Inspector became more pleasant and in fact, we became good friends. Much later, he told me they thought they knew who had been after the morphia but they were never able to pin it on him.

3

DUFF COOPER IN PARIS, 1944

AFTER THE ALLIED INVASION of Normandy, towards the end of World War II and the liberation of Paris, I was, by some fluke, the senior British officer in Paris for a short time after our Ambassador, Duff Cooper, took up his post. One day I received a message that the Préfet wished to see me. (For those who do not know, the Préfet of Paris was a VVIP.) I went to see him and found a tall man with a neat black beard and a swirling cloak. I asked him what the purpose of his request to see me was, and said I was at his disposal. He replied:

> Mon Colonel, je voudrais vous parler d'un sujet assez délicat. Votre Ambassadeur vit ouvertement avec Madame Louise de Vilmorin. Vous savez peut-être que Madame de Vilmorin a collaboré d'une façon notoire avec les Allemands. (It is by no means certain that this allegation was true.) Elle avait un sauf-conduit qui lui permettait de voyager librement en Allemagne. Cette situation est inacceptable; et je suis obligé de vous demander d'en faire part à votre Ambassadeur.

I put on my army hat, saluted smartly and retired.

What was I to do? I felt I had no alternative but to tell Duff Cooper, a close personal friend, about the interview. His reaction was terrifying. His face went dark red, a large vein started to swell on his forehead and he began to abuse me in the most extreme language. He terminated the interview by saying he never wished to see me again. I therefore stopped going to the Embassy at 6 o'clock in the evening to play backgammon, which we regularly did three or four times a week, the score being kept on a lampshade. This lacuna in my life persisted for exactly one week, after which I received a message from Duff Cooper asking why I had stopped coming to play backgammon. I therefore went to the

Embassy at 6 o'clock the next day, and we played our backgammon and had our drink as if nothing had happened. The subject was never mentioned again, Duff Cooper's complexion returned to normal and he continued his relationship with Lulu as if the Préfet did not exist.

4

BERTRAND RUSSELL, 1955

ON THE 28TH OF JANUARY 1955 I wrote the following letter to
Bertrand Russell:

Dear Russell,
I would like to present the manuscript of your recent
broadcast dealing with the Hydrogen Bomb to Trinity
[Trinity College, Cambridge]. Can you suggest any way
in which I might acquire it?

Yours sincerely,

Rothschild

He replied on the 1st February 1955:

Dear Rothschild,
Thank you for your letter of January 28. I should be
very glad to give you the manuscript of my broadcast for
you to present to Trinity if you have any reason to think
that Trinity would like to have it. Have you already ascer-
tained their view about it or do you know what their view
is likely to be?
The broadcast has already been reprinted as a leaflet.
I do not know whether you have any suggestions how to
forward its object. If you have, I should be very glad to
know of them.

Yours sincerely,

Russell

On 21 February 1955, after making the enquiries Bertrand
Russell apparently wanted and having got, needless to say, the
assurances which he required, I again wrote to him:

Dear Russell,
Thank you very much indeed for the manuscript. I am
having a little cloth case made for it and will then hand it

over to Trinity who, unknown to you, already possess one of your manuscripts which I presented to them some years ago. I should very much like to come and have a talk to you; apart from introducing Adrian* into the House of Lords on March 2nd, I shall not be in London for some while, as I am going to a Marine Biological Station to do some work on sea urchin eggs.

Would you be so kind as to let me know on the attached postcard whether you like claret?

Yours

Rothschild

and in response got the following postcard:

'Yes   N̸o

but it disagrees with me and I have had to give it up.'

As a result of this postcard and a further letter from Russell in which he said, 'Mercifully I can still drink whisky', I went round at once to Matthews in Trinity Street – of course it no longer exists – and bought twelve bottles of whisky which I sent to one of the few great men I have known.

---

* Introducing Lord Adrian to the House of Lords was one of the most distinguished moments in my life. We rehearsed (with Lord Moran) for at least an hour beforehand: so that when the time came to perform, we were as good as three chorus girls in the Radio City Rockettes.

5

THE AGRICULTURAL
RESEARCH COUNCIL, 1951

As ALDOUS HUXLEY SAID in another context, the work of the Agricultural Research Council was routine punctuated by orgies – but perhaps everything is routine, including orgies. The orgies were few and far between, but I recall one. There came a moment when the Secretary of the Agricultural Research Council, tactful, genial and efficient Sir William Slater, suddenly became very irritable and covered in eczema. What was to be done? The doctors, including the then Secretary of the Medical Research Council, Sir Harold Himsworth, seemed unable to suggest anything, let alone do it. The Council was in despair, at its wits' end; and, at its annual get-together at Edinburgh, decided to have a private meeting without the Secretary being present. (Neither Sir William Slater nor those civil servants who heard about it forgave me for agreeing to hold this meeting, though it was impossible to avoid.) We discussed the eczema and ill-humour at the private meeting, during the course of which an extraordinary proposal was put forward: that the Secretary should retire because of ill health and that I should combine his job with that of Chairman. I pointed out that this would be impossible, for a number of reasons; and that I had an alternative suggestion. There were a number of agricultural research centres in Canada from which, doubtless, we had much to learn. In addition, Sir William's sister lived in Canada. Might it not be a good thing for him to visit Canadian agricultural research centres and in due course report his findings to the Council? The proposal was accepted, Sir William went, stayed with his sister and visited the agricultural research centres. He returned in excellent humour and without the eczema.

6

DIRECTIONS TO SERVANTS

IN 1946 I ACQUIRED at Sotheby's 28 pages of the original manuscript of Swift's *Directions to Servants* which was published posthumously in London and Dublin in 1745. This manuscript was found among the papers of the 1st Earl of Normanton who became Archbishop of Dublin and Primate of Ireland. (The paper on which Swift wrote his *Directions to Servants* is the same as that used in his correspondence with Charles Ford between 18 June 1724 and 14 August 1725.)

G. M. Trevelyan, the Master of Trinity College, Cambridge, was, as every historian knows, specially interested in England in the eighteenth century and I therefore thought it might interest him to see the original manuscript of *Directions to Servants*. He and one of his oldest friends, my father-in-law, the philosopher and educationalist Robin Mayor, looked at the manuscript together at our house in Cambridge. Trevelyan was deeply moved by it. His hand shook so violently with emotion as he turned the pages over that I became greatly frightened that he might tear a page. In addition, he and Robin Mayor read out parts of the *Directions* to each other, roaring with laughter and slapping each other on the thigh when they came to parts which particularly amused them. One of these was:

> Never wear Socks when you wait at meals, on the Account
> of your own Health, as well as of them who sit at Table;
> because as most Ladies like the Smell of young men's Toes
> so it is a Soverign Remedy against the Vapours.

Trevelyan's emotion and pleasure were one of the factors which prompted me to give my collection of eighteenth-century first editions and Swift manuscripts to Trinity College, Cambridge, where they now occupy one bay in the Wren Library.

7

CAVEAT EMPTOR

BOOK COLLECTORS are much concerned with the condition of the books in their collections, inordinately concerned, some might say. Is it the first or the second issue of the first edition? Original wrappers? Original boards? Are the leaves uncut, that is untrimmed? Or even unopened? Portrait in the first state? Contemporary binding? Re-bound a hundred years later? These are a few of the questions which cause book collectors excitement or anguish and whose answers determine the value and price of a book. There is, for example, an enormous difference between the value of the first issue of the first edition of *Gulliver's Travels*, uncut in the original boards, and the first issue bound in contemporary calf, with the leaves trimmed so that their edges are not serrated but smooth and level.

Some of these factors were responsible for my excitement when the American bookseller Gabriel Wells offered me the famous Jerome Kern copy of *Tom Jones*, sold in the Kern sale (p. 51) in 1929 to the well-known American bookseller Dr A. S. W. Rosenbach for $29,000 or about £6,000. Dr Rosenbach bought the *Tom Jones* at the Kern sale 'for stock', but shortly afterwards sold it to the American steel magnate Owen D. Young. For reasons which are not relevant to this story, Gabriel Wells persuaded Owen D. Young to let him try to sell some of the books, including the *Tom Jones*, and manuscripts from his collection. Wells offered me the *Tom Jones plus* part of the original manuscript of Pope's *Essay on Man*, also in the Kern sale, and refused to sell me the former without the latter, which I did not want. Eventually, after much bargaining, I bought both items, for a great deal less than they fetched at the Kern sale, almost, one might say, at a knock-down price.

Early in 1940, John Hayward, the author and bibliographer – a close friend of mine – examined what by then was my copy of the Jerome Kern *Tom Jones* and concluded that it was a fake, a made-up copy. That is to say that up to a particular but at that time unknown date, this copy of *Tom Jones* was incomplete, but had then had other copies of the missing leaves, taken from another (presumably incomplete) copy, inserted. Some dozen pages were involved. But the inserted leaves were not all that they should have been in that at least some of them were taken from a later edition or editions. Hence John Hayward's discovery.

I asked Gabriel Wells to take back the *Tom Jones* and the Pope manuscript, repaying me what I had paid him for them. He refused and I therefore decided to sue him. This is what I had to say, in 1951, about this episode; later I shall fill in the detail by reproducing the transcript of my examination and cross-examination in court in 1942, a time when it was difficult to concentrate on book collecting – World War II was in full swing.

> A number of book-collecting friends have suggested that the details of this lawsuit would interest book collectors (even, perhaps, booksellers) and should be published. The same friends were really responsible for the lawsuit itself. They told me that few book collectors would dare to bring a lawsuit against a bookseller, however good the grounds; that I should be doing a service to bibliophiles if I were to do so; that I was one of the few collectors who could afford such an action; and that they were sure I would never take their advice. I did, and the reader will be able to judge whether their advice was good or bad, though he will not be able to imagine my feelings in the witness box, nor when I found that my friend Dr A. S. W. Rosenbach was to become involved in the action.
>
> I learnt two things from this case, which took place at a time when it was difficult to concentrate on book collecting and its hazards. First, that if you are a collector, and people like John Hayward or John Carter are your friends, you are bound to have some unpleasant surprises when they have "had a look" at your library. Secondly, that the law is very complicated and, if you try and understand it, you will never buy a barrel of glue, a stallion or a valuable old book again.
>
> The case was settled out of court, on terms which, from my point of view, were entirely satisfactory.

The reader may ask whether any efforts have been made to establish the antecedents of the Kern *Tom Jones*. The information in the following table about other incomplete uncut copies which have passed through the sale rooms may therefore be of interest; but for a number of reasons it is clear that the facts given below cannot shed any light on the previous history of the Kern copy.

TABLE I

	Copy 1	*Copy 2*	*Copy 3*
	Purchased by J. Kern from C. Sessler. Purchased by C. Sessler from F. T. Sabin in 1924	Purchased by W. T. Spencer at Hodgson's, 24. 3. 1927 (Lot 90)	Purchased by F. T. Sabin at Sotheby's, 14. 11. 22 (Lot 385)
Binding	Original boards	Original boards, stripped of grey paper, except Vol. V	Original sheep
Leaves	Uncut	Uncut	Uncut
Vol. I	Sig. K trimmed	Perfect	F4 missing
Vol. II	B8, B9, D3, D4, D5, D6 and D7 inserted from later edition	Perfect	B8, B9, D3, D4, D5, D6 and D7 missing
Vol. III	F10, H4 and H5 inserted from later edition	Title-page and 56 leaves missing	D3 and P9 missing
Vol. IV	—	Title-page missing	O4 missing
Vol. V	—	Missing	—
Vol. VI	L6 and L7 inserted from later edition	Perfect	L6 and L7 missing

What really happened and when? Who did it and how? In 1951, on the advice of my lawyers, I said, 'it is clear that the facts given in Table 1 cannot shed any light on the previous history of the Kern copy.' I did not believe that sentence to be true in 1951. *But*, in 1983, I know it was true, for reasons explained in the *Epilogue* to this chapter, whose contents are amazing, incredible, fantastic – no adjectives are adequate to describe what happened, in 1929 (when the deed was done) and a little later, actually in 1982 (when I discovered when and how it *was* done).

But, first, the table needs some explanation, which is given below in the form of notes, the first being for the non-bibliographer:

(1) The leaves or pages of the first edition of *Tom Jones* were printed twelve at a time on one large sheet of paper which was then folded in such a way that each of the twelve pages were the right way up for reading in book form. This implies, of course, that the twelve pages were not all printed with the same orientation on the large single sheet of paper. Pages on the sheet were lettered and numbered, for example A1, A2, A3, . . ., A12. These were the 'signatures', so that the phrase 'Sig. K' in *Vol I* of *Copy 1* in the table refers to the twelve pages K1, K2, . . . , K12.

(2) The question at issue is whether there are, in *Copies* 1, 2 and 3, leaves or pages which could have been inserted, where necessary, into the Kern *Tom Jones*. The leaves which someone inserted into the Kern copy were: Vol. I, Signature K, which could have come from *Copy 1*; Vol. II, B8 and 9, which could have come from *Copy 1*; Vol. III, F10, H4 and H5, which could have come from *Copy 1*; Vol. IV, B1 (suspect), available from *Copies* 1, 2 or 3; Vol. V, perfect; Vol. VI, Signature F, available from *Copies* 1, 2 and 3; L6 and 7 available from *Copies* 1 and 2 but possibly taken from *Copy* 3. From what is said above it could be concluded that the Kern copy of *Tom Jones* might have been derived from two or even three incomplete copies and the dates at the top of the table are not incompatible with this hypothesis: but it must be rejected, for reasons which constitute the *Epilogue* to this chapter.

This is what happened in court.

Examination and Cross-Examination
of the Plaintiff

Direct examination by MR GERALD GARDINER (later Lord
Chancellor), *appearing for the Plaintiff*

Q   Are your full names Nathaniel Mayer Victor Rothschild?

A   Yes.

Q   Have you for some years been in the habit of purchasing rare
books and Swift manuscripts?

A   Yes.

Q   And have you accumulated a considerable collection?

A   Yes.

Q   In the course of collecting those books and manuscripts, have
you come in contact with a number of dealers in the rare book
and manuscript business in London?

A   Yes.

Q   And also in New York?

A   A few in New York.

Q   Among them has there been the defendant Mr Gabriel Wells?

A   Yes.

Q   Is he an outstanding dealer and expert in books?

A   Yes.

Q   Is he well known to all important book collectors?

A   Yes.

Q   In June of 1937 did you go to the bookshop of William H.
Robinson, Ltd, in Pall Mall?

A   Yes.

Q   Is Mr Robinson of that Company a well-known bookseller
and dealer in rare books?

A   Yes.

Q   In consequence of what he told you, did you go shortly afterwards to Mr Wells' flat?

A   Yes.

Q   Is that next door to Mr Robinson's shop?

A   Very close to it. I think it is next door.

Q Would you tell us what happened when you got there?

A Previously I had seen a parcel of books in Mr Robinson's shop in Pall Mall, and Mr Robinson had said –

Q You cannot tell us what Mr Robinson said, unless my friend raises no objection.

> BY MR HOLROYD PEARCE (later Lord Pearce), *appearing for the Defendants*: I object.

Q (Mr Gerald Gardiner): You must only tell us what happened between you and Mr Wells when you went to his flat.

A Mr Wells said that he had certain books to offer me for sale. He showed me a copy of *Tom Jones* which he said it was not necessary for him to describe in great detail as it would already be well known to me as being the copy which had been put up for sale in the book collection of Jerome Kern. Mr Wells was aware that I was familiar with the sale catalogue.

> BY MR HOLROYD PEARCE: I object to that. I do not know how he can say Mr Wells was aware, unless he said anything.

Q (Mr Gerald Gardiner): Had you previously discussed that catalogue with Mr Wells?

A Yes.

Q Had you at that discussion a copy of the catalogue?

A At that time, do you mean?

Q At the time when you discussed the catalogue with him?

A Yes.

Q Is *that* the one which you had with you when you discussed it with him? (*Sale Catalogue handed to the witness.*)

A This is the copy of the sale catalogue which I discussed with Mr Wells on a previous occasion, though I did not have it with me during the conversation which I am describing.

> (*The Sale Catalogue was marked 'Exhibit 1'*)

Q Are some of the items in that catalogue marked with the letter 'G'?

A Yes.

Q In whose handwriting is the letter 'G'?

A Mr Gabriel Wells' handwriting.

Q In what circumstances did he mark those?

A On a previous occasion I met Mr Wells in Mr Robinson's shop. I discussed the Jerome Kern sale with him, and during the course of the discussion he made certain notes in my copy of the sale catalogue, and he indicated certain other matters to me about the items in that catalogue.

Q What did he say?

A He said that he had been the under-bidder for certain items, had bought certain of the items, and suggested that some of the items in the sale catalogue were fakes or improperly catalogued.

Q Did you yourself then mark in the catalogue the ones which he told you were fakes or improperly described in the catalogue?

A Yes, at the time.

Q Was that in front of him?

A Yes.

Q Did he mark the item of *Tom Jones* in the catalogue as being one of those which he thought might be faked or improperly described?

A No.

Q Did he suggest to you when he was discussing the items –

> BY MR HOLROYD PEARCE: I think, Mr Gardiner, at this stage you had better not lead the witness.
>
> BY MR GERALD GARDINER: I was not proposing to.
>
> BY MR HOLROYD PEARCE: That sentence seemed to me a leading question.
>
> BY MR GERALD GARDINER: I do not think so. If it is, your objection will be noted.

Q Did he suggest to you when he was discussing the items that he thought might be faked or improperly described, that the description in the catalogue of the *Tom Jones* was an improper description?

A No.

Q Or that it was in any way a fake?

A No.

Q Now if I may come back to the discussion at the flat, you were saying that he said to you that he need not describe in great detail the *Tom Jones*. What else did he say about it?

A He pointed out that it was the Jerome Kern copy and that it was a first edition, uncut in boards.

Q Did he say anything about the binding?

A Perhaps I should explain that the phrase I used 'in boards' refers to the binding.

Q What did you understand by that?

> BY MR HOLROYD PEARCE: I submit that he is not allowed to give evidence of that. He is entitled to say what was said, and it is a matter for the Court to decide what effect any matters that were spoken had on the minds of the people to the conversation.

> BY MR GERALD GARDINER: Very well; the objection will be noted.

Q What did you understand by that?

A I understood, on the one hand, that the *Tom Jones* in question was identical with the one sold at the Jerome Kern sale; further, that Mr Wells, when he said that it was not necessary to give any further description other than that it was a first edition uncut in boards, had satisfied himself that the description in the Kern sale was correct and adequate.

Q Did you believe what he told you to be true?

A Yes.

Q Did he also show you another book or manuscript?

A Yes.

Q What was that?

A It was the original manuscript of part of Pope's *Essay on Man*.

Q Did he say what price he wanted for the two?

A He did not specify it exactly, but he implied that it would be in the neighbourhood of the price that those two items fetched at the Kern sale.

Q Did you know how much that was?

A Yes.

Q About how much?

A I think it was of the order of ten thousand pounds for the two.

Q Did he tell you whose property they were or for whom he was acting?

A I think he mentioned in passing that they were Mr Owen D. Young's property.

Q What did you say at that interview?

A I told Mr Wells that I was interested in the *Tom Jones* and would like to buy it, but I was not interested in the Pope manuscript which he wished to sell to me at the same time.

Q Was he willing to sell the *Tom Jones* separately?

A No.

Q After that did he on several occasions ring you up?

A Yes.

Q What did he say on those occasions?

A He pestered me to complete the sale and to buy the two items. I was hesitant because of the price, which I thought was too high, and also because I was not interested particularly in the Pope manuscript.

Q Did you see him again about it, do you remember; and, if so, where?

A I think I saw him once at Claridge's Hotel, but no decision was reached at that meeting.

Q Did you finally ring him up about it?

A Yes.

Q What happened at that telephone conversation?

A I got rather bored with the protracted negotiations and I decided to finish them, as I thought, by offering him what I considered was an insultingly low price. I therefore rang him up and said: 'I will offer you three thousand, five hundred pounds for the two' and in the course of the next few days I was somewhat surprised to find that he accepted that offer.

Q Did you then take delivery of the books?

A No, they remained for some while in Mr Robinson's shop in Pall Mall.

Q Did you then take delivery from there?

A Yes.

Q Would you have bought the books if you had not believed what Mr Wells told you about them?

A Certainly not.

Q Were you yourself competent to form a judgment by examining the books as to whether or not they were the first edition uncut and as described in the catalogue?

A No.

Q Did you in fact attempt to make any such examination?

A No, because I believed what Mr Wells had said.

Q Did you ask him whether the books were genuine or faked?

A No.

Q Would it be usual or unusual for a book collector –

BY MR HOLROYD PEARCE: I object to that.

Q (Mr Gerald Gardiner): Would it be usual or unusual for a book collector to ask a well-known dealer whether books which he was offering for sale for some thousands of pounds were genuine or faked?

A I think it would be an insult to ask that question, and in any case I had reasons for thinking that it was genuine.

Q After the books and manuscript had been delivered, were they placed with the rest of your collection?

A Yes.

Q So far as you are aware, did anyone make any further examination of them until March 1940?

A I am reasonably positive that no one did.

Q At that time was Mr John Hayward staying with you at Rushbrooke Hall, Suffolk?

A He was staying with me at Cambridge.

Q Did you and he go over to Rushbrooke Hall, Suffolk?

A Yes.

Q   Would that be for the day, or a week-end, or what?

A   It was for a week-end.

Q   Is he a well-known bibliographer?

A   Yes.

Q   Did you show him your collection of books?

A   Yes.

Q   After he had examined the *Tom Jones*, did he speak to you about it?

A   Yes.

Q   And make a written report?

A   Yes.

BY MR HOLROYD PEARCE: I object to the report going in. I agree you can have the fact of his getting some report, unspecified, and the date at which the report was made to him, but I object to the report itself.

Q   (Mr Gerald Gardiner): Did you then submit Mr Hayward's opinion to William Robinson Ltd and obtain a report from them?

A   Yes.

Q   In consequence did you write to Mr Wells a letter of the 21 May 1940?

A   Yes.

Q   Did you and your solicitors subsequently have correspondence with Mr Wells?

A   Yes.

Q   Did you send any originals which you received to your solicitors?

A   Yes.

BY MR GERALD GARDINER: Mr Holroyd Pearce, I do not know whether you are prepared to accept it from me that they were all destroyed in the blitz.

BY MR HOLROYD PEARCE: I know that Field Roscoe's unfortunately were.

BY MR GERALD GARDINER: The copies which I was going to produce to the witness are copies which have been obtained in this way: that before Messrs Field Roscoe suffered that tragedy they had sent copies of the documents to New York, and these are the copies of the copies sent back from New York.

BY MR HOLROYD PEARCE: They will decide over there as to their admissibility. I have got copies of Mr Wells' letters to Lord Rothschild and Field Roscoe. You are putting in the letters that they sent to Gabriel Wells, are you?

BY MR GERALD GARDINER: I think they are only the ones from Mr Wells. The ones of which I have here copies are a letter to Mr Wells of the 21st May 1940, and letters from Mr Wells of the 5th and 13th June, 25th October (there being two letters of that date), and 28th October 1940.

BY MR HOLROYD PEARCE: There is one to Lord Rothschild and one to Field Roscoe of the 28th.

BY MR GERALD GARDINER: I have two letters of the 25th, one to Lord Rothschild and one to Field Roscoe, a letter of the 28th, being one to Lord Rothschild, and then a letter of the 19th November 1940 from Lord Rothschild's secretary to Mr Wells.

BY MR HOLROYD PEARCE: I have got one of October 28th.

Q (Mr Gerald Gardiner): I do not suppose for a moment that you will be able to remember the exact terms of any of these letters but will you look through them and tell me whether they appear to you to be substantially accurate copies of letters the originals of which you saw? (*Letters handed to the witness.*)

A Yes, I am familiar with those letters in a general way.

(*The letters were marked 'Exhibit 2'*)

Q In the course of this action were you requested to forward the six volumes of *Tom Jones* to your lawyers in New York for use in the action?

A Yes.

BY MR GERALD GARDINER: Mr Holroyd Pearce, is there any dispute that the volumes which were received were those which were sent?

BY MR HOLROYD PEARCE: They have been identified out there. There is nothing we can do about identifying the volumes. So far as I know, there is no difficulty, but I am not in a position to make any admission.

Q   (Mr Gardiner): Was the despatch arranged through your bankers, the Foreign Branch Office of the Westminster Bank?

A   Yes, I believe so.

Q   And were they sent in August 1942?

A   That would be about the time, I think.

Q   Were they sent to your New York solicitors, Messrs Spencer, Ordway & Wierum?

A   Yes.

Q   Until they were so sent, had they been in your sole possession from the time when they were delivered to you?

A   Yes, except that I think they were sent to Messrs Robinson's for examination after Mr Hayward had examined them.

Q   Subject to that, they have been in your sole possession?

A   Yes.

Q   And were they in the same condition as when you had taken delivery of them?

A   Yes.

Cross-examination by MR HOLROYD PEARCE

Q   You are alleging that Mr Wells deliberately lied to you and swindled you, are you?

A   I do not think I put it quite like that, no.

Q   How would you put it?

A   I should put it that Wells had evidently examined books which were sold at the Kern sale with some care, because he was aware that certain of them were fakes or improperly described in the Kern sale catalogue; and that therefore when he offered me a book from the Kern sale, I naturally assumed that the book he offered, he had examined with the same care

34

as I knew he had examined others. When he offered it to me he on the one hand said that no elaborate description was necessary because it was in fact as described in the Kern sale. On the other hand, he also mentioned the fact that it was a first edition uncut and in original boards. That is the situation as I see it, and subsequently it transpired that the book was a fake. That is in reality all that I can say about it, which I think are the facts.

Q I suggest that you can answer my question, which is this: Are you suggesting that Wells deliberately swindled you?

A I do not know.

Q You have pleaded that Wells made representations about this book when he knew it was a fake, have not you?

A I do not think so.

Q 'Nineteenth: At the time defendant Wells made said representations and warranties of the nature and character of said *Tom Jones*, he knew that the said representations and warranties were untrue'. What does that mean except that it was a swindle?

A I am afraid that is not my language. I do not know what a warranty is.

Q You know what a representation is?

A Certainly.

Q That when he made the representation as to the nature and character of *Tom Jones* he knew the representation was untrue. How does your knowledge of what a warranty means affect that? That is an allegation, is it not, of a lie and a swindle?

A Yes.

Q Let us face the facts. I have asked you this question: Are you saying you were lied to and swindled?

> BY MR GERALD GARDINER: I object to the questions on the ground that the witness has already answered.
>
> BY MR HOLROYD PEARCE: He has not answered it and I want an answer. He says he does not know.
>
> BY MR GERALD GARDINER: Exactly.

35

A   I cannot tell myself personally whether Mr Wells knew that these books were faked or did not. I can only make an inference in view of Wells' eminence as a bookseller and the remarks he made to me at the time. I cannot dogmatize as to whether he knew.

Q   (Mr Holroyd Pearce): You know it is a very serious suggestion to make?

A   Yes.

Q   And you are basing it on the fact that you say he had examined some of the Jerome Kern items?

A   Yes.

Q   And that he must have known about this?

A   I find it difficult to believe that a person in Wells' position could not have known.

Q   Rosenbach is one of the cleverest dealers there is, is he not?

A   I should have said the most famous.

Q   Is he the most famous, or one of the most famous, dealers there are?

A   Yes.

Q   He had bought this book after a sale at which he had an opportunity of examination, had he not?

A   Yes.

Q   He had bought it for a very large sum, had he not?

A   Yes.

Q   And then resold it a few months later to Young?

A   I do not know when the transaction took place.

Q   At any rate we know he bought it and we know he resold it?

A   Yes.

Q   So I suppose he was lying and swindling, too, when he sold it, was he?

A   I do not know.

Q   I am suggesting that this charge of fraud put here is made quite recklessly and that there is no reason whatever to suggest that Mr Wells acted in bad faith.

A Am I to answer that?

Q Yes.

A I understand the suggestion but I find it difficult to agree with it.

Q You do not think the charge was put in to frighten a person of Mr Wells' eminence so that he would pay up if you were weak on the case with regard to warranty?

A I do not think a person of Mr Wells' eminence need be frightened.

Q But it is very distasteful to have a charge of fraud brought against you, is not it?

A Not if you are completely innocent.

Q Do you seriously suggest that you would not mind having a charge of fraud fought out against you; you would not dislike it?

A I think the proceedings would be distasteful, certainly.

Q Frightening proceedings in which there is a charge of fraud made against you must be very distasteful to any man of honour.

A I think very much less distasteful if you really were not involved.

Q That was not my question. My question was that they must be distasteful to any man of honour, must they not?

A Yes.

Q I suggest a charge of this kind might be thought by you to make Mr Wells more likely to accept liability on the contract?

A No.

Q Let us see really how much you remember about these matters. The offer of the books was made at your first interview with Wells on the occasion of this visit of his to this country, was it not? Have I made it clear? What I mean is that on the first of this sequence of conversations that you had with Wells, the books were offered to you?

A Yes.

Q You were asked for particulars of the offer that you alleged, because you have pleaded that the books were offered to you as being such and such?

A Yes.

Q And your answer was this: 'The offer was made to the plaintiff orally or by telephone to Merton Hall, Cambridge, or at Claridge's Hotel.'

A I am sorry. I am a little confused about which offer you are talking about. Is that my offer to Mr Wells?

Q No. Wells' offer of the books to you.

BY MR GERALD GARDINER: The offer referred to is put telescoping the entire transaction: 'During the year 1937, the defendant Wells, being then in London, offered to sell to the plaintiff a set of the first edition of Fielding's *Tom Jones* in six volumes and also an autograph manuscript of the first three books of Pope's *Essay on Man* for the price of £3,500 and the plaintiff agreed to buy them at that price. The said volumes and the said manuscript thereupon were delivered to the plaintiff who paid the defendant Wells the agreed price of £3,500'. That is telescoping what happened at a series of interviews and telephone conversations.

BY MR HOLROYD PEARCE: You think that referred to Wells' offer?

A May I explain what did happen?

BY MR GERALD GARDINER: There was not any offer from Mr Wells of £3,500. It is really telescoping the entire transaction which took place over a period of some months and several telephone calls and two interviews.

Q (Mr Holroyd Pearce): Let us see where you say this interview took place – at Mr Wells' flat, the first interview?

A Yes.

Q You say that he told you it was not necessary to describe it, as the copy was put up for sale?

A Describe it in detail.

Q That, you know, has never been suggested in the Pleadings, that he said that. You accept that, do you?

A I am afraid, owing to ignorance of the law, I am not quite sure what the word 'pleadings' means.

Q It is the thing that sets out your case. The case you have put against him is that he offered a set of the first edition of *Tom Jones* in six volumes. Then you say that at the time of making the sale he referred to the volumes as 'the Jerome Kern copy of *Tom Jones*', intending that you should understand that they were the books that had previously formed part of Kern's library. What I suggest to you is that that which is set out there, namely, that he referred to the volumes as 'the Jerome Kern copy of *Tom Jones*' is an accurate description of what happened.

BY MR GERALD GARDINER: Is it quite fair to put that without also putting the Seventh?

Q (Mr Holroyd Pearce): That I suggest is the case put against my client in the Pleadings. I think it can be dealt with by those who will be dealing with the rest of the case, but what I am suggesting to you is this, Lord Rothschild, that your case when it started was this, that you had been offered the Jerome Kern copy of *Tom Jones* and that that meant certain things?

A That is not the complete case.

Q I am suggesting that the case has altered somewhat now from what was put forward in the Pleadings.

A I understand the suggestion entirely.

Q And that it is inaccurate to say that Mr Wells told you it would not be necessary to describe it as it was a copy which was put up for sale?

A That is accurate.

Q In fact apparently you and he had discussed the Jerome Kern sale before.

A Certainly.

Q I suggest all he said was that that was the Jerome Kern Fielding, or Jerome Kern *Tom Jones*?

A   That was not all he said.

Q   We agree that he said that the books belonged to Owen D. Young, do not we?

A   Yes.

Q   When did this first interview take place?

A   In 1937.

Q   At what date?

A   Some time in June.

Q   In the beginning or end of June?

A   I am not certain.

Q   You appreciate what I suggest was the purport of this conversation, that he just said they were the Jerome Kern copy of Fielding's *Tom Jones* and that is all there was to it?

A   I appreciate the purport, but I do not think it is correct.

Q   It was a long time before you had occasion to throw your mind back to this interview was it not?

A   Yes.

Q   This was in 1937?

A   Yes.

Q   And you first thought of it after the war had intervened?

A   I first thought about it again.

Q   But you had had no occasion to reflect on this particular conversation until it had been found the books were fakes?

A   I think anybody who has had a conversation with Mr Wells rarely forgets it.

Q   Lord Rothschild, that is surely not dealing with my point for the moment. I was asking you why you were suggesting that you would ever throw your mind back to Mr Wells' conversation before you found the books were fakes.

A   No reason whatsoever.

Q   And we have no reason to suppose you did ever throw your mind back to that interview?

A   I did not.

Q   That was the question I asked you before. So over three years had passed before you threw your mind back to it?

A Yes.

Q And many things had happened?

A Are you talking about book collecting or the war?

Q Both.

A Not much had happened in book collecting, but a great deal otherwise.

Q A great deal in your private life, no doubt, like every other Englishman's?

A A great deal.

Q It would obviously be very difficult for you to recollect it in any detail?

A Yes.

Q I suggest that at this interview you took the books yourself, took them away with you?

A At this interview which we are discussing?

Q The first interview, yes.

A That is quite incorrect.

Q And that you had them for two or three months before the deal was actually concluded?

A I did not have the books, but it took some while before the deal was concluded. The books remained as before, in Mr Robinson's shop.

Q Perhaps I asked you two questions at once. It was two or three months, was it, before the deal was concluded?

A Some while.

Q Would that be far wrong, two or three months?

A I am afraid I cannot remember the time.

Q During that time were not the books in your possession?

A Certainly not.

Q Did not you come over to Mr Wells' flat and get them there?

A No.

Q Is that all then that was said at the first interview?

A The interview was a long one and what I have said is all I am afraid I can remember after the lapse of time.

Q I suggest nothing was said about the books being uncut, and so on. You have told us that he said the books were uncut. First of all you said he said it was not necessary to describe it, as the copy was put up for sale. Then a little later in your evidence, as I understood it, you said he said that he need not describe it in detail, because it was the Jerome Kern copy and was the first edition uncut in boards?

A I think you are commenting on the length or shortness of the description that Wells thought it necessary to make. What I say is that he said that it was unnecessary to describe it in detail; booksellers very often go in for very long descriptions in their catalogues.

Q The long and short of it really was this, was not it: You were buying a book which you had heard of which had come out of a famous collection, and he just referred to it as the Jerome Kern *Tom Jones*? That was the substance of your conversation, was not it?

A I do not think so.

Q You were asked whether you could have asked him whether it were genuine, and so on. You said, 'I thought it would be an insult'. There would not be the slightest reason would there, why you should not say to him, 'Lots of books are fakes, I suppose you are satisfied that this is all right?'

A There would be a reason, yes.

Q Why?

A Wells was offering me some books at a very large price, and I think it reasonable to assume that a transaction involving as much money as that must have received very careful attention on the part of the bookseller.

Q Would not it be fairer, if you are going to allege that he gave you a warranty that the books were so and so, to say, 'Are you satisfied that the books are so and so?'

A In the circumstances of the sale I considered such a question quite unnecessary.

Q You were speaking to him as the mouthpiece of Owen D. Young?

A   I do not think that gives quite a fair impression of the sale, to say that.

Q   He was the agent for Owen D. Young?

A   I had certain discussions with Mr Wells about that aspect which put rather a different complexion on it. He told me later that Mr Young was not particularly keen on selling these books, and it was Wells who was anxious to get them, because he was so anxious to effect a sale with me which up till then he had been unable to do.

Q   You added, after saying it would be an insult, which I challenge, 'and in any case I had reason for believing it was genuine'?

A   Yes.

Q   Your reason for believing it was genuine was that it had come from Jerome Kern's collection, I suppose?

A   No. My reason for believing it was genuine was that I knew that Wells had great knowledge about the genuineness or otherwise of books in that particular sale and had indicated certain items in the catalogue which he believed to be false or improperly described, and amongst the ones he indicated there was not the *Tom Jones* in question.

Q   I suggest that is not the meaning of what you told us before. Just listen: 'I thought it would be an insult and in any case I had reason for believing it was genuine.' Surely that was something separate from any assurances Wells had given you?

A   No.

Q   You meant it was the same thing, really?

A   I was referring to the episode which occurred previously when Wells indicated to me certain fakes in this sale catalogue.

Q   You are assuming then, that because Wells knew of some fakes in that sale, he knew of all fakes that might be in that sale, is that it?

A   Yes.

Q   That is rather a difficult assumption to make, is not it?

A   It is an assumption.

Q   You are making an assumption, Lord Rothschild. I want to show you how serious it is, possibly, in connection with a book which has deceived quite a lot of distinguished people – Jerome Kern?

A   I do not know.

Q   You assume so, don't you?

A   Not necessarily.

Q   You think he deliberately had this fake among his collection?

BY MR GERALD GARDINER: I object to the question on the ground that it is quite irrelevant to any issue in the action.

A   I do not know. I do not think it was deliberate or accidental. I just have no information on the subject.

Q   (Mr Holroyd Pearce): And then Rosenbach?

A   I do not know.

Q   And then Owen D. Young?

A   Again I do not know. I have got no information.

Q   Let us come now to the position after the first interview. You say you had not got the books?

A   No.

Q   But they were at Robinson's?

A   Yes.

Q   Did you not look at them?

A   No.

Q   Never until the deal was concluded?

A   I looked at them in Mr Wells' flat, and in view of what he said, that was enough and I did not bother to look at them again.

Q   Who took them to Mr Wells' flat?

A   Somebody from Mr Robinson's shop, I imagine.

Q   While you were at Mr Wells' flat?

A   No.

Q   Before you came there?

A   Yes, because they were there when I arrived.

Q   So they were not among the parcel of books at Robinson's shop?

A Yes.

Q But between the time when you saw the books at Robinson's shop and the time you went to Wells' flat, the books were taken there?

      BY MR GERALD GARDINER: He has not said he saw them at Robinson's shop.

Q (Mr Holroyd Pearce): Did you not say you saw a parcel of books at Robinson's shop?

A Yes.

Q And I said to you, 'Were they among the parcel of books at Robinson's shop?' and you said 'Yes'.

A I cannot tell, because the parcel was done up. I was only told by Mr Robinson.

Q How many conversations on the telephone did you have with Mr Wells after the first interview?

A I should think four or five.

Q Was not five thousand pounds the price he was asking for the two?

A I cannot remember the exact figure.

Q I suggest five thousand pounds was the price he was asking for the two.

A I am afraid I cannot remember. I only remember that I considered it excessive.

Q I think it is clear from your evidence, that nobody was present at your interviews with Wells in his flat. You were both alone were you?

A Yes.

Q How soon do you think was the first telephone conversation after that?

A I am afraid I cannot remember that.

Q Did you have any further interviews face to face?

A I think that I met Wells once at Claridge's Hotel, where we had a brief discussion about it.

Q And you think nothing of importance was said then?

A I do not think anything other than further discussions as to whether I should or should not buy and at what price.

Q I think it is implicit in what has been said, that any sale was subject to Owen D. Young's approval, was it not? The price had to be agreed by him?

A Yes.

Q Again I think it is agreed between us that no separate price for the two items was ever mentioned?

A No.

Q They were bought as one transaction?

A Yes.

Q I do not think you would dispute that the bargaining went on over about two months?

A No.

Q But you cannot give any idea of the dates of these things beyond saying that the first interview was in June?

A I have seen recently the date upon which I paid him a cheque.

Q What is the date of that?

A That, I am afraid, I cannot remember.

Q I suppose the cheque will be disclosed. I thought you said you saw recently the date on which you paid him a cheque? Is that your passbook you are referring to?

BY MR GERALD GARDINER: It is the 23rd September 1937.

BY MR HOLROYD PEARCE: I could call for that now.

BY MR GERALD GARDINER: I do not know that the cheque is here.

Q (Mr Holroyd Pearce): You were referring to your passbook, were you, where you saw the date of the cheque?

A I saw it in certain papers when discussing the matter.

BY MR GERALD GARDINER: The information has been obtained from the Manager of the Bank.

BY MR HOLROYD PEARCE: I do not want to deal with it if it will appear from anything that will be given on discovery, but if it will not I think we had better have the date from this witness when he alleges the cheque was drawn.

BY MR GERALD GARDINER: He has said he does not know.

BY MR HOLROYD PEARCE: You are going to help him.

BY MR GERALD GARDINER: I said I was quite prepared to agree that it was the 23rd September.

Q (Mr Holroyd Pearce): Do you think that was possibly the date?

A I should think that was about the date.

Q How many interviews do you think you had with Wells on the 'phone?

A Including ones on the telephone?

Q I meant conversations on the telephone.

A I should think about three, and two face to face.

Q Was the final agreement reached on the telephone or face to face?

A On the telephone.

Q Assuming the date of the cheque was the 23rd September, when do you think the date of the final interview was?

A Would it be satisfactory if I say some little while before that?

Q I only want your recollection of the matter. Do you mean the beginning of September – that sort of thing?

A I am afraid I cannot remember the date.

Q Beyond his agreeing to take three and a half thousand for the books, nothing was said of interest on the final telephone conversation, was it?

A At the final telephone conversation nothing else was said, as far as I can remember.

Q When did you first receive these books in your possession?

A It was some while after the transaction had been concluded. I should explain that I have been in the habit of leaving my books, sometimes for quite long periods, in Mr Robinson's shop.

Q Does he act as your agent in any way in dealing with books or caring for them or handling them?

47

A I have made a lot of purchases of books through him, but he is not my agent.

Q But he sometimes holds books on your account?

A I have sometimes left books that I have purchased from him in his shop for a very considerable time.

Q Have you ever left books you have purchased from someone else in his shop?

A Yes.

Q So he has then been holding them on your account as your agent?

A He has just kept them there for me.

Q Did you have the books examined at any time by anybody?

A After Mr Hayward had stated in 1940 that he thought they were fakes, yes; before that, no.

Q But during all the time the bargaining was going on with Wells, you say that the books were in Robinson's possession.

A Yes.

Q And you could easily have had them examined there?

A Yes.

Q Is Mr Robinson an expert?

A Yes.

Q So he could have examined them, obviously?

A Yes, but I did not consider it necessary.

Q So that you suggest that an effort was made to get you to buy these books by a fraudulent representation or representation known to be untrue to Wells. That is so, is not it? We have agreed that that is what your case means?

A Yes.

Q And that in order to do that he leaves them in the hands of an expert who acts on occasion as your agent. Do you agree?

A I am not quite happy about the word 'agent', I am afraid. I do not quite know exactly what is meant by that. In these circumstances there was no question of Robinson examining them at all.

Q What I mean is this: He leaves them with a person who has frequently acted for you?

A   Wells had the habit of leaving his books in Mr Robinson's safe because he had no safe in his flat.

Q   Just think. You were a regular client of Mr Robinson's were not you?

A   Certainly.

Q   And there is no reason to suppose that Mr Robinson would not use the utmost good faith towards you?

A   I think he would.

Q   And he is an expert who could detect any fraud in a book?

A   Yes.

Q   So for something like two months, or even more, Mr Wells goes on trying to get you to buy a book which on your case he knows is a fraud, leaving it where it can easily be examined by your expert, Mr Robinson, or any other expert?

BY MR GERALD GARDINER: I object to that question.

Q   By your friend, the expert, Mr Robinson, or any other expert?

A   It could have been examined by Mr Robinson if I had instructed Mr Robinson to examine it, but I had no reason to instruct him to examine it.

Q   What I am suggesting is that it is a monstrous charge to make against a man when he has left the books like that, available for inspection, in the hands of an expert who used good faith towards you. Do you not think so?

A   I understand the suggestion, but I cannot agree that it applies in these circumstances.

Re-examination (direct) by MR GERALD GARDINER

Q   Before you had bought the books or agreed to buy them, if you had wanted Mr Robinson to examine them, would you have had to have obtained Mr Wells' consent?

A   Yes.

Q   As far as you know, when Mr Wells left a parcel of his books in Mr Robinson's safe, had Mr Robinson any right to undo his parcel and look at his books?

A   None whatever.

Q   You say that you do not think that you would be likely to forget a conversation with Mr Wells in particular. Why is that?

A Mr Wells is a rather eccentric man and has a very peculiar and excitable way of conducting conversations which impress themselves on one's mind rather vividly.

Q You have been asked your view of Mr Wells' knowledge. Can you conceive of a well-known expert such as Mr Wells having these books in his possession for the purpose of sale without making any examination of them?

A I cannot conceive it.

SALE NUMBER 2307
ON PUBLIC EXHIBITION FROM TUESDAY, JANUARY FIRST
〚WEEK DAYS 9‑6 P.M.——SUNDAYS 2‑5 P.M.〛

THE LIBRARY OF
JEROME KERN

NEW YORK CITY

〚 PART ONE 〛

A‑J

TO BE SOLD BY HIS ORDER
AT UNRESERVED PUBLIC SALE
MONDAY EVENING, TUESDAY 'AFTERNOON & EVENING
WEDNESDAY & THURSDAY EVENINGS
JANUARY SEVENTH, EIGHTH, NINTH, TENTH
AT TWO O'CLOCK AND EIGHT‑FIFTEEN

THE ANDERSON GALLERIES
〚MITCHELL KENNERLEY, PRESIDENT〛
489 PARK AVENUE AT FIFTY‑NINTH STREET, NEW YORK

1929

Page from the sale catalogue

Epilogue

The true facts are completely at variance with the hypothetical explanation given earlier and are as follows: Neither Jerome Kern nor the Anderson Galleries which sold the Jerome Kern Library in 1929 checked ('collated') the *Tom Jones*. Consequently the fact that some twelve pages were missing was not mentioned in the catalogue. Dr Rosenbach, who bought the *Tom Jones*, did not examine it carefully, as he himself admitted. But one of his associates did. Furthermore, what no one seemed to have noticed was that the *next* lot in the Kern sale, p. 51, was another copy of *Tom Jones*, also uncut except for the top edges of the pages which were trimmed and gilt. This copy, the second issue, was also bought by Dr Rosenbach, for the comparatively small sum of $1,700, small enough to warrant its dismemberment in the interest of rectifying the mistake, which cost $29,000, of buying a defective copy of the first issue, uncut in boards.

But how was the job done? And how, particularly, were the trimmed and gilt top edges dealt with? I learnt the answer in the autumn of 1982. Lot 512 was dismembered, the pages needed for lot 511 were removed and, with a razor blade, an extremely thin slice was cut off the top gilt edge of each of the twelve pages needed for lot 511. While doing this operation, the bibliosurgeon deliberately made his hand shake so that the new top edges of the twelve pages were serrated, as if they had never been trimmed. Then they were inserted into the defective Kern copy, which of course had also to be dismembered before the insertions could be effected. When put together again, Dr Rosenbach, who may well not have known what had happened, sold the Kern *Tom Jones* to Owen D. Young for $29,000 + 10%. From the time of the Jerome Kern sale, no one had to tell any lies. All that had to be said was: 'Look at the sale catalogue: it speaks for itself': or nearly.

Even if not a bibliophile, the reader may wish once more to glance at the title of this chapter.

8

A GOOD INVESTMENT?

VIRTUALLY ALL MY FAMILY have collected something: French furniture, butterflies, coins, fans, irises, snuff boxes, fleas, Renaissance jewellery, rare books, tortoise shells, carpets, French buildings, Limoges enamel, bumble bees, engravings, bird skins, antique silver, stamps – you name it, they collected it.

People rarely collect things as investments – I certainly did not. But recently I indulged for a few moments in that most useless but entertaining of pastimes: jobbing backwards. Was my passion for English eighteenth century first editions and Swift manuscripts just collecting mania? Or was it the expression of another gene, which I call the chrysogene, that the Rothschilds, or some of them, are supposed to have had? Put another way, were these books and manuscripts, a few of which are described later, a good investment; or would I have done better to buy the equivalent number of shares in, for example, Royal Dutch? I have chosen a relatively conservative investment because so many of the more glamorous go-go shares, as IBM and Polaroid were some forty years ago, have now disappeared without trace (though not, of course, IBM or Polaroid).

Before comparing the value of Royal Dutch shares between 1933 and 1981, two other comparisons are worth mentioning. First, £1 in 1935 was worth 5.8p in 1981, that is about 1/17th of its value in 1935. Secondly, in 1938, my wife, after graduating from Cambridge University and taking a course in shorthand and typing, became private secretary to the manager of a well known but not very generous publisher. She was paid £156 per year whereas the other girls in the firm, who had not got a degree, were paid ten shillings less per week, that is £130 per year. In 1981 a girl aged 22 with the same qualifications as my wife had a starting pay of £5,000 per year, 32 times as much.

It is, therefore, interesting to compare the cost, in 1933–1948, of some English eighteenth century first editions – and a few manuscripts – with what they were worth in 1981, according to an expert book valuer, Mr Hans Fellner. Brief descriptions of the books and manuscripts are given in the table below. But before that, the contents of the table need some interpretation. In the first entry, the 1981 valuation, £7,000, is followed by the factor 70, by which the original purchase price in 1937, £100, must be multiplied to reach the current value. The third number, £1,700, is the value this book would have had to reach, just to keep pace with the devaluation of sterling. The last figure, is the value of a Royal Dutch shareholding in 1981 which cost £100 in 1937. As a matter of fact it would not have been possible to buy £100 worth of Royal Dutch in 1937 because one share was worth more than that sum. This has been taken into account in the calculations and does not affect them.

Both in the case of the devaluation of sterling and the appreciation of Royal Dutch shares a straight line relationship between the value in 1933 and in 1981 has been assumed. In other words the decrease or increase takes place by the same amount, or is constant, each year. This is, of course, an over-simplification and gives rise to some errors. One has only to note that in 1933 one Royal Dutch share was worth £185 whereas in April 1981 one of them was worth £18 to realize that all sorts of share splits and scrip issues took place during the 48 years in question. These 'jumps' make anything other than a straight line approximation virtually impossible.

Account, has, of course, been taken in the calculations of the fact that the books and manuscripts were not all bought in the same year.

The table shows that, relative to the value of sterling, there were five 'good' buys, three 'very bad' and two 'fairly bad' buys. If, however, the actual total value, in 1981, of the ten items is compared with what they would have had to be to keep pace with the devaluation of sterling, £52,500 *v*. £69,100, various points emerge. First, from an investment point of view, there was one particularly bad buy, Swift's annotated copy of his and Pope's *Miscellanies in Prose and Verse*. Without this gaffe the performance of the 'portfolio', relative at any rate to the value of sterling, would have been reasonable though in no way spectacular; secondly, professional valuations take no account, apparently, of romantic considerations. I am thinking of the *Decline and Fall* inscribed and presented by Gibbon to Lord Sheffield. Bound in contemporary red morocco, what could be a more desirable collector's piece? *But*, it was the third edition and it was that, presumably, which did the damage. Thirdly, if one had wished to buy books and manuscripts solely as investments, it is hard to decide, even with hindsight, what to have bought or not bought, apart from original manuscripts of world famous writers such as Jonathan Swift.

The first edition of *Pamela*, for example, bound in contemporary calf, is a very rare book and desirable from a literary point of view; but in real terms it is now only worth one third of its cost. To sum up, on the basis of comparison with sterling, these books and manuscripts were not good investments – and of course generated no income – though I dare say one could have done worse.

Comparison of the total value of the books and manuscripts in 1981 with that of the appropriate number of Royal Dutch shares bought in 1933–1948, £52,500 *v.* £140,000, needs no comment.

Reference was made earlier to glamorous 'go-go' shares such as IBM. I suppose your parents or grandparents did not by any chance put those savings, say £1,000, into IBM in 1935? If they did, they would be worth half a million pounds now. What a pity they did not. Or did they?

TABLE 2

Books/Manuscripts	Purchase Price/Date	Value 1981	Sterling	Royal Dutch
THE LIFE OF SAMUEL JOHNSON, LL.D. By James Boswell, first edition, uncut in original boards.	£100/1937	£7,000 (×70)	£1,700	£3,352
EVELINA By Francis Burney, 1788; first edition, contemporary calf.	£220/1933	£2,000 (×9.1)	£3,900	£8,044
THE HISTORY OF THE DECLINE AND FALL OF THE ROMAN EMPIRE By Edward Gibbon, 1777; third edition, contemporary red morocco, presentation copy to Lord Sheffield.	£260/1936	£1,000 (×3.8)	£4,400	£8,912
MISCELLANIES IN PROSE AND VERSE By Alexander Pope and Jonathan Swift, 1726–1732; first edition, contemporary calf, Swift's annotated copy.	£1,674/1935	£9,000 (×5.4)	£28,800	£58,655
PAMELA By Samuel Richardson, 1741–1742; first edition, contemporary calf.	£600/1935	£3,500 (×5.8)	£10,300	£21,023
A SONG TO DAVID By Christopher Smart, 1763; first edition, uncut.	£265/1937	£10,000 (×37.7)	£4,400	£8,882
TRAVELS INTO SEVERAL REMOTE NATIONS OF THE WORLD By Jonathan Swift, 1726; first serial printing, in the *Penny London Post*.	£150/1936	£2,000 (×13.3)	£2,500	£5,142
ATLAS By Jonathan Swift, 1712, Original manuscript. At the end, there is a note in Alexander Pope's handwriting: 'This is the Original, in Dʳ. Swift's hand.' A. Pope.	£140/1945	£4,000 (×28.6)	£1,900	£3,839

Books/Manuscripts	Purchase Price/Date	Value 1981	Sterling	Royal Dutch
TO CHARLES FORD ESQ^r. ON HIS BIRTHDAY Original manuscript of poem by Jonathan Swift, 1722.	£133/1935	£4,000 (× 30.1)	£2,300	£4,660
LYRICAL BALLADS By William Wordsworth and Samuel Coleridge. 1798–1800, first edition, mid-nineteenth-century calf. Coleridge's copy with an additional stanza and a correction, both to the *Ancient Mariner*.	£700/1948	£10,000 (× 14.3)	£8,900	£17,596

9

AN UNEXPECTED GIFT FROM
AN UNEXPECTED QUARTER

DURING WORLD WAR II it became known that I was engaged in bomb disposal. One day, I was in the world-famous jewellery shop, Cartier, in Bond Street. I forget why. A member of that firm, whom I knew well, asked me some questions about my bomb disposal work. Was it difficult? Was it frightening? I replied that although from time to time I was nervous, particularly at the beginning of World War II, the work was so interesting and required such concentration that there was not much time to be nervous. I also mentioned that there was one problem during the War: it was difficult to get hold of the first class screw drivers that were necessary to undo the extremely small screws in the delay mechanisms which were often made by professional watchmakers. It was important that the screw drivers should not slip during a de-fusing operation.

I thought no more about this discussion. About a month later, I received, as a gift from Cartier, a case containing a superb set of seven hardened steel, rustless screw drivers of varying sizes, including some marvellously small ones.

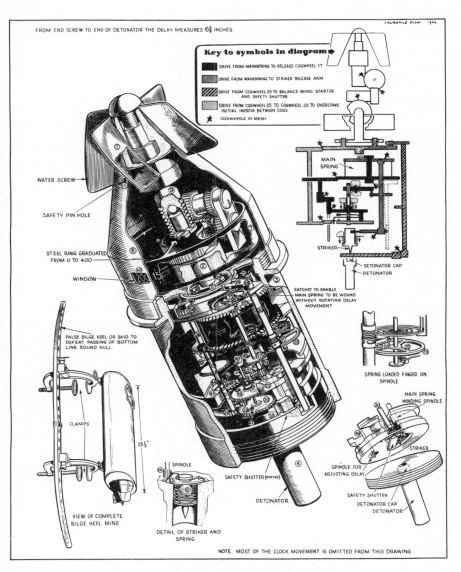

Fuse of an underwater sabotage bomb

10

FISH JUNIOR

DURING WORLD WAR II some twenty sabotage fuses with their delays were in use, directly or indirectly, by the German Secret Service. Where the delays included clock mechanisms, these sometimes came from Switzerland. One day I was belly-aching in my office to a police officer, Inspector Donald Fish, who had been seconded to our organization, about the difficulty of finding a draughtsman whose drawings *explained* to a layman how the fuse worked; for many of those who might have come across sabotage bombs were not technically trained and experienced difficulty in visualizing the fuse mechanisms – and how to dismantle them. What we wanted but could not get, I said to Inspector Fish, was someone who could make perspective drawings to scale, with parts of the casing and innards removed or opened up, to show how the fuse worked; and how to undo it without activating any booby trap that might be incorporated to prevent, by exploding it or the whole bomb, an understanding of how in fact the fuse did work. We did not want a conventional professional draughtsman skilled in making sectional diagrams for the initiated. Apart from that, the person undoing the fuse would be maimed or killed if the booby trap worked. Inspector Fish said that his son Laurence was in the RAF, was quite a good draughtsman and might be able to help. I set to work. The Air Ministry was not unduly cooperative but eventually I was allowed to meet Fish junior. What was he doing? Needless to say, literally peeling potatoes. I showed him a sabotage bomb fuse. He said: 'If you explain to me how it works, I think I can draw it.' I tried him out and the result was beyond my most optimistic expectations. Somehow or other I managed to stop Fish junior peeling potatoes and get hold of him. One result is reproduced on page 59.

Some years after World War II, I was interested in the metabolism of fern spermatozoa and wondered whether a set of electron carriers called the cytochromes were involved in their metabolism and their movements. Fern spermatozoa were difficult

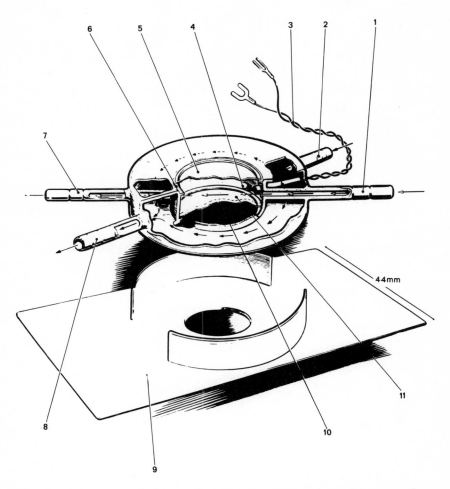

Cell for examining bracken spermatozoa in a known gas mixture, under the microscope

1. gas inlet
2. circulating water inlet
3. thermojunction leads
4. thermojunction
5. upper cover-slip
6. support for upper cover-slip
7. gas outlet
8. circulating water outlet
9. supporting base of gas chamber
10. lower cover-slip
11. water layer above lower cover-slip.

to examine spectroscopically at that time, so I decided to study the involvement or otherwise of the cytochrome system in their movement by a different method. The action of cytochrome oxidase, the last in the chain of cytochromes which passes electrons on to oxygen, is inhibited by carbon monoxide in the dark but, obviously, in such circumstances the sperm could not be observed or photographed. Fortunately, green light is equivalent to darkness from the point of view of cytochrome oxidase, so I conceived the idea of photographing the fern spermatozoa, through a microscope of course, in an atmosphere of 94% carbon monoxide and 6% oxygen, in green and in white light, the latter reversing the inhibitory action of carbon monoxide. The experiment needed a rather fancy cell to place on the microscope stage and, as the results were so interesting[2], I decided to ask Fish junior if he would draw the cell, for inclusion in my paper which was published in the Proceedings of the Royal Society[3]. The elegant and sophisticated result is reproduced on page 61.

ARE I.Q. TESTS USELESS?

RECENTLY MR BRYAN MAGEE referred in a letter he wrote me to the very high I.Q. of a mutual friend, the philosopher Bernard Williams, now Provost of King's College, Cambridge. This reminded me of an episode in World War II which left me permanently sceptical as to the value of intelligence tests. In 1944 I was seconded to the American army to facilitate the transmission of certain technical information that we had but the American army did not. When joining the American army one had to take an I.Q. test under examination conditions. The test was not very difficult. I completed it and thought no more about it.

Some days later I was summoned by General B. Conrad, in charge of the Paris Communications Zone – I never understood exactly what that meant. He said, 'Colonel Rothschild, I have a serious question to put to you, which I hope you will answer with complete frankness.' I replied, obviously, 'Of course, General.' He then said, 'You did our I.Q. test a week ago; can I have an absolute assurance from you that you had not seen the papers before, nor discussed their contents with anyone?' I replied truthfully, 'I can give you that assurance, General.' He then went on, 'Colonel Rothschild, you have an I.Q. of 184. There is only one person the U.S. army has ever examined with as high an I.Q. and that is Dr Schacht, at present interned.' There did not seem to be anything to say so I saluted as smartly as I was able and left.

Dr Schacht was, of course, Hitler's Finance Minister and we knew he was considered a financial wizard with God knows how many different exchange rates operating simultaneously in Germany. In the I.Q. test, however, there were no questions to do with finance, nor exchange rates.

One can, I think, conclude from this episode that such I.Q. tests for people *above* a certain fairly low level of intelligence are of questionable value. I think I remember hearing that Dirac scored zero in an I.Q. test in the Psychology Laboratory at Cambridge. That speaks for itself and at least succeeds in demonstrating the differences between the two examinees.

12

STANDARD OF LIVING, 1980

ONLY ONE POLITICIAN, John Biffen, has had the courage to say in public, on television of course, that no one has the right to expect a particular standard of living, let alone a gradually rising one. None of the tablets Moses brought down from his Summit Meeting on Mount Sinai had on them anything to that effect.

I can't remember if it was Sid Weighell or Bill Sirs who was reported in one of the dailies as saying, 'If our lads' standard of living goes down they'll be at the barricades.' Reading these courageous and patriotic words, I wondered what they meant by 'standard of living.' Did they just mean that the cost of a pound of bangers had gone up? Ditto school meals, ditto the telly licence, ditto petrol, ditto almost everything you can think of including, of course, funerals.

But there is more to a decline in the standard of living than bangers and funerals. Let me give you a few examples. I telephoned my wife. On the first go after dialling, nothing happened. After the second go, I get the number unobtainable sound. Shall I try a third time? Or shall I dial 100 for the operator? And if I do, and if he or she answers in measurable time, will I be charged extra for my troubles? The frustrating inadequacy of our telephone service is just one other example, not of the bangers-funeral type, of the decline in our standard of living.

My train may well be late, cancelled and almost certainly dirty. A cup of char is hellishly expensive. My tube is dirty and I may be mugged. My bus was taken off my route recently, without notice. Before that, it was usually late and always dirty. We can't afford to repair our roads, even when the gas man has taken them up with a pneumatic drill at thirty-yard intervals along the road or street; and, of course, the pavements are covered in dog shit and other forms of litter. Our daily paper is not always available, some Chapel or other having gone on strike. And, if it does come, there are far more misprints and nonsense sentences than there were five years ago. Perhaps that has also got something to do with modern technology. Fings ain't wot they used t' be on the telly either. They can't afford so many live shows, so we get more old movies: nostalgic to some, paralytic to others.

I don't think most people identify what is said above with a decreased standard of living, any more than they identify those holidays in Spain with its Legionnaire's Disease, or Majorca with its clapped out tenement blocks masquerading as hotels, as an increase in standard of living. The decrease in standard of living associated with those holidays is only perceptible when you have been three nights at Heathrow or Gatwick because 'they', baggage handlers, traffic controllers, stewardesses or simply 'airline employees' wanting more pay, shorter hours, more holidays with pay and more free meals, are on strike.

So, one's standard of living is not just that pound of bangers or the cost of your funeral. It is, virtually, everything, as my few examples show.

13
EMINENT SCIENTISTS

EMINENT OLD SCIENTISTS (not old eminent scientists) pose serious problems: their eminence lingers on when old age has eliminated the usefulness of their eminence. Governments should be more aware than they are of the dangers of relying on any eminent scientist aged 55 or more, particularly in those branches of science, or technology for that matter, which are active, for example biotechnology, chippery, and materials technology, to mention a few. The danger is not so great, though it may exist, in such fields as organic chemistry or taxonomy.

The adjective eminent carries with it a hint of middle if not old age. But I use it here as a synonym for outstanding or brilliant. People rarely go on being outstanding or brilliant when they are 55 or more. (Yes: I have heard of Gauss, Yeats and Renoir). By the age of 55, committees, councils, administration and the loss of brain cells have taken their toll.

The fact that the old often get recognition for work they did when they were much younger is no reason to think that their creativity and ability to absorb new concepts, even in their own field, has kept pace with the ravages of old age. Even Einstein could not take quantum theory; and like others before him, he found the inevitability of uncertainty indigestible to the point of rejection.

14
LONDON AIRPORT, 1980

IF YOU ARE A VIP or a VVIP you will have no idea what the ordinary traveller has to put up with at London Airport. You, the Secretary of State, the Minister, the Cabinet Secretary, or even perhaps the Permanent Secretary, will be allowed to drive right up to your aircraft and board it. It may mean climbing quite a few steps in the case of a Jumbo, but that is nothing in comparison with what the ordinary mortal has to do. Alternatively, you will be conducted to a special waiting room, called Alcock & Brown or something like that, where you will be plied with canapés, Scotch, gin and tonic or, if you behave youthfully enough, a glass of white wine. After all that and negligible formalities, you will be in your seat, first class of course, and possibly even curtained off, before anyone else is allowed to get near the aircraft.

What happens to ordinary folk is very different. If there is any common sensation other than anxiety, frustration or misery, it is of a bullock on the way to the slaughterhouse. The probability of any particular ticket counter being closed is quite high; and when it is open, there will of course be a queue before you. When your turn comes don't be so stupid as to ask if you can have an aisle seat or a non-smoker. All that is dealt with a couple of miles away in the satellite lobby, you will be told. There was a moving pavement to it, but once again it is out of order. Having had your ticket certified, endorsed, condemned or whatever is done to it at the first counter, you pass more or less easily, but often with an unnecessary feeling of guilt, through Passport Control, Immigration Control and the Security Checks. Don't look at his fingernails while he rummages through your briefcase. You then find yourself in the *main* waiting room, usually characterized by three or four Indian ladies or gentlemen lethargically sweeping up the half-eaten hot-dogs and sandwiches, plastic cups and paper wrappers left or thrown on the floor by your fellow travellers. In due course there comes a seemingly important moment in the journey. A loudspeaker announces, more or less comprehensibly, that you are to board your aircraft at Gateway 19, if you are lucky. After a long walk – you stupidly thought it a good idea to carry your small suitcase – you arrive at the satellite lounge where many who arrived before you are either sitting, exhausted after their long walk, or languidly propping up the walls of the lounge. Here, of course, your ticket is re-examined and you may get an answer to your questions about aisle seats or non-smokers. You may stupidly have thought that when, earlier, the loudspeaker told you you were to board your aircraft, it really meant it. Disillusion comes quickly. There is no sign of activity in the satellite lounge and questions are rebuffed with the 'a few more minutes' platitude. In due course, naturally, the bullocks are herded into the aircraft, by seat numbers of course, because there are so many of you. Economy first; club (whatever that means and if it exists) second; and then, if you have been stupid enough, first class last. As the hairdresser said when pulling out some of your eyebrows, 'il faut souffrir pour être belle.' But the only belle is a glass of acid champagne followed by a typical BAC meal, re-heated previously roast duck after a special sort of smoked salmon mixed with grade 3 foie gras and followed by a 1,000 calorie per slice cake.

No wonder more and more people over-fly London airport, if they possibly can, and land near Paris, Amsterdam and Frankfurt. 'Nothing can be done to improve London Airport. It is in the wrong place and badly designed. It is useless to compare it with other airports in Europe or the United States. And as the number of people who use it grows, it will get worse.' This I was told by a London Airport official.

15

A HOLIDAY AFTER HARD WORK, WITH KISSINGER AND CHARLIE SCHULTZ THROWN IN, 1974

WHEN PRIME MINISTER HEATH told me I had been appointed head of the Central Policy Review Staff or the Government's 'Think Tank', my first reaction (which displeased him) was to say I had to have three months' holiday. I did this on the advice of Jhr John Loudon, 'Chief Executive' of the Royal Dutch-Shell Group, who said to me, 'Victor, you will not realize until you have left Shell the pressure under which you have been working for the last five years. To Holland and back by air each week with other air travel in between, and two offices, one in London and the other in the Hague, make quite a mouthful even for the toughest of us. When you leave you will certainly get all sorts of offers and invitations to do this and that. Don't accept any of them for three months. Take a holiday instead.'

To begin with, I was under the impression that my new job had some similarity with the Office of the President and, as I intended to take my holiday at Mauna Kea, I decided to stop off in Washington DC and see two people: Kissinger, who at that time was in charge of the Office of the President, and Charlie Schultz, then a member of the Brookings Institution.

Kissinger was both helpful and informative; and it became clear that, at that time at any rate, there was no similarity between the Office of the President and the Government's 'Think Tank'. When taking me to his club for supper, Kissinger said, 'Don't be alarmed if you see two men in mackintoshes following us about 20 yards behind. They are only my bodyguard, or part of it.'

Charlie Schultz made a remark which is engraved on my memory. He drew a graph on a blackboard (actually a whiteboard) in his office showing the rise in public expenditure as the years went by. He said, 'Sooner or later you are certain to be confronted with the problem of public expenditure. Don't ever imagine it will be possible to reduce it except by a virtually infinitesimal amount – about this much.' He then drew a line under his graph but so close to it that there was a negligible space between the new line and the original graph. I have often wondered since then whether anyone has done better than Charlie Schultz expected.

16

PREPARATIONS
FOR AN OPERATION, 1980

WHILE, IN 1980, I was in a nursing home being cured, I hope, of endocarditis, like many other men I chatted-up the nurses, among other things to satisfy my curiosity about medical matters, having no knowledge of them.

Going for a stroll along the corridor I happened to pass someone being wheeled into an operating theatre. I wondered how one was prepared for an operation and asked Luan, an intelligent and attractive Chinese nurse from Singapore. What she told me seemed so extraordinary, at any rate to a layman, that I noted down what she said:

Name-band on admission, and religion
Remove head lice if present
Urine analysis, blood pressure, temperature chart, pulse rate
    and respiratory rate
Chest X-ray
Electrocardiogram
Haemoglobin and blood electrolyte assay
Blood test for Australia antigen (hepatitis)
Shave chest, groin and legs (if operation in these parts)
Two glycerin suppositories (not always)
Sign Consent Form
No food or drink for 8 hours before general anaesthetic
Mogadon (if requested, at night)
Diamorphine or Valium if operation delayed (not always)
Bath with antiseptic
Paint from neck to ankles with Betadine containing iodine
    (bright orange in colour)
Into gown
Omnopon plus scopolamine (pre-anaesthetic)
Heparin injection (subcutaneous) – not always

Visit by physiotherapist
Visit by anaesthetist
False teeth and all jewellery removed except wedding ring, to
    be taped to finger
Koran, miniature bible or amulet under pillow
Arterial cannula (intensive care, often by doctor)
Urinary catheter (intensive care, often by doctor)
Mechanical lung ventilator (intensive care, often by doctor)

After these preliminaries the nurses have concluded their duties and in due course the fun begins.

17

IN AND OUT OF THE
THINK TANK

Address to the Press Club, 7 September 1977

AFTER I HAD THANKED your Chairman for the great honour you conferred on me by your invitation I asked him what, by analogy with previous speakers, I should *not* do this evening. He said, 'Don't pontificate'; so I shall endeavour to conform with his admonition. But first, I must say something about my appearance. My cousin, Mrs James de Rothschild, who has had some experience of listening to me addressing audiences, says from time to time: 'Can't you smile?' I don't think I can on occasions such as this; but I hope you will not be misled by my dead-pan features into thinking that I am not laughing from time to time at myself or even, more rarely, at you. This inability to smile has got me into trouble with the press in the past. When I first became head of the Government Think Tank, Donald Maitland, at that time Chief Press Officer at No. 10, conceived the idea of a Press Conference to get the Think Tank off the ground (or wherever it was). At the conference a foreign member of your profession said to me, 'How does it come about that your son is so good at finance while you are said to be so bad?' I replied, with my dead-pan look, 'Jacob is so brilliant at finance and I so much the reverse that some people think it casts doubt on his legitimacy.' I think all the newspapermen present knew I was joking except for that one foreign correspondent, whose misinterpretation of my remark had adverse consequences, fortunately of a temporary nature, on my relationship with my son. You will, I am sure, understand that I am determined not to make such a mistake again, least of all with you who are so adept at causing innocent characters such as myself to step out of the dead-pan into the fire.

Talking about the Government Think Tank reminds me that when I first became head of it I visited a number of ministers and said to them, 'You now have a new machine; is there anything it

73

can do for you?' (because the Think Tank served the Cabinet and not only the Prime Minister). Sir Alec Home, then Foreign Secretary, said, 'You couldn't reduce the amount of paper that comes onto my desk could you?' Mr Heath had his eye on this question, as he has recently said, but we did look a bit into an allied problem, form-filling: we never got very far with it because other things intervened. All I remember now is that the envelopes the Health Service designed for people's medical records were such that any X-rays they had taken could not be fitted into them. I am sure someone has changed that by now. I am equally sure that form-filling is still a national disease and one which is more than ready for surgery. Some industrial concerns have reduced their use of paper by prodigious amounts without any loss of efficiency – in fact just the opposite; and I don't see why the Government should not consider taking a similar risk.

When I put the same question – how can the Think Tank help you – to the Home Secretary, Mr Maudling, he replied, 'You should take a long hard look at the List of the Great and Good', the catalogue in which are recorded those considered to be suitable or, if not suitable, deserving or desirable for public appointments. I may be wrong, but I thought I detected some resistance on the part of the authorities to the Think Tank studying this subject. Patronage is, as we all now know if we didn't before, a very precious and delicate commodity, and the List of the Great and Good is jealously guarded, no doubt for good if not great reasons. Patronage is not for outsiders. As one of the civil servants concerned with administration in the Cabinet Office said to me soon after I went there: 'We have quite a few of your sort through here. They come and they go.' Clearly, they came too often for him, and could not go soon enough.

Another conversation with a Cabinet Minister whom I shall *not* name went along somewhat different and unexpected lines. As the Minister began to talk, before I could say why I had come, I started to have a very curious feeling, somewhat akin, I fancy, to that experienced by people who have taken LSD. I felt I was floating upside down. I thought of D. D. Home's levitation in 1868 during which he floated out of a window in Ashley House and back through an adjoining one. He, however, was horizontal whereas I felt I was vertical, with my head downwards. Gradually it dawned on me that the Minister was under the impression I was Solly Zuckerman. Overwhelmed as I was by this unexpected and undeserved compliment, it made communication on the subject I had in mind rather difficult. Nor was I capable of reproducing Solly's Svengali-like power to manipulate ministers to his way of thinking: no Sollycisms came to mind. Not even a Sollypsism.

Mr Wedgwood Benn and I had rather similar views about secrecy – views so often enshrined in the phrase 'More Open Government': and I was grateful for the help he gave the Government Think Tank in this field. If, as I think I perceive, there is now a good deal less secrecy about the work of the Think Tank than in 1973, Tony Benn must certainly have some of the credit for this state of affairs. But, of course, we must not go too far; otherwise that well known firm of advisers to the Foreign Office, Blackstone & Mortimer, may find themselves in the hands of a Receiver.

I could not, of course, tell you about the reactions of Sir Alec, Mr Maudling and Mr Benn to my questions without getting their permission, which I have done; and this prompts me, again with permission, to describe my first meeting with Mr Heath, which, of course, took place at No. 10. The conversation went as follows:

Mr Heath 'It's funny we have never met before.' Then there was a sort of row of dots. I could not think what to say; after a while, I said, rather desperately: 'Prime Minister, do you not think it would be better to have an economist in charge of this Unit?'

Mr Heath 'I did economics at Oxford.' Another row of dots. Again after a while, I said rather desperately: 'Prime Minister, could you give me an example of the type of problem you want the Unit to tackle?'

Mr Heath 'Concorde.' At that moment I thought, perhaps wrongly, that I detected some anguished vibrations emanating from Sir Burke Trend and Sir William Armstrong, as they then were, who were hovering in the background. There was some justification for their anguish, if I did not imagine it, because an hour beforehand they had told me it was precisely things like Concorde that the Government Think Tank would *not* be expected to study.

75

While I was still feeling the vibes, a Secretary came in and handed the Prime Minister a piece of paper which he read with some signs of displeasure, and said, 'Oh well, I had better see him.' Turning to me, he concluded the interview by saying, 'Let me know if there are any other points.' Those 'other points' came quickly enough and I found Mr Heath to be a careful listener with, of course, a very sharp mind. In spite of one row and a number of arguments, my relationships with him were and still are excellent.

There *is* something alarming or disequilibrating about having to see Prime Ministers at No. 10 and this went for Mr Wilson, as *he* then was, just as it did for Mr Heath. When Mr Wilson became Prime Minister, some members of the Think Tank were quite worried lest it should suddenly be liquidated, several important people in the Labour Party having previously said that the Tank was a joke, that they did not need anyone to think for them, and so on. I could not relieve the members of the Think Tank of their anxiety, although I knew, in confidence, before Mr Wilson became Prime Minister, that he was not going to liquidate us: I had met him at luncheon six months before the Labour Party came into Office and, at the end of it, he said to me 'When we win the Election I do not intend to make any institutional changes at the centre'. I must add that I found Harold Wilson punctiliously reliable and helpful in all my dealings with him.

Running the Think Tank was, of course, intensely interesting though from time to time I felt I was threading my way through a minefield; and I sometimes wondered whether I had been selected *because* of my knowledge of bombs acquired during World War II.

The first bomb, or to be more precise, fuse, I took to pieces made me rather nervous. The only person who had previously dismantled this type of fuse, a Lieutenant in the Royal Navy, sadly lost an eye and an arm while doing so. That raised the suspicion that the fuse was booby-trapped to prevent it being undone. One of these fuses, which until then had only been found abroad, appeared in England. I decided that my eyes were more valuable than my hands and I therefore took it to pieces while kneeling behind a well padded arm chair. I should explain I *thought* I understood what had gone wrong on the previous occasion, so, though nervous, I was fairly confident.

This fountain pen I am wearing is a revolver (inactive now of course, otherwise I could not wear it) which a German agent gave me as a present. This fourteen-day time fuse was given to me in rather curious circumstances. Some German saboteurs landed from a submarine off the coast of the United States with various types of camouflaged bombs. Some looked like pieces of coal. At that time the Americans did not have any specialists in this sort of warfare and asked the British to lend them one; so I was sent for ten days to the FBI in Washington DC, and a very enjoyable time it was. J. Edgar Hoover, a hero then, the object of odium since, gave me this fuse as a 'thank you' and 'goodbye' present.

More frightening than bombs was an earlier experience, to do with cricket. My career in first-class cricket was brief, something not unconnected with the fact that it coincided with the era of bodyline bowling. Northants, for which I used to play, had two lines of defence against bodyline bowling, mainly inflicted on batsmen then by Larwood who played for Notts, and by the famous Australian fast bowler MacDonald, who played for Lancashire. (He once hit me on the funny bone.) Our captain, V. W. C. Jupp, explained to the captain of Notts that he quite often made wild swipes to leg and inadvertently let go of his bat. With two or three silly short legs when Larwood was bowling, he did hope that none of them would get hurt. If that propaganda did not work, we made generous use of an extremely fast, ill-tempered, left hand bowler called Nobby Clark who, with the slightest encouragement from Jupp, could terrorize any batsman. In spite of these advantages, it was not much fun playing against Larwood and I well remember my first ball batting against him. The wicket keeper was standing some twenty yards back behind the stumps. I played a normal forward shot on the offside and as my bat, so I thought, was about to connect with the ball, I heard it smack into the gloves of the wicket keeper – so much had I misjudged the pace. I lasted for about an hour after that but I felt my first-class cricket days were numbered and indeed they were.

As well as being told not to pontificate, some of those concerned with my appearance this evening have said to me 'Don't you have a theme?' Certainly I have no political theme. Nearly four years in the Cabinet Office turned me into a political eunuch or hermaphrodite. Nor, having read a few months ago in *The Times* Professor Friedman tearing a strip off Lord Kaldor as if he was a small boy who had not done his prep. properly, could I possibly have an economic theme. There *are* themes, of course: Energy (may God preserve us from too many 'wide-ranging debates'), Waste, Water (whatever happened to the Minister for Drought? Must we always be either praying for rain or for the floods to abate?), the Miners (why can't politicians remember Stanley Baldwin's aphorism?), Union bashing and Union beatification, Hyper-taxation, Melanophobia (a new word coined for this occasion), and the creaking, groaning and crumbling machinery of Whitehall and Westminster so much revered by that Darby and Joan of constitutionalism, Michael Foot and Enoch Powell, these are all potential themes; but not for me this evening, talking to so knowledgable and hard-headed an audience as you.

Many years ago Lord Boothby, I think, coined a political slogan 'Give the people a rest'. Perhaps it is a sign of our national vitality, so conspicuous at football matches, that we do the opposite. The British people are *never* given a rest. They are constantly lectured, hectored, criticized, taxed (taxed and taxed again as Hugh Gaitskell might have said), and reminded, *ad nauseam*, of the sacrifices to come, but rarely of those already endured. So if I were forced to have a theme tonight it would be 'Give the people a rest'. I don't mean we haven't got to work very hard: of course we must and many of us know it. But need we be lectured so interminably about the things we know too well? If the answer to this question is 'No', the press, the telly and the steam radio will be in a very difficult position and one which deserves all our sympathy. For if you curtail the amount of pontification to which we are subjected, if you reduce the number of times we have to read or hear the words Bullock, the Social Contract, Free Collective Bargaining, Devolution, the Money Supply and that hoary or should I say hairy favourite, British Rail, you will be accused of failing to bring before the public the important issues of our time. If, on the other hand, you allow us to be endlessly lectured, some of us, like me, get fed up and cry 'Give us a rest'. That is not easy for the ordinary man and woman when things are as difficult as they now are and, I'm afraid, are going to be for some time to come, in spite of North Sea oil – because we must be very careful how we spend or rather, I hope, *invest* our capital. But even if the press manages to steer a safe course between the Scylla of too much exhortation and the Charybdis of too little, it can *still* get into trouble, as I learned when I was actually writing these words. I had switched on the telly to watch my double (Kojak) but, being a bit too early, I was privileged to see two of our bosses, Jack Jones and David Basnett, explaining how vile and biased the whole press, irrespective, it seemed, of political persuasion, was against them.

So, gentlemen, you the newspapermen cannot win. And I admire you for not letting the knowledge of your dilemma get you down. The result is that though the British press, unlike all other institutions in this country, is not, I believe, perfect, and perpetrates the odd clanger, it is, by and large, as good as any press in the free world. I emphasize in the *free* world. *You* can be criticized. In the other world the press is *never* criticized. It is *beyond* criticism. The Soviet press never offends its Government nor its readers because they only know what the press tells them. They are pleased with their newspapers just as Eskimos are pleased with their snow – they know nothing else. But in the free world, the world of collisions, revelations, exhortations, yawns, bodyline bowling and eccentricities like thinking in a tank, there is always a dilemma, because democracy itself is a dilemma – where should one be between that Scylla and Charybdis I mentioned a few minutes ago? Steering the right course between what we would like to do and what we ought to do is a formidable challenge. You, gentlemen, greatly help to keep us sailing in the right direction. I only hope you keep your compasses calibrated.

18

ONE THAT GOT AWAY

IT IS A VERY SERIOUS OFFENCE, a gross violation of the Official
Secrets Act, to remove official documents from the Cabinet Office,
let alone minutes from a Prime Minister. Nevertheless, the one
reproduced below did get away and in spite of the possible
penalties, seemed to me worth preservation.

10, Downing Street,
Whitehall.

Prime Minister's
Personal Minute
No. M 13 W/74

LORD ROTHSCHILD

    In view of the current economic crisis, I would be
grateful if you would give consideration to the following
figures:

Population of the United Kingdom	54,000,000
People aged 65 and over	14,000,000
People aged 18 and under	18.000,000
People working for the Government	9.000,000
The Armed Forces	2,300,000
Local Government employees	9,800,000
People who won't work	888,000
People detained at Her Majesty's pleasure	11,998
TOTAL	53,999,998
Balance left to do the work	2

    You and I therefore, must work harder, especially you,
as I have felt no evidence of your considerable weight
since I took office.

1 April 1974

H.W.

19

DEATH OF THE TANK

I COME NEITHER TO PRAISE nor to bury the Think Tank: just to make a few fairly obvious remarks about it.

When I accepted Mr Heath's invitation, conveyed by the Cabinet Secretary Sir Burke Trend (as he then was), to become the first head of the Government's Think Tank, I had no idea what it was intended to be or do in spite of the characteristically sonorous prose in which its future activities were described in the inevitable White Paper. Nor did anyone else seem to have much idea, such phrases as 'long term strategy', 'trans-departmental problems', 'not the rate of exchange', or 'not the Office of the White House' being bandied round. We spent quite a time during the first six months arguing about what we were supposed to be doing and, if the members of the Tank had no other virtues, they certainly knew how to argue.

These arguments, however, were quickly and abruptly interrupted by instructions from the Prime Minister who, at very short notice, requested us 'to take an interest in' a Rolls-Royce engine, the RB211, for not more than twenty-four hours. I shall explain the curiously opaque phrase 'take an interest in' a little later.

We had an excellent start because, on D-day, Sir Burke injected into the Tank Dick Ross, the distinguished economist, and two young, top-class civil servants, John Mayne and Robin Butler. In one case, the injection was made somewhat earlier than D-day. It never passed through our minds, of course, that any of these had been planted in the Tank for more Byzantine or Smileyesque reasons. Had that been the case, some of us knew a bit about turning people round, *and* round.

I was not particularly convinced by the *bons mots* of Robert Wade-Gery – 'sabotaging the smooth working of the Whitehall machine' – or of Dick Ross – 'thinking the unthinkable'. From the start, it seemed to me that our job was to analyse problems and proposals and for that we needed excellent analytical brains: so that was what I tried to get. I thought we needed about sixteen graduates, half from within the Civil Service and half from outside. But so small an organization made it essential to have outside consultants, so we built up a network of these, none of them paid. When, for example, we 'took an interest in' the British computer industry, the team consisted of three members of the Think Tank and two outsiders, one of whom was Brian Flowers, at that time Chairman of the Computer Board. The other, I say rather archly, came from within the Government service.

At that time some emphasis was placed on the need to brief each Cabinet Minister about matters which were *not* the concern of his or her department but on which the Cabinet was expected to take decisions. The idea was that as the Cabinet was collectively responsible for such decisions, it might be a good thing for Cabinet ministers to know a little about the subjects on which agreement or disagreement was sought. Accordingly, the Think Tank prepared what were called 'Collective Briefs'. Dick Ross had a genius for preparing these which more often than not consisted of half a page of apparently innocent questions which one minister might put to his colleagues. All this sounds fairly pedestrian and obvious; but quite frequently ministers were rather unconcerned about matters which had no special interest for their department. I remember sitting next to a Cabinet Minister at a Cabinet Committee meeting and improperly reading the brief he was given by his Permanent Secretary. It said: '5. This item is of no interest to you.' Collective Briefs were intended to counter such parochialism.

I said earlier that I would explain the peculiar phrase 'taking an interest in'. When the Think Tank first came into existence and for a long time afterwards, people were very curious as to what we were doing; and we were tormented by questions from all quarters. 'Victor, if forced by circumstances to answer,' Sir Burke said, 'you may say that the Central Policy Review Staff is taking an interest, or has taken an interest, in such-and-such a subject. That is as far as you may go. You may not say that you are writing a report on any subject, nor that you have written one.' We did our best to conform with these instructions but of course we were sometimes tricked. At other times leakages were ascribed to the Tank when in fact they had come from elsewhere. On one occasion, when we were under attack for leaking, Donald Maitland, then the No. 10 Press Secretary, strongly and successfully defended us.

Death of the Tank

It is hardly necessary to say that the most efficient way of fairly or unfairly damning any Whitehall institution is to accuse it of being leaky. But can the CPRS be blamed if a minister accidentally leaves his brief-case in Tante Claire?

As I am on the subject of leakages, I believe they would be an excellent subject in which the Think Tank, or rather a Think Tank, could usefully take an interest, with, of course, recommendations: and I have some ideas as to how to reduce leakages. If anyone is interested they are welcome to what have been held, on various occasions, to be jejune or impracticable ideas.

Well, what *did* we take an interest in? Who asked this question? On this occasion I asked myself, and came up with a few answers dredged from an imperfect memory. We took a repeated, not to say continuous, interest in the economy, counter-inflation, and public expenditure. We took an interest in a number of industrial problems – I seem to recollect particularly the construction industry and the newspaper industry, and relations between the Government and the nationalized industries. We took an interest in Concorde; and in various energy issues, including North Sea oil, nuclear power (and safety) and energy conservation. And we took an interest in a certain number of social issues like early retirement, services for the elderly and help for the disabled.

I expect I have forgotten quite a few and there are some which must not be mentioned. Please remember that we only 'took an interest in' the ones I have listed.

People often asked me then, nearly ten years ago, and still now, if I thought we were successful: whether our deliberations and recommendations changed Government policy. My answer was invariably the same: 'We have not been fired.'

You must not think that there is only one way, by having a Government Think Tank, to get complex issues objectively analysed. There are other ways which it is hardly necessary to enumerate. But there is one difficulty. It will not be easy or even perhaps possible to get this input without those responsible for it first, having the confidence of ministers and of the Civil Service; and secondly, having access to classified and often highly classified material. That is more difficult though not impossible to achieve outside Whitehall. But one thing is certain: if the Prime Minister of the day does not feel the need for a Think Tank or does not think its existence is worth the cost, the sooner it is disbanded the better.

After all, there is nothing to stop a Tank being dusted down and resuscitated, temporarily or otherwise.

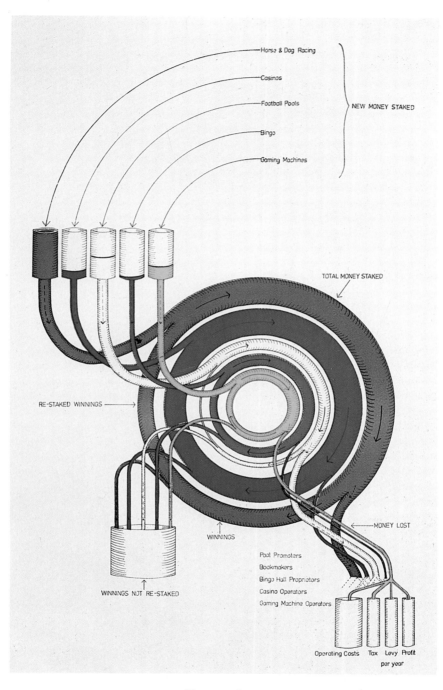

FIGURE 6
Hydrodynamic model of gambling in Great Britain, 1976

20

ROYAL COMMISSIONS

An Address to the British Academy,
29 June, 1978

MAY I SAY how much I appreciate being invited to address you this evening. I should at once utter a warning. In the past you have, I believe, been regaled by Sir Harold Wilson on the Machinations of Government; by Sir Frederick Dainton on the University Grants Committee and Education; by Mrs Williams on Education and Liberty; and by Mr Macmillan on Patriotism and how nice it is to be reported dead. But tonight the next few minutes will not, as in the cases just cited, be taken up with discussion of a topic objectively chosen as a means of celebrating or solemnizing the purposes of this Academy. I trust, nevertheless, that my subject will not be unworthy of this distinguished audience, some of whose members are or certainly will be also members of Royal Commissions.

Those few of you who know me will be only too aware that my recent life has consisted of a series of obsessions, sometimes connected with each other but in any case of so demanding a nature as to overcome any temptation to express an interest in things of general concern, or of an academic nature. My present obsession is with gambling or, more accurately, with what is officially described as an inquiry 'into the existing law, and practice thereunder, relating to betting, gaming, lotteries and prize competitions', with particular reference to such matters as the restrictions placed upon the provision of facilities for gambling, the financial structure of the gambling industry, the publication of information about gambling and the contribution from gambling to the sports on which it is in some cases based. As a result of this inquiry my colleagues and I are bidden to produce recommendations. The establishment of the Royal Commission on Gambling was announced in the autumn of 1975. There then followed an incubation period of some four months during which, I assume, the task of killing three statutory birds with one stone – finding, for example, a female Scottish accountant of appropriate standing – was started and abandoned. So our work began in February 1976 and we are now about to publish our report. The Commission, it seems, was established in response to demands for an inquiry into what is variously considered to be anything from a social evil to an enjoyable way of wasting money and, very occasionally, of making it. You may be surprised to learn, and I certainly was when the statistics first came to my notice, that gambling is an enormous industry. In Britain it now enjoys an annual turnover – a phrase to be interpreted with caution – in excess of £8,000 million, a little under the recently announced Public Sector Borrowing Requirement, and it provides employment for about 90,000 people. It is indulged in, in one form or another and at some time or another, by more than 9 out of 10 adults in this country, which gives it a participation index almost equal to that of sex and, as with sex, there is little evidence to suggest that it does the majority of its participants any serious harm. Unlike sex, however, it has not received much publicity from government, press or people. In fact the Home Office's Research Unit concluded that too little was known about gambling to enable government policy on the matter to be formulated.

It is some three and a half years since I left Whitehall so I am, inevitably, rather rusty about Whitehall procedures, particularly those involving the right hand of a department not, apparently, knowing what the left hand is doing. It is therefore hard for me to understand what the point is of setting up a Royal Commission, sponsored by the Home Office, to study gambling, if that department mounts its own investigation into gambling (under the disguise of a review of gambling literature – which incidentally was excellent) at about the same time and publishes its results independently. I have just mentioned two hands, the left and the right, but in this case there was a third hand: while our Royal Commission was labouring – and parturition has occasioned much labour – a Select Committee of the House of Commons made an investigation in depth into one important aspect of gambling, the Tote, which, for obvious reasons, we were also studying. Is there not something incomprehensible about such prodigality, such overkill?

If one starts with the findings of the Home Office's Research

Unit, several thoughts spring to mind. It may be said that a more detailed study of the subject should be undertaken to allow firmer conclusions to be drawn about the place of gambling in our society. If this were done it might be possible to crystallize government thinking on the matter. The question could then arise: how should these detailed studies be carried out, and one obvious answer would be to say that the Home Office should be requested to probe further. In fact, however, this was not what was done. *Before* it became clear from the work of the Home Office Research Unit that more work was needed, the Royal Commission was set up with the terms of reference I have already mentioned. Its task was to a certain extent a replica of the Home Office's research but we have gone somewhat further. The purpose of a commission is to make recommendations which the Government may implement, or simply forget. The question which several people have put to me is: Why do we do things this way? What is the rationale of a Royal Commission? Why appoint people from different walks of life with no apparent qualifications for the task, and little or no practical experience, to consider and determine issues of public importance which ultimately require the cooperation of government to be translated into legislation; and issues which could, some argue, be quite adequately determined by the Government or the appropriate minister, on the basis of information provided by a departmental research unit? In short, they say, why bother to have Royal Commissions at all? They can hardly expect me to agree with the implication of this question, after two and a half years' hard labour.

A. P. Herbert once noted that 'a Royal Commission is generally appointed, not so much for digging up the truth, as for digging it in: and a government department appointing a Royal Commission is like a dog burying a bone, except that the dog does eventually return to the bone.' He might have added that another reason governments are said to set up Royal Commissions is to facilitate answers to awkward parliamentary questions: 'the Right Honourable Member may have forgotten that the Royal Commission on Confusion in Public Life is considering this question among others, and is expected to report within three years.' A. P. Herbert was highly critical of the use made of committees of inquiry in general. It was in his opinion tantamount to a failure to govern.

Against this one can argue that such a committee is a desirable means of achieving a conclusion since it is not dependent upon the cooperation of Parliament or the parliamentary timetable; but there are those who assert that there is nothing in this line of reasoning which favours a Royal Commission over a research unit of the type I have described. Others would emphasize the independence of a Royal Commission and the ability of government to select a body of experts not to be found within its own ranks. Expertise may strike some as a strong argument in favour of Royal Commissions in general, but not a necessary characteristic of any particular Royal Commission.

Experts, moreover, have their disadvantages. For gambling and its closely associated sports I estimate that my Royal Commission would need at least 50 members if the experts and interested parties were to be represented on it. The last time an overt enquiry was made into Royal Commissions, as recently as 1910, the Balfour Committee of Enquiry said: 'it is of equal or greater importance that those selected as commissioners should, as far as possible, be persons who have not committed themselves so deeply on any side of the questions involved . . . as to render the probability of an impartial enquiry and an unanimous Report practically impossible. . . . A commission selected on the principle of representing various interests starts with a serious handicap against the probability of harmony in its work, and perhaps even of practical result from its labours.'

None of the members of the Royal Commission on Gambling is a hardened or experienced gambler (indeed few of us indulge in it at all), and there seems to be no particular reason why a philosopher, a sports commentator, a specialist on office organisation, an ex-scientist, an Olympic Medallist, a trade unionist, a journalist and two practising barristers should be any better qualified to pronounce on the particular subject of gambling than any nine members of the Cabinet; except that the latter are known not to have time whereas the former are assumed, for some obscure reason, to have the time, the energy and the capacity to learn an entirely new subject and become expert on it. The interesting thing about all the people on my Commission is that each is employed whole-time on a job which has nothing to do with the Royal Commission. They are not, of course, paid a serious amount and even the red, black or blue cabinet boxes which members of Royal Commissions used to be given – and greatly treasured – may now have been withdrawn, so rumour has it, though I am told that commissioners can, if they wish, buy them, at a price. Why on earth should these hard-pressed people give up what spare time they have, in our case almost invariably after 4.30 in the afternoon, if only so that our two barristers can hurry out of court and attend our meetings? Can a system which relies on the goodwill, the evenings and the weekends of hard-pressed people be viable in the 70s and after? 'What about your secretariat?' I hear someone ask. 'They should prepare all the papers for your consideration. They should write your report. You are just the jury and the judge.' It is true that Royal Commissions are serviced by able civil servants, seconded or retired; and some of them, as in our case, are recognized authorities on the subject in question. But I do not believe that is how Royal Commissions are intended to work now, or in the nineteenth century when commissioners had the time and even, on occasions, the means to do much more than merely be inquisitive members of a rather unusual sort of jury. *Is* there a case requiring study, that Royal Commissions are out of date and should be replaced by something else or something different in form? The question is what?

To answer that question one should first pose another: what is it about Royal Commissions which gives them their cachet? I think governments *like* Royal Commissions because they believe they have popular support, and that support comes from the widely held view that Royal Commissions are *independent*, which I believe they are (if they want to be). The British as a nation are rather suspicious of inquiries by civil servants and prefer to place their faith in people with no obvious hand in government: a righteous band of apostles dedicated to the discovery of the public good. The criticism so often levelled at Royal Commissions, and which is echoed by A. P. Herbert in the words I have quoted, is not so much that the commissions have failed to produce any effective recommendations, as that the government has failed to implement them. I suspect that much of this disappointment stems from a feeling on the part of the public that a Royal Commission is bound to produce a report which will solve the problem, assuming there is one. I have little doubt that those who support the appointment of the Royal Commission on Legal Services, or who have called for a Royal Commission on the Use of Animals in Experiments, hope and possibly expect that their own view will be adopted. They regard the commission as an instrument of truth and therefore a purveyor of justice whose siren song no government will be powerful enough to resist.

Much of the confusion probably stems from a failure to appreciate the purpose of a Royal Commission. In the report of the Balfour Enquiry which I have already mentioned, the Committee expressed its unanimous belief that 'the appointment of Royal Commissions is useful for the elucidation of difficult subjects which are attracting public attention, but in regard to which the information is not sufficiently accurate to form a preliminary to legislation. That this view is generally held is obvious from the fact that the number of Royal Commissions has been greatly increased in recent years. But we have some doubts whether in all cases the practical results achieved have been commensurate with the time, labour and expense involved. And we are disposed to deprecate the appointment of Royal Commissions on subjects as to which there is no reasonable prospect of early legislation'.

This caution has not by and large been heeded and, as the report implies, it is indeed true that the future of any Royal Commission recommendations rests ultimately with the government, and to a lesser extent, perhaps, with Parliament. The value of the Royal Commission over the departmental research unit is held to be that it seeks both to inform and to guide and, when a subject is a delicate or complex one, it may be of importance to a government for the matter to be seen to be reviewed in as impartial a manner as possible. But though the burden of making a decision is placed on the commission's shoulders, the acceptance and implementation of that decision remains a political choice. A. P. Herbert was therefore right to question the purpose of a Royal Commission but wrong when he castigated its appointment as a failure to govern and simultaneously criticized the government for failing to implement its recommendations.

The success or failure of a Royal Commission should not, therefore, be measured by the legislation which may follow, but its usefulness may be so measured. The Report which one aims to produce must be thorough, constructive, hopefully imaginative but above all clear in its reasoning. It should also in my opinion be free from dissenting opinions (though there are dissenting opinions about that). A government should not be interested in a sample of views whatever their individual merits. It has ordered a series of recommendations for action which constitute the end-product of the Commission's deliberations. If the individual and uncoordinated views of different people were what was needed, there would be little need for a Royal Commission. The Home Office, for example, could simply send the evidence it had gathered to a number of people and ask for their comments.

The Balfour Committee considered that the difficulties facing a Royal Commission have usually been overcome by the exercise of tact and patience. The ideal chairman is one who is able to blend the discordant views of his or her colleagues into a harmonious tune. If the chairman attempts, the report says, 'to take the position of a despot, however intelligent his despotism might prove, he will not only add greatly to his own burden, but there will be a constant strain against his authority. By taking the former position and through the good will of his colleagues he in practice obtains real power; by taking the latter position he may assume to himself great powers, but in practice he acquires much less real control.' In order to produce a useful report, long hours of discussion, sometimes amusing and interesting, on other occasions boring, repetitive and tedious, have been necessary. One pressurizes some of one's colleagues to contribute a chapter to the final report by ceaseless cajoling, while at the same time hoping, as another Royal Commission Chairman told me, that others will desist from putting pen to paper. Ultimately, one hopes that this Royal Commission will succeed within the definition of success which I have attempted; and I believe, optimistically, that this Royal Commission *has* had some success in producing a practicable and feasible programme for change and action. Whether that optimism is justified or not will only be known after July 12th. Thus it remains to be seen whether the reliance which has been placed upon us is less an act of faith than – if I may say it – a gamble.

21

ANNUAL DINNER OF
H.M. CUSTOMS AND EXCISE,
10th MAY 1978

MR CHAIRMAN, Sir Ian[4], M. le Directeur[5] Ladies and Gentlemen,
Being neither a clergyman, a politician nor Lord Mancroft, I
am not a professional speaker. This not only means that I speak
with difficulty and apprehension, but also that I have to find out
as much as possible beforehand about the audience I am to
address: what they like to hear, what they do not, and so on. It
therefore seemed desirable to have a chat with an expert, a member of H.M. Customs and Excise who had attended your annual
dinner, actually on the last four occasions. I shall call him Colonel
B. 'Where would the dinner take place?' I asked. 'How many
people would be present? Microphones?' Colonel B. was not sure
about this last point but he *was* sure that it would be easy to
arrange – or not – as the speaker wished. After these preliminaries
I turned to the real reason for the chat. 'What had last year's
speaker talked about?' 'I'm afraid I don't remember.' 'Was it
interesting?' 'Again I'm afraid I don't remember.' 'Was it amusing?' 'Not particularly, so far as I can remember.' 'What about
the speakers in the previous *three* years?' 'I'm afraid I'm not prepared for these questions. I remember that the Chancellor spoke
one year. He made a joke and gave us a pat on the back which was
very welcome at the time. Perhaps I can deal with your questions
in another way, by telling you why we invited you to speak. You
have had a rather unusual life, more like someone two hundred
years ago. You have changed your job so often.' '25 years in a
laboratory at Cambridge studying the biophysics of reproduction,' I protested. 'Yes but you were for 10 years the Research
Director of Shell; and then you became a *sort* of civil servant. And
you're a banker.' 'Banker,' I protested again: 'Never.' 'But you
are called Rothschild.' Stunned, I was not quick enough to remind

Colonel B. that the London telephone directory contains Roths-childs who are dentists, accountants, doctors and one who simply calls him or herself 'Trading Company'. The New York telephone directory contains 138 varieties.

The conversation led me to one conclusion. I must, I must say something which Colonel B. will remember, if only for the sake of next year's speaker. Perhaps I have already said something that a few of you will remember. If not, I nevertheless suspect that some of you who are here tonight will remember one thing I shall say: it is a statistic which, because of my previous scientific research and my present preoccupation, I am rather well qualified to record.

But first I must revert to having been 'a *sort* of civil servant', as Colonel B. put it. He referred to my fairly recent stint, nearly four years, in the Cabinet Office, though earlier than that, I was a civil servant for five years; and in that capacity I used to give lectures to members of H.M. Customs and Excise, at a place euphemistically called the Patriotic Schools, on how German saboteurs camouflaged their bombs, or parts of them, when bringing them into this country. Detonators embedded in coat hangers, raincoats made out of flexible high explosive, thermos flasks with real tea in them but which in fact were bombs, and so on.

On both these occasions I developed a great respect and ad-miration for the Civil Service; much more, I must tell you in strict confidence, than for the great majority of ministers. From Perma-nent Secretaries downwards, I found a far higher level of intelli-gence, loyalty to their political bosses, and selfless attention to duty than I believe one could find in any other segment of the community. I have no patience with the strictures of that Select Committee – Michael English is its chairman I think – and less than no patience with the immature malevolence of one of the committee's members. Of course, in such a large organization as the Civil Service the Central Limit Theorem *requires* that there will be a sprinkling of peculiar characters, some 6 foot 5 inches tall, others under 5 foot (both in stature and other human charac-teristics); and this also goes, of course, for H.M. Customs and Excise, with its 29,000 members. But in my experience the distri-bution of characteristics in the Civil Service is what the mathe-

93

maticians describe as being skewed to the left, which means that, on average, civil servants are a good deal better than they ought, on a strict mathematical basis, to be. This pat on the back may be more labyrinthine than the one the Chancellor gave you a few years ago according to Colonel B., but it is nevertheless sincere and bestowed with gratitude.

My most recent job, for the last two and a half years, has been to be chairman of the Royal Commission on Gambling. It has proved to be a most arduous and complicated job. Not being a gambler and never having been to a race-meeting or casino, there was much for me to learn. Napoleon, I think, said we were a nation of shop keepers. A nation of gamblers would be more appropriate, for reasons I shall now justify. The percentage of our adult population that gambles some time or other is about the same as the percentage of adults who engage in sexual intercourse. That, of course, is the statistic which I thought some of you might remember for a few moments. But there is more or worse to come. In the calendar year 1977, the amount of money we staked on our various forms of gambling was a little less, about 10% I think, than the Chancellor's recently announced Public Sector Borrowing Requirement. Of course one must treat the statistic 'money staked' with caution. It is not the amount of money *lost* by gamblers, which is about 11% of the money staked, though, as you all know, H.M. Customs and Excise takes $7\frac{1}{2}$% of all money *staked* off-course on horse and dog racing.

In a survey of the whole, rather monstrous, spectrum of gambling in the United Kingdom, two sorts have struck me as being worthy of attention. The first is one-armed bandits or, as they are often called, fruit or jackpot machines. There are a vast number of these in the country and the punter gets a lousy deal from them, although he does not realize it. A one-armed bandit has to have a notice on it saying how much of the money put in is returned to the players. Not a single one of these notices is truthful, but that is partly the fault of the Gaming Board which does not understand elementary probability theory. Moreover, there are several ways of fixing a one-armed bandit so that it pays out less than it should, or sometimes more for a very short time, followed by less, a procedure which stimulates play and therefore profits for the owner of the machine. We describe some of the ways of fixing one-armed bandits in our report, together, of course, with recommendations for neutralizing such activities.

There is no way of removing one-armed bandits from the British scene: they are now an integral part of British life. The profits that owners make from them support some 4,000 Working Men's Clubs, 1,400 Conservative Clubs, a number of British Legion Clubs and a sizeable percentage of our 4,000 Golf Clubs. Remove the one-armed bandits and many of these organizations will become insolvent. I suspect that quite a few of you in this room belong to a particular Working Men's Club. Even a casual glance at its annual accounts will show you the extent to which it depends on the proceeds of its two one-armed bandits, which, as usual, have untrue notices on them relating to their pay-out.

The second sort of gambling which I think is of special interest is lotteries. Because the very recent lottery legislation was cobbled together in great haste, it has many deficiencies. Lotteries are now out of control all over the country. The Gaming Board, which is supposed to supervise or look *after* them, is overwhelmed with paper to *do* with them. Local Authorities, who also have a responsibility, pay no attention to them, apart from themselves running lotteries. Entrepreneurs have moved in in a formidable way, to the extent that they now not only promote lotteries all over the country, but also quite often determine, indirectly, the good causes for which lotteries are run. When one sees the scintillating operation of Mr Cyril Stein of Ladbrokes in this field, with his Cashcade lotteries, it makes one sad that this brilliant entrepreneur cannot be pointed in another direction of more value to the country, for example to the renaissance of Merseyside.

Apart from the entrepreneurs, there are, naturally, the bent boys. I know of one case where the so-called commission and running expenses of the lottery amounted to the staggering figure of 65% of the proceeds, leaving only 35% for the prizes *and* the good cause.

Then there is the rather interesting phenomenon of some lottery promoters requiring the printers of instant tickets to send separately from the others those tickets with winning numbers or symbols. I am sure you can guess the reason. If you are a friend of the promoter, there is no problem in these circumstances about your getting a winning ticket.

In the case of casinos the dangers of a gambling free-for-all were well understood by 1968; so that it is now very difficult for someone to open a new casino. The result is, of course, that those who *do* own casinos have a very lucrative franchise: so much so that I said to my son Jacob, who, unlike me, *is* a banker, that he was mad to go on banking and ought to try and buy a casino – if he was interested in profit.

So the legislator is on a tightrope. Everyone is said to agree, in this country at any rate, that free-for-all gambling is to be deprecated. But if the controls are too harsh, you drive gambling underground, with the usual consequences of criminal invasion. Alternatively, if you have rationing, the promoters are given a lucrative franchise.

Perhaps I have said enough to indicate that the promoters of gambling may not like our report which will be laid before Parliament fairly soon. The Commission will no doubt be said to be naive, muddled, amateurish, biased, puritanical, ambivalent, long-winded, incomprehensible and purveyors of inaccurate information. You may not always realize, when you hear these criticisms, that they will have mainly come, often by a circuitous route, from gambling promoters.

The trouble is, from the promoters' point of view, that for the first time in the history of this country there has been an investigation in depth into the finances of gambling, coupled with a particular concern to let the punter know what is probably going to happen to his flutter.

Someone was telling Hugh Cecil, Provost of Eton, a long story and said 'Am I boring you?', to which Hugh Cecil replied 'Not yet'. Let me hope I have reached that point and that the time has therefore come for me to propose the health of Her Majesty's Customs and Excise.

22

A CHILD'S GUIDE TO
BIOTECHNOLOGY

MANY PEOPLE ASK what the meaning is of the word biotechnology. Accordingly, I prepared what might be called a Child's Guide to Biotechnology, an account which assumes no scientific knowledge on the part of the reader. This account originally appeared in the *Financial Times* on 13th November 1981, in unreadably small typeface ($5\frac{1}{2}$/$6\frac{1}{2}$ pt.). With the help of Dr Sydney Brenner, FRS, it has therefore been updated.

First, the meaning of some words.

The cell. All living matter consists of cells most of which can reproduce themselves by dividing into two. They go on to divide many times more. Some living matter consists of a single cell, for example a bacterium, often called a germ or bug, though these words have a harmful connotation whereas many bacteria are harmless or positively beneficial.

Chemical reaction. An example of a chemical reaction is:
$$\text{hydrogen} + \text{oxygen} \rightarrow \text{hydrogen peroxide}$$
The arrow means produce. Hydrogen peroxide is a *molecule* which is something that consists of *atoms* such as hydrogen and oxygen. In the case of hydrogen peroxide two atoms of hydrogen combine with two atoms of oxygen – hence H_2O_2, the formula of the molecule of hydrogen peroxide.

Catalyst. Some chemical reactions proceed very slowly, hardly at all. But it may be possible to accelerate a reaction by means of a catalyst which therefore is a substance which accelerates a particular chemical reaction, without forming part of the products of that reaction. A catalyst might be a metal such as magnesium or platinum.

Enzyme. Enzymes are catalysts produced by living matter. They are very complicated molecules whereas catalysts not derived from living matter, as in the case of magnesium, may be quite simple.

Molecular genetics and molecular biology. Every cell continually engages in the chemical reactions required to maintain its life processes such as respiring, reproducing, excreting and producing special substances. The study of molecules engaged in these chemical reactions is biochemistry and the further study of how the ability to engage in these reactions is passed on to future generations is called *molecular genetics*, genetics referring to the inheritance, by future generations of cells, of the ability to do the same things as their parents, grandparents, etc. The whole subject (biochemistry and molecular genetics) is also called *molecular biology*.

DNA and genetic information. DNA is a complicated molecule which carries the information specifying the cell's chemical or biological processes. Like the cell in which it is contained, DNA is reproduced every time the cell divides.

The information in DNA is contained in the particular arrangements of the chemical units of which it is formed. It is like a tape in a teaching cassette to which the cell can 'listen' and carry out the instructions on the tape. Short lengths of DNA, which control and direct particular operations, are *genes*. Each gene specifies the structure of a particular protein, the molecule which signals the existence of life. All enzymes are proteins and many of the specialized functions and structures of different cells depend on different proteins.

As mentioned above, DNA reproduces itself, so when a cell divides, each daughter will contain an exact copy of the original genetic blueprint and will therefore have the capacity to perform the same chemical and biological tasks. However, higher organisms have different sorts of cells because different genes are 'switched on' – and off – in different cells.

Antibodies. These are special proteins found in higher animals. They recognize the shape of other molecules and form part of the animal's defence mechanisms by reacting to foreign invasion, for example by bacteria, and producing antibodies which recognize the invaders, clamp onto them and help to neutralize their harmful action. Each antibody is highly specific for its target and each animal has the capacity to make an enormous number of different antibodies.

Biotechnology is the application of biological processes to the production of a wide range of substances. It is a very old technology: fermentation for example, in which single cells are used to produce alcohol and many food products, goes back to the dawn of man's history. We have also learnt to use such cells to make chemicals like citric acid on an industrial scale, and antibiotics such as penicillin. They are also grown as sources of enzymes which are used in a wide variety of industrial processes.

In the last few years, scientists have developed new methods of modifying the genetic structure of cells. This promises a whole new biotechnology. Cells can be artificially joined together so that the new, fused cell acquires genes from both parents. This, for example, enables one to select just one line of antibody-producing cells from the many present in an animal, and achieve the production of single, specific antibodies from immortal lines of cells outside the body. These are *monoclonal antibodies* and provide a wide range of important diagnostic reagents. They may, in the future, be important in the treatment of human disease.

Even more powerful are the methods of 'gene splicing'. Scientists have discovered how to dissect DNA with micro-scissors – enzymes which in fact cut DNA molecules at specific places – and how to put the DNA together again in new and useful ways. This has made it possible to insert new genes into living cells. Gene splicing has been used to put genes which 'order' the production of human insulin, and interferon which attacks viruses, into bacteria and yeasts which can then produce these important human proteins in large amounts. Scientists can now also modify genes in a test tube and, incredible as it may seem, synthesize them by chemical methods: and then put them into cells. These are the beginnings of genetic engineering. In the future, it may be possible to create drought-resistant and disease-resistant plants and even, for example, make bacteria convert carbon dioxide into petrol.

It is impossible to predict the range and number of applications of biotechnology. Molecular biological research, on which it depends, is still in the phase of rapid development with a constant flow of new facts, ideas and methods. The new biotechnology, which feeds on molecular biology, may well have an impact on agriculture, waste disposal, food processing, industrial processes and medicine. Specific applications in these fields will develop from the mid-1980s onwards.

FIGURE 7
Gutle Rothschild

23

GUTLE, 1753–1849

GUTLE[6], the daughter of Baruch Schnapper[7], a Frankfurt tradesman, married the Rothschild, Mayer Amschel, whose five sons settled (and triumphed financially) in London[8], Paris, Vienna, Naples and Frankfurt. They held their mother in the deepest respect and visited her regularly. The street in which she lived in Frankfurt, the Judengasse, was so narrow that the coaches of the five brothers could not get into it, so they had to walk to number 148, where Gutle lived. In spite of repeated efforts by the five sons to persuade her to move to a larger and inevitably more luxurious house – inevitably because 148 Judengasse was humble in the extreme – Gutle refused to move. What was good enough for Mayer Amschel and his ancestors was good enough for her. Gutle was a formidable woman, obstinate, warm-hearted, pious, quick-witted and dominating. I believe that Golda Meir, Prime Minister of Israel, was very similar to her, in spite of being a world famous politician. Heine had this to say about her:

> The old Mother Rothschild could tell the Germans a thing or two about real patriotism. Look over there on the left, there's a small house – she lives there; she is called Laetitia, mother of so many financial wizards, the family of money lenders, and in spite of her sons' world famous reputations and wealth, she does not want to leave her tiny family stronghold in the Judengasse. Today she's decorated her window with white curtains to note this festival of joy. How lovely it is to see the tiny candelabra which she lights herself when celebrating a festival – especially on a day like today, the Festival of the Maccabees, when Judaea was freed from the tyranny of Antiochus Epiphanes by the Maccabees, our brothers – a heroic and brave feat matched by the deeds of Friedrich Wilhelm, Alexander and Franz II of our time.
>
> Whenever this dear old lady looks at the candelabra,

tears glisten in her eyes, as she remembers with melancholic delight all the times in her youth when Mayer Amschel celebrated the Festival of the Maccabees with her, when her sons were mere babies – when they put little candles on the floor, which shed lively shadows capturing the children's enthusiasm for the festival.

Gutle died on the 7th of May, 1849, aged two months less than ninety six. The Frankfurt Archives show that on the 9th of May of that year the City Treasurer of Frankfurt, Dr Burckard, visited 148 Judengasse and reported to the Frankfurt City Court II, as follows:

Estate of the deceased widow
Gutle Rothschild, née Schnapper,
regarding surviving children of age

    1 Mrs. Jeanette Worms, widow
    2 Amschel Meyer von Rothschild
    3 Salomon von Rothschild in Vienne
    4 Mrs. Betty, married to Sichel
    5 Mrs. Babette Beyfus, widow
    6 Carl von Rothschild in Naples
    7 Mrs. Henriette Montefiore in London
    8 James von Rothschild in Paris
    9 the children of a deceased son, Nathan Meyer von Rothschild in London
    10 the son of a deceased daughter, Mrs. Julie Beyfus in Paris

The estate is located in house No. 148 in the Judengasse, where the following items were sealed on the 9th May 1849 in the presence of the heirs named under 1, 4 and 5, then in the presence of Messrs. Leopold Goldschmidt, David Lipmann and Dr. Reinganum.

    a) an iron cash-box containing money.
    b) 1 suit case with a silver device.
    c) 1 pot containing all sorts of objects.
    d) 1 little chest of drawers and clothing.

e) 1 cupboard with fittings.
f) 1 cupboard with a silver device.

The keys were handed over into official custody together with the following household effects:

1 settee	1 screen
6 chairs	Various porcelain items
1 bedside table in glass	1 oval table
1 mirror	3 bedsteads and beds
1 chest of drawers	1 mirror
2 alabaster vases	1 settee
1 firescreen	3 arm-chairs

6 chairs
1 small table
1 mirror together with a small table
2 brown pendulum clocks
1 sofa
6 chairs
1 arm-chair
1 mirror

A will of the deceased is lodged with the Court. Real property does not form a part of the estate.

This gives the proper report required by law.

Frankfurt, 9 May 1849

The City Treasurer

Dr. Burckard

This is all we know about her.

FIGURE 8

The Shadow of a Great Man

24

THE SHADOW OF A
GREAT MAN

Introduction

THIS ESSAY is about Nathan Mayer Rothschild, who founded the English branch of our family. He was born in Frankfurt in 1777, emigrated to England at the age of 21 and died at the height of his powers when not yet 60. He is referred to throughout as NM.

Although so short a sketch must be a mere shadow of the great man, it does examine in detail one episode which clings like a burr to his reputation: how and when news of the Battle of Waterloo reached London, and to what extent NM may have taken advantage of it. Some attention is also paid to his financing of the Duke of Wellington's campaigns and of Britain's Allies: one of the many services he rendered his adopted country.

The task of tracing NM's financial career imposes unusual difficulties on the historian, whether amateur or otherwise. In the early nineteenth century, the care and classification of records seems to have been the exception rather than the rule. NM, moreover, was by temperament secretive. That remarkable memory which, during his reign at New Court in St Swithin's Lane, daily enabled him to recall every Stock Exchange transaction and its price also allowed him to dispense with much of the paper work of banking. It is true that some of the confidential correspondence he exchanged with his brothers has survived. But he would often write in Yiddish, using Hebrew letters and therefore from right to left; but even then, certain key words and phrases were put into a code which has been only partially broken.

It is thus under certain handicaps that a biographer of NM embarks on his labours. And always, ringing in his ears, is that daunting retort of his subject, who, when asked to what he owed his extraordinary success, replied 'To minding my own business.'[9]

What sort of man was he?

NM was short and fat, with blue eyes, reddish hair and a strong German accent. He was not interested in titles or high living, although he wished intensely to be accepted by the City of London. He could justly feel that he had arrived when he achieved one of his earliest ambitions in England: to dine in State with the Lord Mayor. We are fortunate to have an account of a more informal evening which he spent in 1834 at Ham House, home of the Tollemache family. A fellow guest, Sir Thomas Fowell Buston, wrote to his daughter on the following day[10]:

> We yesterday dined at Ham House to meet the Rothschilds; and very amusing it was. He (Rothschild) told us his life and adventures. He was the third son of the banker at Frankfort. 'There was not,' he said, 'room enough for us all in that city. I dealt in English goods. One great trader came there, who had the market to himself: he was quite the great man, and did us a favour if he sold us goods. Somehow I offended him, and he refused to shew me his patterns. This was on a Tuesday; I said to my father, "I will go to England." I could speak nothing but German. On the Thursday I started; the nearer I got to England, the cheaper goods were. As soon as I got to Manchester, I laid out all my money, things were so cheap; and I made good profit. I soon found that there were three profits – the raw material, the dyeing, and the manufacturing. I said to the manufacturer, "I will supply you with material and dye, and you supply me with manufactured goods." So I got three profits instead of one, and I could sell goods cheaper than anybody. In a short time I made my £20,000 into £60,000. My success all turned on one maxim. I said, I can do what another man can, and so I am a match for the man with the patterns, and for all the rest of them! Another advantage I had. I was an off-hand man. I made a bargain at once. When I was settled in London, the East India Company had £800,000 worth of gold to sell. I went to the sale, and bought it all. I knew the Duke of Wellington must have it. I had bought a great many of his bills at a discount. The Government sent for me, and said they

must have it. When they had got it, they did not know how to get it to Portugal. I undertook all that, and I sent it through France; and that was the best business I ever did.'

Another maxim, on which he seemed to place great reliance, was never to have anything to do with an unlucky place or an unlucky man. "I have seen," said he, "many clever men, very clever men, who had not shoes to their feet. I never act with them. Their advice sounds very well, but fate is against them; they cannot get on themselves; and if they cannot do good to themselves, how can they do good to me?" By aid of these maxims he has acquired three millions of money.

"I hope," said ——, "that your children are not too fond of money and business, to the exclusion of more important things. I am sure you would not wish that." Rothschild. – "I am sure I should wish that. I wish them to give mind, and soul, and heart, and body, and everything to business; that is the way to be happy. It requires a great deal of boldness, and a great deal of caution, to make a great fortune; and when you have got it, it requires ten times as much wit to keep it. If I were to listen to all the projects proposed to me, I should ruin myself very soon. Stick to one business, young man," said he to Edward; "stick to your brewery, and you may be the great brewer of London. Be a brewer, and a banker, and a merchant, and a manufacturer, and you will soon be in the Gazette. . . . One of my neighbours is a very ill-tempered man; he tries to vex me, and has built a great place for swine, close to my walk. So, when I go out, I hear first, grunt, grunt, squeak, squeak; but this does me no harm. I am always in good humour."

The daughters are very pleasing. The second son is a mighty hunter; and his father lets him buy any horses he likes. He lately applied to the Emperor of Morocco, for a first-rate Arab horse. The Emperor sent him a magnificent one, but he died as he landed in England. The poor youth said very feelingly "that was the greatest misfortune he ever had suffered"; and I felt strong sympathy with him. I forgot to say, that soon after M. Rothschild came to England,

Bonaparte invaded Germany; "The Prince of Hesse Cassel," said Rothschild, "gave my father his money; there was no time to be lost; he sent it to me. I had £600,000 arrive unexpectedly by the post; and I put it to such good use, that the prince made me a present of all his wine and his linen."

Proud as he was of his achievements and obsessed by his business enterprises, NM nevertheless had sufficient sense of humour to laugh at himself, and he sounds to have been a clubbable guest.

He was a devoted husband, too, who after the fashion of his time apostrophized his dearest Hannah in his Will:[11]

> All my Children Sons & Daughters are to treat her with true Love, kind affection and every possible respect which she deserves in the highest degree, having shared with me Joy and sorrow during so great a number of years as a fond, true and affectionate Wife.

Less formal testimony to their shared love is to be found in a letter from their daughter Louise to NM:[12] 'I suppose you are rather impatient to see Mama as you can scarcely be a day without her.' NM's lifelong regard for Hannah was all the more fervent in that he had not won her hand without a struggle. When first he proposed in 1806, her father, a rich London merchant, doubted whether NM was a man of enough substance to marry his daughter. The suitor replied that if Mr Cohen were in search of wealth and character, he could not do better than give him *all* his daughters in marriage.[13a]

Yet there was a more abrasive and even churlish side to his character, acquired during those early years when he was struggling to make his mark in a strange and sometimes hostile country. Even after he had established himself as a financial potentate both in England and on the Continent of Europe, he remained a master of the wounding phrase. Certainly he did not spare his brothers, three of whom were to follow his example in seeking their fortune outside Germany: Salomon in Vienna, Carl in Naples and James in Paris. His fourth brother, the pious Amschel, continued to live in Frankfurt. A somewhat sanctimonious letter of June 1814 from one of his brothers-in-law, Myer Davidson, who worked for the Rothschilds, reveals how much NM's sharp pen was resented: [14]

With God's help

Amsterdam 24th June 1814
Honoured Mr. Rothschild:

Two of your letters arrived today, even though only one post got here. You can easily imagine with how much impatience your brothers, especially dear Mr. Salman, may he live long, waited for your letters. Finally Cullen arrived here at 6 o'clock in the morning and handed your letter from the 17th of this month over to brother Salman, who was still in bed. Following this he came immediately downstairs. But he was so sad and depressed that I got frightened, so that I asked him why. To this he answered me: Read our letters from brother Nathan, which, instead of being commercial reports, contain nothing but rude insults, reproaches and troublemaking against our whole family. He showed me the letters and I have to confess sincerely, dear Mr. Rothschild, that I was embarrassed for your own brother when I found these serious insults in your letters. Really, you call your brothers nothing but idiots. This, my dear Mr. Rothschild, is in all sincerity unjust on your part. It also has a negative effect on the big transactions between the brothers. It makes your brothers completely confused and sad.

Now God gave you the good fortune to carry out large scale transactions, such as, I think, no Jew has ever done before. So you should be happy about it together with your brothers. Justice should be done to each of you for his work, so that one continues to work with pleasure and joy, instead of spending the whole day writing letters which cause only ill humour and nuisance. By now I really know your family relations a little bit closer and I know that you as well as your brothers like to work, even though you do not need to for bread, thank God, but you just do it out of enjoyment for the business, which does not recur every day.

The most unpleasant part for me in these sad letters is

that I cannot defend you at all. You write about Frankfurt, because a too low rate of exchange was accepted, without taking into consideration that your brother could not possibly dream then about the increase in the rate, which was as stable as a wall here for two months at 28/10.

As long as a house is like yours, and as long as you work together with your brothers, not a house in the world will be able to compete with you, to cause you harm or to take advantage of you, for together you can undertake and perform more than any other house in the world. But if such a family disintegrates, it makes a big difference – and through your correspondence it could, God forbid, come to it, that your brothers will feel too insulted.

I hope you will excuse me for giving you my opinion so freely. You know I always did it and, thank God, you never had reason to regret what I did for you. Especially though because of brother Salman, may he live long, who really does not deserve that you should write one bad word to him but should always be cheered up with good, agreeable and flattering letters.

That is what I really ask you to do.

Your most sincere servant.

M. Davidson

The brothers quarrelled intermittently throughout 1814. On the same day in June, Salomon wrote to NM:[15]

Your letters make me feel ill. It is impossible for me to send such letters to Frankfurt. I cannot for one moment believe that even if I were to be "the learned Nathan Rothschild" the other four brothers could be stupid schoolboys and that I would be the only wise one. Let us, however, forget all this. I do not wish to be upset any more and made more ill than I already am. To put it quite bluntly, we are neither drunk nor stupid. We have something that you in London obviously do not have – we keep our books in order and are therefore able to tell that I personally remitted to the "learned Nathan Rothschild" about £700,000. Until today I have only received back from my good learned Nathan Rothschild about £500,000. I can certainly tell from the cash situation that I advanced these considerable amounts to you. If my tears were black I would write a lot easier than with ink.

This was followed in August by a reproach from Amschel, who concluded:[16]

> Your brother who asks you not to lose your temper so quickly: we only lose business because you seem to get annoyed whenever payments have to be made over here.

Even NM's father, Mayer Amschel Rothschild, was not immune. He wrote to his clever but wilful son:[17] 'My dear Nathan, you must not be angry with your father.'

In NM's defence it must be said that some of his brothers were no less contentious. Both sides of these fraternal correspondences were peppered with insults, and NM was justly incensed when Amschel wrote of his 'dirty little speculations.'[18]

Business associates and strangers suffered no less severely from NM's brusqueness. The most famous episode concerns his reception of Prince Puckler Muskau (known at New Court as 'old pickles and mustard'), who was announced while NM was working on some papers. NM said curtly: 'Take a chair.' After a minute or two, the Prince said: 'I do not think you heard who I am. I am Prince Puckler Muskau.' NM raised his head from his papers. 'Well, well,' he said sardonically, 'take two chairs.'[19a]

Another unheralded visitor at New Court was Audubon, perhaps the greatest painter of birds there has ever been. He presented NM with an envelope containing his credentials. 'Is this a letter of business,' NM asked, 'or is it a mere letter of introduction?' After reading it, NM went on: 'This is only a letter of introduction, and I expect from its contents that you are the publisher of some book or other and need my subscription.' Audubon continued:[20]

> Had a man the size of a mountain spoken to me in that arrogant style in America I should have indignantly resented it; but where I then was it seemed best to swallow and digest it as well as I could. So in reply ... I said I should be honored by his subscription to the *Birds of America*. "Sir," he said, "I never sign my name to any subscription

list, but you may send in your work and I will pay for a copy
of it. Gentlemen, I am busy, I wish you good morning.''
We were busy men, too, and so bowing respectfully, we
retired, pretty well satisfied with the small slice of his
opulence which our labour was likely to obtain.

A few days afterwards I sent the first volume of my work
half bound, and all the numbers besides, then published.
On seeing them we were told that he ordered the bearer to
take them to his house, which was done directly. Number
after number was sent and delivered to the Baron, and after
eight or ten months my son made out his account and sent
it by Mr. Havell, my engraver, to his banking-house. The
baron looked at it with amazement, and cried out, ''What,
a hundred pounds for birds! Why, sir, I will give you five
pounds, and not a farthing more!'' Representations were
made to him of the magnificence and expense of the work,
and how pleased his Baroness and wealthy children would
be to have a copy; but the great financier was unrelenting.
The copy of the work was actually sent back to Mr. Havell's
shop, and as I found that instituting legal proceedings
against him would cost more than it would come to, I kept
the work, and afterwards sold it to a man with less money
but a nobler heart. What a distance there is between two
such men as Baron Rothschild of London and the merchant
of Savannah!

There is something odd about this story, because the following entry appears in the 'Catalogue of the books belonging to the
principal Library of Baron N. M. de Rothschild, London, 1835',
at New Court: 'Audubon's Birds of America 2 Vol. Text & 2 Vol.
Royal folio.' When did NM get them? If he thought them gro-
tesquely expensive when Audubon offered them to him, why
should he have changed his mind later when a bound set of the
Birds of America would have been even more expensive? Did
Audubon invent the story? Did NM ignorantly dislike books in
their original condition, partly unbound as these were? No one
will ever know and, needless to say, no one knows whether NM's
copy of Audubon's *Birds of America* still exists.

A more agreeable anecdote about a visitor to New Court concerns Louis Spohr, the composer, who arrived with a letter of introduction from Amschel. When Spohr asked NM whether he was interested in music, he answered by jingling a pocketful of sovereigns, saying, 'This is my music.'[19b]

If, as the story continues, NM asked Spohr to dine,[13b] we can be sure that the composer was treated to the best. Although NM himself liked soda water,[21] he bought only the finest wines for his guests. Among his known purchases were 13 dozen Chateau Margaux 1822,[22] for which he paid £5 a dozen: £14.70 a bottle in the currency of 1982. It was a family custom to keep a good cellar. NM's son Lionel in 1859 gave Macaulay a vintage 'beyond all praise', together with *Ortolans farcis à la Talleyrand*. Naturally it was not one of those occasions on which Macaulay, as he wrote, expected to be given 'pork in all its forms.'[23]

Very occasionally it was NM rather than the visitors to New Court who was disconcerted. Here is an account of two strangers who called on him:[24a]

> Rothschild greeted them with a slight inclination of the head which the visitors met with a profound bow, without any of them saying a single word. Instead of speaking they felt nervously in their pockets, as if to extract something. Rothschild became as pale as death. On that very morning he had received a number of threatening letters, and he thought that his visitors were assassins. His face was tense, and he swiftly seized a large book and flung it at the men. With desperate energy he laid hold of everything within reach and threw it at them, shouting for help at the top of his voice. His servants rushed in, and it was found that the visitors were small bankers who had been struck dumb in the presence of the great prince of finance. The feeling that they were actually face to face with Nathan Rothschild, on whom their fate depended, had so overcome them that they were not only unable to speak, but could not find the letter of introduction to him which they had in their pockets.

Was the astute NM ever worsted? One such story is too improbable to be believed, yet deserves a place in the apocrypha of family history:[24b]

At that time he lived some distance from the city, at Stamford Hill, where he had his offices. One day, late in the evening, a wealthy and well-known stockbroker named Lucas noticed that his carriage was waiting for him in front of the house. Lucas, who would very much like to find out Rothschild's plans, suspected something; he said to himself that there must be some serious reason for driving out at that late hour. He ordered his own carriage at once, and watched if Rothschild really left the house. After a time he saw Rothschild, accompanied by two friends, and heard him call to the coachman before he joined them in the carriage – "Drive to the City!"

Lucas had now no doubt that there was question of some business of importance. He jumped into his carriage and followed Rothschild who made at a gallop for New Court, his town residence. A few moments later Lucas, apparently drunk, staggered through the doorway, and, in spite of the protests of the servants, entered Rothschild's study, where he fell to the ground like a heavy sack. Rothschild and his friends, not a little disturbed by this unexpected visit, sprang upon the apparently unconscious man, lifted him on the couch, sprinkled him with cold water and perfume, and rubbed his limbs to bring the blood back to them. It was all in vain; and, as the conversation which had been interrupted by the appearance of Lucas was extremely important, and the quiet and regular breathing of the man seemed to show that he had fallen into a healthy sleep, they continued the discussion. It was a matter of great urgency, as important news had come from Spain and provided an opening for some good business, if they could buy up certain stock at once without attracting attention. They drew up a plan of campaign and went their various ways, intending to enter upon the business the following morning. They did not, of course, forget the sick man, and Rothschild told the servants to take him home as soon as he recovered.

There was no need to do this. As soon as Rothschild had gone Lucas left the house, in spite of the clamour of the servants, though he still seemed to be very weak, and his gait was uncertain and staggering. He had, of course, no idea of returning home; he hurried to his office, and made arrangements to snatch up the stock in question before Rothschild could get them. He completely succeeded, and made an enormous profit. It was the last time that Rothschild sprinkled Lucas's forehead with perfume.

So much for those anecdotes and legends which cluster round the memory of all great men. What of those hard-headed operations which raised him to a near-impregnable place in the financial world of his day? We can scarcely do better than begin with the informed and apparently authoritative memoir of NM which *The Times* printed on 3rd August 1836 after his death on 28th July of that year:

> The death of this gentleman, which was made known yesterday morning, is one of the most important events for the city, and perhaps for Europe, which has occurred for a very long time. His financial transactions have certainly pervaded the whole of the continent, and may be said for years past to have exercised more or less influence on money business of every description. No operations on an equally large scale have existed in Europe previous to his time, for they were not confined to his own capital and resources, which are well known to have been immense, but were carried on in conjunction with his brothers in Paris, Frankfort, Vienna, and Naples, all of whom possess colossal fortunes of their own. Besides this essential co-operation, he had agencies in almost every city either in the old or the new world, all of which, under his directions, conducted extensive business of various kinds. He had also, as well as his brothers, hosts of minor dependent capitalists, who participated in his loans and other extensive public engagements, who placed implicit confidence in the family, and were ready at all times to embark with them in any operation that was proposed. Nothing, therefore, was too great or extended, provided the project was a reasonable one for him to undertake. Within the last fifteen years, the period during which his character for sagacity may be said to have been fully established, there

has been, in fact, no limit to his means, taking the indirect as well as the direct means into account. All the brothers of Mr. Rothschild are men of great capacity and knowledge of business, but it is generally admitted that they deferred to his judgment in all their undertakings, and that he was the moving principle of the great mass of capital they represented. Mr. Rothschild may be said to have been the first introducer of foreign loans into this country; for, though such securities did at all times circulate here, the payment of the dividends abroad, which was the universal practice before his time, made them too inconvenient an investment for the great majority of persons of property to deal with. He not only formed arrangements for the payment of the dividends on his foreign loans in London, but made them still more attractive by fixing the rate in sterling money, and doing away with all the effects of fluctuation in exchanges. All these operations were attended with a most remarkable degree of good fortune; for though many of the countries which made loan contracts in this country became bankrupt, not one of those with whom Mr. Rothschild entered into contracts ever failed in their engagements. For this he was indebted occasionally as much to his own good management afterwards as for his judgment in the original selection. If the dividends were not ready at the time appointed, which was the case in some few instances, his resources always enabled him to make the requisite advances, while his influence and perseverance afterwards uniformly enabled him to recover the money which had been advanced. Whatever may be said, therefore, of the ruinous effect of foreign loans cannot with any justice be charged on Mr. Rothschild; on the contrary, they have proved to be the source of great national profit, as nearly all the stocks of the continental Powers originally created here have passed over for investment into the countries for which they were raised at an advance of 20 or 30%, or more, on the contract price. Besides his loan contracts, Mr. Rothschild was a purchaser and a large dealer in the pre-existing European Government securities. Stock of any description, however unmarketable elsewhere, could always be bought or sold at his counting-house, and at fair prices. Besides his contracts with foreign Governments for loans in money, he entered into numerous others, for conversion into stocks, bearing a lower rate of interest, and had various projects for further reduction under consideration at the time of his death, which he probably was alone able to carry through, and which will therefore fall with him.

Mr. Rothschild's loan contracts were not uniformly successful in the first instance. He was exposed to several very severe reverses, which would have proved fatal to houses of inferior means. One of these was Lord Bexley's loan or funding of Exchequer-bills in a $3\frac{1}{4}\%$ stock, the first of that denomination introduced into the English market, and by which alone he is said to have lost 500,000. At the time of the Spanish invasion by France, in 1823, he was largely engaged in the French loans of that period, by which he was placed in great jeopardy, but his resources enabling him to hold the stock, he came off ultimately without loss. The same cause shook violently the contracts with other European States then in progress in this market, and the stock of Naples in particular underwent so severe a depression that most of the subscribers, after the deposit, refused to go on with the instalments. The London house was left, in consequence, to bear the whole weight of that contract. Another event by which he was exposed to great danger was the project of M. de Villele for the conversion of the Rentes. Fortunately for him, the measure was lost by a single vote in the Chamber of Peers; but had it been carried, the convulsion in the money-markets of Europe which shortly followed it would probably have proved fatal to him with such a burden on his shoulders, notwithstanding all his vast resources. Indeed, it was a common remark of his own at the time, that neither he nor the houses engaged in the undertaking with him could have stood the shock. Another most perilous contract for Mr. Rothschild was the 4% French loan made with M. de Polignac, just previous to the 'three days', and which fell afterwards 20 or 30% or more. In fact, the stock was for some time in such bad odour, that no purchasers could be found for it. This contract was more detrimental in proportion to his subscribers than to himself, as the greater part of it was distributed among them, and it was at the time a matter of severe reproach against him that he did on this occasion leave his friends completely in the lurch. But this was answered by the remark that he had always been in the practice of dealing liberally with his subscribers in sharing his contracts among them, and that the revolution which followed and made this so ruinous an operation was one that could not possibly have been foreseen by him. Since that period he has been in a constant course of successful operations, with the exception perhaps of that in Portuguese stock, which, however, was to him of very small amount and consideration.

Mr. Rothschild's great success in loan operations made it a matter almost of rivalry with all those States who wanted to borrow money to obtain his co-operation. He uniformly refused, however, to enter into any such contracts for Spain, or the American States, previously the colonies of Spain. He contrived literally to steer clear of all the bad bargains which were made during the 15 years, which may be called the zenith of his career as a banker and a financial merchant.

Mr. Rothschild also avoided with great care the numerous joint-stock companies which had their rise and fall in his time. He might be said, however, to take the lead in their formation, by the introduction of the Alliance Insurance Co. which took place in 1824, just before the general mania, and which was peculiarly successful; but, with that exception, we are not aware of any in which he has been directly engaged.

Mr. Rothschild's operations in bullion and foreign exchanges have been on a scale probably little inferior to his loan contracts, and, devolving wholly upon himself and the family circle of his transactions of a similar kind, have formed, we suspect, a still more important feature in his general scale of profits. They continued at all times and under all circumstances, and were subject to none of those reverses which occurred in his foreign loan contracts. His management of the business in exchanges was one of the most remarkable parts of his character. He never hesitated for a moment in fixing the rate, either as a drawer or a taker, on any part of the world, and his memory was so retentive, that, notwithstanding the immense transactions into which he entered in every foreign post day and that he never took a note of them, he could dictate the whole on his return home with perfect exactness to his clerks. His liberality of dealing was another conspicuous feature of these operations, and many merchants whose bills were objected to elsewhere found ready assistance from him, and his judgment was proved by the very small amount of loss which he incurred in consequence of such liberality. To this class at any other time his death might have been productive of considerable embarrassment, but as trade is prosperous, and the state of credit good, little inconvenience is anticipated. This is under the supposition, too, that the business would now cease, but, though no arrangements can of course be yet made, it seems to be expected that it will be continued under the management of his sons, who have been for some time attached to the house, and have acquired, notwithstanding their immense prospects in point of wealth, the habits of the best trained commercial men. . . .

The rise of Mr. Rothschild's fortune is all within the present century, and it did not make any decided progress till some time after it had commenced. It was not until the breaking out of the war in Spain, in 1808, that his extraordinary means, which were displayed in making the remittances for the English army in that country, were developed to any extent, so as to be known to the mercantile world in general. He came to England in 1800, where he acted as agent for his father in the purchase of Manchester goods for the Continent. Shortly afterwards, through the agency of his father, for the Elector of Hesse Cassel, and other German Princes, he had large sums placed at his disposal, which he employed with extraordinary judgment, and his means went on at a rapid rate of accumulation. His youngest brother, James, then coming to reside in Paris, Mr. Rothschild was induced to fix himself permanently in London, where he has ever since remained. He was one of ten children, eight of whom survive him – four brothers, two older and two younger than himself, and four sisters.

Financing the war against Napoleon

As the author of that perceptive obituary notice remarks, it was the outbreak of war in Spain which in 1808 first brought the financial genius of NM to the notice of the mercantile world. It is from this point that we may take up the narrative of his operations.

Between 1793 and 1815, Britain was almost continuously at war with France. During the early years of the conflict with Napoleon, the emphasis of British policy was on ruling the waves and capturing French colonies such as French Guiana, Martinique, Guadeloupe, Senegal, Mauritius and Réunion: what Sheridan called 'filching sugar islands'.[25] But once Britain had decided to mount a major offensive on the Continent of Europe while simultaneously subsidizing Austria, Prussia and Russia, the burden on her Exchequer escalated enormously. In fact the greater part of the vast sums which it cost to defeat Napoleon were incurred between 1808 and 1815.

Throughout the Peninsular War, the Duke of Wellington was haunted by the fear that there would not be ready money enough with which to pay his troops. Officers were obliged to accept at least part payment in devalued paper money, with a purchasing power often one quarter less than its face value. The other ranks, however, insisted on being paid in gold or silver coins. Unless they received such specie they would not fight; or if they did fight, they would make good their loss by looting. By the end of 1813 Wellington had pursued the French armies to the Pyrenees. Whether he could carry the war across the mountains into France depended on hard cash. The outlook was sombre. Specie was obtainable only on impossibly unfavourable terms and the Government had to pay through the nose for the little it could get from such distant sources as China and India. By August 1812,

Wellington needed £100,000 each month, in addition to what could be raised locally. Three months later his armies faced paralysis. On 21st November he wrote to Lord Bathurst, Secretary for the War Department: [26a]

St. Jean de Luz, 21st Nov., 1813

My Lord,

I am concerned to be obliged to draw your Lordship's attention again to the want of money with this army. The paymasters of the regiments have received the balances due on the regimental estimates only to the 24th of May; and, in the course of three days, the arrear will have grown to one for six months; and in the ordinary course of the service, the balance of the estimates to the 24th of December ought, in a few days, to be in the course of payment, making a seventh month. I cannot say, however, that the British troops are yet in any distress. Owing to the circumstances detailed in my dispatch of the 2nd instant, the officers commanding companies have still money in their hands to make the daily payments to the 3rd or 4th of next month; but unless your Lordship should have sent out money, we shall have none after that period.

The amount of money now received at Lisbon for bills is but small, and has lately only served to pay the Portuguese subsidy, which I have promised shall, from the month of December inclusive forward, be paid in this part of the country. It is most convenient to the Portuguese Government that it should be so, and equally convenient to our departments.

I beg leave to remind your Lordship, however, of the necessity that there should be ships of war at Lisbon, to convey the treasure, raised in that city by bills upon the Treasury for the army, to the north coast of Spain.

While writing upon this subject, I must mention that the soldiers' great coats were still at Oporto on the 7th instant, embarked, and waiting for convoy; although it is most desirable that at this season they should have them.

The money raised at Cadiz by bills upon the Treasury has, within these last six months, done no more than defray the expenses there, and pay the Spanish subsidy. I am apprehensive, indeed, that the produce of the bills has lately much diminished, as a sum of three hundred thousand dollars, which I had requested early in September His Majesty's Minister at Cadiz to send round by the 1st of November, for the use of the Spanish troops in this quarter, has not yet arrived; neither has any money been lately procured from Gibraltar. From this statement your Lordship will see that, unless this army should be assisted with a very large sum of money at a very early period, the distress felt by all the troops will be most severe; and that, however desirable that I should continue in operation, and however favorable the circumstances of the moment and the season, it will be quite impossible for me to do any thing.

> I have the honor to be, &c.
> Wellington.

Wellington wrote to Lord Bathurst again, on the same day:[26b]

I must tell your Lordship, however, that our success, and every thing, depends upon our moderation and justice, and upon the good conduct and discipline of our troops. Hitherto these have behaved well, and there appears a new spirit among the officers, which I hope will continue, to keep the troops in order. But I despair of the Spaniards. They are in so miserable a state, that it is really hardly fair to expect that they will refrain from plundering a beautiful country, into which they enter as conquerors; particularly, adverting to the miseries which their own country has suffered from its invaders. I cannot, therefore, venture to bring them back into France, unless I can feed and pay them; and the official letter which will go to your Lordship by this post will show you the state of our finances, and our prospects. If I could now bring forward 20,000 good Spaniards, paid and fed, I should have Bayonne. If I could bring forward 40,000, I do not know where I should stop. Now I have both the 20,000 and the 40,000 at my command, upon this frontier, but I cannot venture to bring forward any for want of means of paying and supporting them.

Without pay and food, they must plunder; and if they plunder, they will ruin us all.

I think I can make an arrangement of the subsidy to cover the expense of 20,000 Spaniards; but all these arrangements are easily settled, if we could get the money. Where we are to get the money, excepting from England, it is impossible for me to devise; as the patriotic gentlemen at Lisbon, now that they can buy no Commissariat debts, will give us no money, or very little, for the draughts on the Treasury, and the yellow fever has put a stop to the communication with Cadiz and Gibraltar; and if we had millions at all three, we could not get a shilling for want of ships to bring it.

On 21st December 1813 Wellington once more wrote to Lord Bathurst:[26c]

Your Lordship is also acquainted with the state of our financial resources. We are overwhelmed with debts, and I can scarcely stir out of my house on account of the public creditors waiting to demand payment of what is due to them. Some of the muleteers are 26 months in arrears; and only yesterday I was obliged to give them bills upon the Treasury for a part of their demands, or lose their services; which bills they will, I know, sell at a depreciated rate of exchange to the sharks who are waiting at Pasages, and in this town, to take advantage of the public distresses. I have reason to suspect that they became thus clamorous at the instigation of British merchants.

Then, in February 1814 there came a remarkable change which prompted Wellington to write on 22nd February to Lord Bathurst from the South of France:[26d]

I am obliged to Your Lordship for the supplies of money which are very ample.

What had caused this sudden improvement in the financial fortunes of Wellington's Army? It sprang from the confidence established between J. C. Herries and NM. Three years earlier, on the recommendation of Wellington, Herries had been appointed the Government's Commissary in Chief, responsible for the pay of the Army in an acceptable form[27], as well as for horses, equipment and food. Towards the end of 1813 he conceived the plan which revolutionized the supply of specie to the Army and which prompted Wellington's letter of 20th February 1814; it was secretly to entrust the business to NM, lock, stock and barrel, with the proviso that he should keep the Commissary in Chief continuously informed of what he was doing. A letter from the Chancellor of the Exchequer, Vansittart, to Herries, dated 11th January 1814, illustrates the free hand which the Government was prepared to give NM, in spite of his having no official position.[28]

It being of the utmost importance to the public Service at the present moment that the commander of His Majesty's forces in the South of France should speedily be supplied with a larger sum in specie, applicable to his expenditure in that country, than it has been found practicable to procure through the Bank of England or any other usual channel. It has been judged expedient by Lord Liverpool and myself, upon consideration of your report to me of the substance of the conferences, which you have had with Mr. Rothschild, to authorize you to employ that gentleman in the most secret and confidential manner to collect in Germany, France and Holland the largest quantity of French gold and silver coins, not exceeding in value six hundred thousand pounds sterling, which he may be able to procure within two months from the present time. We are aware, however, that Mr. Rothschild cannot be expected precisely to estimate the sums which his different agents may be able to procure in various and distant places and that it may therefore be reasonable not to consider the sum I have mentioned as the strict limit of his commission, but you will express to him our expectation that he will endeavour to confine himself as nearly as possible to that amount.

In furtherance of this object, I am to desire that you would give Mr. Rothschild such information and instructions as may be necessary to ensure the most speedy delivery by his agents of such money as may be thus collected, on board ships of war, which will be stationed at Helvoetshuys for the purpose of receiving it, the amount of which is to be paid by you to Mr. Rothschild in this country upon producing to you the invoices and proper certificates of the delivery on board His Majesty's ships. In order, however, to prevent the publicity and other inconveniences which might attend a minute examination of the packages in the first instance, you will be satisfied with certificates which the commander of His Majesty's ships will be directed to furnish of the metal and weight of specie which they contain, reserving 5% upon the amounts of the invoices, as a balance, in order to secure the public from loss by any deficiencies which may be discovered when the specie shall come to be counted by the officer of the Commissariat, to whom it may be delivered in France and you will take care that it will be distinctly understood by Mr. Rothschild, not only that he is to take upon himself all risks and losses, which may occur, prior to the delivery on board His Majesty's ships, but that he will be held responsible for any deficiencies which may be discovered upon the final delivery and inspection of the packages to the consignee, unless reasonable suspicion shall exist of their having been opened and fractured subsequently to their reception into the custody of the officers, employed to convey them to France.

Upon consideration of the magnitude of the object in view of the dispatch and secrecy which it requires and of the risks which may be incurred, it is not thought unreasonable to allow Mr. Rothschild a commission of 2% with all charges necessarily incurred on the sums actually delivered, and in case of his requiring money to enable him to commence his operations, you will be at liberty to advance him such a sum as may be found necessary, upon his depositing with you Government securities to the same extent. You will apply to the Treasury for this and the further sums, which will be necessary in the progress of the business, without specifying the particular service, but in general terms for the purchase of specie.

It is felt that the details of the service may be safely confided to your experience and direction, but if you should find further instructions necessary upon any material points, you will communicate confidentially with me, taking care to keep me fully informed of the actual state of the transaction throughout the whole of its progress.

On the very same day Herries wrote to NM:[29]

In the event of your experiencing any molestation or impediment from the civil or military authorities in those parts of the Continent in alliance with Great Britain where you may be purchasing and transferring specie under the directions which I have given to you you will be at liberty to produce this letter as a testimony that you are employed on account of the British Government.

NM, particularly with James in Paris, but also in concert with his other brothers at key points in Europe, was able on the one hand to buy up Wellington's Bills of Exchange (Annex 1) at a huge discount, get them smuggled back to England and cashed at the Bank of England; and on the other hand, to send gold profitably to Wellington *via* James. Simultaneously, the other brothers, at NM's behest, were buying all the gold they could lay their hands on throughout the world, with the certain knowledge that it would end up in the pockets of Wellington's troops or those of the Allies.

It seems likely that NM started to work unofficially for Herries before 1814; but apart from the correspondence quoted above, the earliest hard evidence, signed by NM, dates from 4th April 1815. Some of the entries in NM's accounts, those for part of July, August, September and October, are given in Table 4 (pp. 224–5). NM's total account with Herries for the year 1815 amounted to £9,789,778.15.10.

As gold then cost about £5 per ounce this was equivalent to some £390 million in 1982 (silver dollars being excluded from the account). The maximum amount of gold sold to Herries on any one day was on 22nd April 1815 and was worth £79,879.2.9. That is equivalent to about £3 million of gold in 1982.

For all his patriotism, NM saw no reason why he should cease to be a man of business. He wrote to the Treasury on 11th November 1817:[30]

My Lords,

About a year ago I had the Honour to receive from the Commissary in Chief, the Commission to invest in our Funds, the Monies arising from the French contributions; and I accordingly purchased at various times, Consols, and Reduced to the Amount of about Six Hundred and fifty Thousand Pounds, the whole at an average price of less than 62 per ct.

Within the last month I have sold about Four Hundred and Thirty Thousand Pounds of this Stock, at an average price of about 82 3/4 per cent., leaving, at this rate, a Net profit of upwards of 20 per ct., or about One Hundred and Thirty Thousand Pounds upon the purchase [see Annex 2].

For these operations, so advantageous to His Majesty's Government, I have declined making any charge whatever, either in the shape of Remuneration to myself or for discounts & other expenses, incident to the heavy Bill Transactions to which these operations have given occasion, leaving it entirely to your Lordships' consideration to award whatever you may deem an Equivalent, for my exertions in the prosecutions of this Business.

I shall therefore merely take the liberty to add, that with whatever Arrangement your Lordships may be pleased to make, I shall readily acquiesce, and have the honour to be &c.,

N. M. Rothschild

No more delicately phrased request can ever have reached that least romantic of institutions.

NM at Waterloo?

If NM's name continues to be associated with the Battle of Waterloo, it is not because of the financial acumen with which he laid the foundations of Wellington's most notable triumph. Unhappily he has become the subject of a myth which falsely accuses him of having used his early knowledge of victory to speculate on the Stock Exchange and so pocket a vast sum almost by fraud. It is, as I shall hope to show, a malicious slander.

The legend was invented by the antisemitic French journalist Georges Marie Mathieu-Dairnvaell, who wrote under the pseudonym 'Satan'. His account of NM having been in person at the Battle of Waterloo was brief:

> Nathan Rothschild était en Belgique les yeux fixés sur Waterloo. Il avait d'avance organisé des relais jusqu'à Ostende; lorsqu'il vit tomber foudroyée cette garde impériale qui mourait et ne se rendait pas, il partit lui-même à francétrier. Arrivé à Ostende, il voit mugir la tempête, les marins déclaraient la traversée impossible; mais est-il quelque chose d'impossible à la cupidité? A force d'or Rothschild détermina quelques hommes à partir avec lui dans une barque, comme César: Meinherr Nathan risquait sa fortune. Le succès couronna son audace: il arriva à Londres, 24 heures avant l'arrivée des nouvelles; il gagna d'un seul coup vingt millions, tandis que ses autres frères le secondant, le bénéfice total fait dans cette fatale année s'éleva à 135 MILLIONS!

Dairnvaell had earlier approached NM's brother, James, in Paris and told him that unless he was paid a certain but now unknown sum of money, he would publish the story about NM, together with other equally derogatory and untrue tales about James himself. James refused to be blackmailed, with the result that in 1846 Dairnvaell published a pamphlet entitled 'Histoire édifiante et curieuse de Rothschild Ier, Roi des Juifs' (p. 129) containing libels about both brothers. It is possible that Dairnvaell was also the author of a second pamphlet called 'Première réponse officielle de M^r. le Baron James Rothschild',[31] published in the same year; it presented an unconvincing defence of the two brothers that was in fact a forgery and totally fictitious.

The next account of NM's supposed presence at the Battle of Waterloo, so far as I am aware, was in Hebrew. It appeared in a journal called *Magid* ('The Narrator') issued on 6th April 1868. *Magid* was published in Lyck, East Prussia, and edited by someone called David Gordon, of Polish origin. Here is a translation:

> On the 18th of July [sic] 1815, Nathan rode on an Indian horse at the side of the hero Wellington, commander

HISTOIRE ÉDIFIANTE ET CURIEUSE]

DE

ROTHSCHILD Ier,

Roi des Juifs,

[PAR

SATAN,

Prix : 30 centimes.

PARIS.

CHEZ L'ÉDITEUR, RUE COLBERT-VIVI   NE, 4.

Et chez tous les Libraires.

—

1846.

—

Anti-semitic pamphlet, 1846

129

of the English armed forces which encamped that day in
the village of Waterloo. Nathan continually enquired as
to the results of the fierce battle that was in full force on
that day. Throughout the battle, Nathan was astride his
horse near the Hougoumont Palace whence the commander of the English army led his forces in battle against
Napoleon. The prince of finance observed the battle as
attentively as did the commander, with all its changing
trends of victory and defeat. Several times he saw the
French army advance strongly, only to be beaten back.
Towards evening the condition of the English army was
very bad. Napoleon had the upper hand. His tired and
weary enemies began to retreat. Suddenly, news reached
the English camp that the Prussian army, commanded by
the hero Blucher, was approaching, to renew the battle
against Napoleon. This news infused new life into the
English camp. At sunset, Wellington and Blucher met on
the peak of [La] Belle Alliance. Nathan now had no doubt
that the end was near for Napoleon. He quickly mounted
his horse and rode through the night to Ostend. When he
arrived the seas were very stormy. He could not find anyone willing to take him across to Dover. In vain did he offer
500 francs; no boat-owner was willing to risk his life on the
stormy seas. At last, he found a seaman who transported
him for the sum of 2,000 francs. The moon had not yet
risen when Nathan reached Dover that night. From there
he hurried to London before dawn. That day, he came to
the Stock Exchange where word went out that the English
armies had suffered a heavy defeat on the evening of 18th
June. The last minute help of the Prussians was not
revealed to anyone in the city, nor to Ministers of the
Crown. Only Nathan Rothschild knew of this, and kept
the secret. Following the rumours of the defeat of England,
the value of England's currency and securities declined
sharply. There were no purchasers. Only Nathan told his
close associates and representatives to buy as much as they
could throughout that day. That night the true results of
the battle, the victory of England, were conveyed by the
commander to the Government. At once the value of

English currency and securities rose greatly, and Nathan
made a profit of many millions of English pounds.

Within a few years, a far more polished version of the myth
was published in England. Its author, John Reeves, drew lavishly
on Dairnvaell, on an article about the Rothschilds in the 'Gentleman's Magazine' of November 1871[19a] and on his own highly
developed imagination:[13c]

> In connection with Waterloo an interesting little
> romance [see Annex 3] has been written upon the immense
> sum Nathan Mayer gained by his early knowledge of the
> victory of the Allies, which his financial strategy enabled
> him to use to the fullest advantage on the Stock Exchange.
> Many of his large speculations had been based on the
> presumed success of the English arms, and he was perhaps
> congratulating himself on his shrewd foresight and the
> soundness of his calculations when the sudden and treacher-
> ous return of Napoleon from Elba shattered at once his
> golden dreams and renewed all his previous anxiety and
> fears. No man, indeed, had greater cause to tremble at the
> reappearance of the mighty despot than had Nathan
> Mayer; when the fruits of his victory seemed almost within
> his grasp, they were at a blow removed, and he was left
> surrounded with doubts and contingencies. In the midst
> of its rejoicings, the whole of Europe was startled with
> alarm and dismay.
> That the deposed Emperor should ever return to
> harass and devastate Europe, had never occurred to men's
> minds; it was a possibility of which no one had ever
> thought. The public alarm was only increased as the news
> of the glad welcome Napoleon received on his way to Paris
> became known. So upset was Nathan Mayer by the news,
> and so intense became his anxiety to learn how matters
> progressed and were likely to end, that it would not allow
> him to rest satisfied with the speed of his couriers, but
> drove him to go himself to the Continent to watch the
> course of events with his own eyes. He accordingly pro-
> ceeded to Belgium and followed close in the wake of the
> English army. When at length the Duke took up his

position at Waterloo, and quietly awaited the French forces, Nathan Mayer felt that the critical moment on which hung the fortunes, not of Europe alone, but of the Rothschilds also, had arrived. He had such an immense stake dependent upon the issue, that his feverish anxiety would not allow him to remain in the background. He proceeded to the battlefield and took up a position commanding a view of both armies. We can imagine how eagerly he scanned the field, and noted the disposition and strength of the opposing forces. Those under the command of the Iron Duke must, we should fancy, have struck him as being outmatched and standing but a poor chance with the French army, which included the famous and hitherto invincible Old Guard. Turning to the distinguished personages around him, among whom were to be seen Count Pozzo di Borgo, Baron Vincent, General Alava, Baron Muffling, and others of equal note, Nathan Mayer questioned eagerly and wistfully all who cared to give him a hearing. The answers he received were discouraging and but increased his fears, for all were too well aware that the struggle between two such remarkable commanders would be long and stubborn. Though hoping for victory, none felt confident enough to predict such a result. The battle began. A dense smoke from the furious cannonade, soon enveloped the whole field in a cloud; but Nathan Mayer's straining eyes were able from time to time to see the fierce charges of the French cavalry, by which the safety of the English lines was more than once imperilled. Cold steel, however, conquered, and the assailants recoiled before the bristling hedge of bayonets. And so the battle grew and waxed fiercer as the day progressed. On the opposite hill of Rossomme, Napoleon was seated with a map outstretched before him, and from there he issued the orders for a last and desperate charge, on which all his hopes of victory were placed. The Old Guard, with the gallant Ney at their head, rushed forward to retrieve the fortunes of the day; but in vain. They had met their masters. They were driven back by the British bayonets, and were soon to be seen making their way from the battlefield in the greatest confusion and disorder. With a ringing cheer that told which side had won, the English forces rushed after their foes, whilst Nathan Mayer, his anxiety allayed and his spirits restored, spurred his horse back towards Brussels. It was dusk as he quitted the field, and his solitary ride in the darkness must have been intensely exciting to his already highly taxed brain. It was a ride he cannot readily have forgotten. Having reached Brussels, he procured, after some difficulty, a carriage to convey him without delay, and at all speed, to Ostend, where he arrived, travel-stained and weary, on the morning of the 19th June. Tired as he was, he would not stay to rest. In spite of the tempestuous sea, and the threatening weather, he wished to make his way across the Channel, but even the fishermen shrank from the attempt. In vain he offered bribes of five hundred, six hundred, eight hundred francs to the poor fellows; they would not venture. It was not until the offer reached two thousand francs that one of them consented to brave the tempest, and endeavour to take Nathan Mayer across to England, on condition that the money was paid to his wife before starting.

They set sail, and before they had gone far the threatening weather changed for the better, whilst a favourable breeze sprang up and considerably accelerated their passage. In the evening they sighted Dover and shortly after Nathan Mayer dragged his weary limbs ashore. Even here he would not rest, but, after procuring the swiftest post-horses to be had, resumed his journey to London. The next day he was to be seen leaning against his well-known pillar on the Stock Exchange, apparently broken in health and spirits, and looking as if he had been overwhelmed and crushed by some direful calamity. The greatest gloom and despondency had for days prevailed in the City, and as men looked at Rothschild, and then significantly at each other, they seemed to come unanimously to the conclusion that their hopes had been blasted, and that the worst was yet to be known. Had not Rothschild travelled post-haste from the Continent, and were not his agents selling out? The Stock Exchange, generally so full of life and noise, was unusually silent; speculators moved about in a listless, aimless way, now and then stopping to discuss in low whispers the cause of the great financier's sales. The gloom and despondency was not lessened when a rumour became current that Rothschild had told a friend in confidence that Blucher with his 117,000 Prussians had been defeated on the 16th and 17th June at Ligny, and that Wellington could not hope with his handful of soldiers to arrest the progress of Napoleon's victorious and far larger forces. The evil news spread through the City like wildfire. The Funds dropped rapidly, and the greatest uneasiness and despondency prevailed. The change was so violent and so sudden. It seemed as if it were but yesterday that Europe had been exulting over the discomfiture of Buonaparte and the restoration of peace. The public thanksgiving, the grand reviews, the public rejoicing, the fireworks, had hardly yet finished, and now, – the whole was in vain, – the scourge of Europe was loose again. And so the day closed, with not a ray of hope to brighten the all-pervading gloom. But the next afternoon a sudden, wild reaction set in. It was everywhere reported, with sparkling eyes and heightened colour in men's cheeks, that Wellington was victorious, and the French defeated. Nathan Mayer had himself been the first to announce the good news with undisguised delight and satisfaction to his friends on the Stock Exchange. When the glad tidings received official confirmation some hours later the public joy knew no limits. The Funds rose again at a bound. Many pitied Rothschild for the enormous losses he had, as they thought, suffered; they little suspected that, while his known agents had been selling openly, his unknown agents had bought up secretly every piece of scrip they could secure. Far from losing, he had by his manipulations pocketed nearly a million sterling.

Is there any reliable evidence to support this highly dramatized tale? None whatsoever: it is a work of sheer fantasy. There is not the remotest possibility of NM having been present at

Waterloo. The battle took place on 18th June 1815, near Brussels. Yet in the 1815 Letter Book at New Court there is a copy of a letter, alas severely mutilated, written by NM from London between 16th and 20th June. We also know that on 20th June, NM was in London, writing to his brother Carl in Amsterdam.[32] His alibi is complete.

In only two respects does the narrative of John Reeves contain a kernel of truth: that NM was in possession of the news from Waterloo before it was known officially in London – and that he made good use of it. The Duke of Wellington entrusted his victory despatch to Major the Hon. Henry Percy, who delivered it to Lord Bathurst, the Secretary of State for the War Department, at 11 p.m. on 21st June. So exhausted was he from his arduous journey that he fell asleep while being questioned by the Chancellor of the Exchequer, who was dining that night with Bathurst (or perhaps Lord Harrowby)[33] to await the despatch. (On the following day Percy's dedication to duty was recognized by promotion to the rank of lieutenant-colonel.) Yet swift as he had travelled, someone had reached London before him with the news. How do we know? Because five weeks later, on 27th July, a Rothschild employee called John Roworth wrote to NM from Paris:[34]

> I am informed by Commissary White you have done well by the early information which you had of the victory gaind [sic] at Waterloo.

That tantalizingly sparse sentence remains uncorroborated, and all the subsequent sagas about NM and Waterloo rest on hearsay and speculation. What precisely happened between Brussels and London during those June days of 1815 remains an enigma. Yet at least we can apply certain tests of probability to the many conflicting accounts of how the news of Waterloo reached New Court.

There are only two possibilities: pigeon post or a personal courier. It is well known that NM used carrier pigeons to obtain early intelligence of events on the Continent of Europe, and that he took a personal interest in their performance. There is no evidence that they were kept at New Court, but NM did pay £8,750[35] for the purchase of Burmarsh Farm, near Hythe, in

Kent and this may have been their base. Some slight support for this theory is to be found, as we shall see, in *The Times* of 3rd August 1836. The newspaper reported that the first intimation in England of NM's death in Frankfurt was when a pigeon shot down in Kent was found to have attached to its leg a roll of paper inscribed with the words: 'Il est mort'.

That the Rothschilds used carrier pigeons is certain. But the earliest evidence is in a letter dated 1st October 1824, from Agie and Insinger, in Antwerp, to NM:[36] 'You are probably informed that the pigeon-post has been stopped since a few weeks. A few trials have been made, but it appears that the season is too much advanced.' But apart from the weather, there were other problems as Thomas Raikes observed in his Paris diary for October 1836:[37]

> The English papers state that the members of the Stock Exchange in London are so indignant at the early information obtained in certain quarters by pigeon-expresses from Paris, that they have collected a certain number of hawks, falcons, and other birds of prey on the Kentish coast to waylay these carriers. It has not, however, wholly put a stop to the practice.

It is conceivable but most unlikely that part of the journey from Brussels to London was undertaken by pigeon post: from Calais, for instance, to Burmarsh Farm. But why should the news of Waterloo have been sent overland to Calais when Ostend was so much nearer? The pigeon-post hypothesis must be discarded.

The true nature of NM's intelligence system was different and more prosaic. He relied on his own couriers and boats, with extra rewards for speed and reliability. In 1813 NM set up agencies in Dover, Calais and Ostend both to communicate with his couriers on the Continent and to facilitate the transmission of money across the Channel. He also had an 'unrivalled stud of horses distributed along the line from the coast to London'.[38a] The ultimate effectiveness of NM's courier service may be measured from Charles Greville's diary for 1830. Greville records that during a fast journey to Naples he had spent 236 hours on the road, including stops totalling 20 hours; Rothschild's man did it in 168 hours.[39]

It must, therefore, have been a courier who brought the news of Waterloo from either Brussels or Ghent to London. Perhaps he was the 'gentleman' who, as reported in *The Courier* of 21st June 1815, left Ghent for Ostend on 19th June, boarded the Nymph and arrived in Deal on the following day. But he cannot now be identified.

There is, however, no shortage of candidates for the role, phantom messengers who float this way and that on the tide of history. Let us examine what we know of their identity, one by one.

The Jew at Ghent. On 19th June, the day after Waterloo, the Duke of Wellington sent a handwritten note to Louis XVIII at Ghent, telling him the result of the battle. According to 'J.Mn.' in *Notes and Queries*,[38b] the Duke later told 'J.Mn.' that a Jew had been present when the message was delivered to the King at breakfast; and to discover the cause of the obvious excitement, 'made his way into the house, and having heard the important news, he set out instantly for Ostend, and getting on board a vessel ready to sail to England, he hastened to London, where he first went to Change Alley and transacted business; which done, he immediately carried the news to Lord Liverpool, some hours before the arrival of Captain Percy with the despatches.' The Duke of Wellington was not at Ghent at the time, so if he did tell this story to 'J.Mn.', whoever he may have been, he must have heard it from someone else; and the same applies to the rest of the story. It seems idle to speculate about the identity of the Jew. He may never have existed except in 'J.Mn's' imagination.

Another Courier from Ghent. Jennings,[40] the editor of the Croker Papers, says that a courier bearing the news from Ghent was sent to Lord Liverpool, who did not believe it to be true and asked J. W. Croker, Secretary to the Admiralty, to cross-examine him. Croker did believe the courier because, in answer to a question, he referred to Louis XVIII being in his dressing gown: the King would not have been taking his ease unless an Allied victory was assured. But Croker himself makes no mention of this episode. Nor do I believe that NM would have sent his courier alone to see the Prime Minister. He would have accompanied him, and Jennings does not record NM's presence. If the courier was not NM's employee, whose was he? And would he have been admitted to Downing Street? I suspect that Jennings invented this episode, or may have misunderstood something which Croker told him.

The Knight of Kerry. The Right Hon. Maurice Fitzgerald, who bore the Irish title of Knight of Kerry, was a friend of the Duke of Wellington. According to the *Quarterly Review* (1845),[41] he is said to have left Ghent for England on 19th June, at the request of Admiral Sir Pulteney Malcolm, to deliver some confidential information to Lord Castlereagh, the Foreign Secretary. This is odd, because Admiral Malcolm arrived at Dover on the same day, 20th June, as the Knight of Kerry.[42] Why then did the Admiral not bring the confidential information for Castlereagh himself? Be that as it may, Fitzgerald did not know the result of the battle: only that the Duke was very confident. But the account continues: 'After we were under weigh a gendarme, with some mail bags in a boat, overtook the vessel and said reports had just arrived that the Duke of Wellington was driving the French at all points.'[41] The Knight arrived at the Admiralty at 4.30 p.m. on Tuesday, 20th June, from where he went to the House of Lords to see Lord Liverpool. To save repeating information already known to the Prime Minister, the Knight asked him how much he and the Cabinet already knew. Lord Liverpool replied that the Cabinet knew nothing. (The same may not have applied to Lord Liverpool.) Fitzgerald may have been first with the news, if this story is true; yet it is highly improbable that a man of such background was also one of NM's couriers.

Mr Assheton Smith. An unknown contributor to *Bell's Life in London*, quoted by a certain Haughmond in *Notes and Queries*,[38c] claimed that a Mr Assheton Smith was the first person to bring the news of Waterloo to England. It is said that he was cruising off the coast of France in his yacht in June 1815, but there is no evidence to support the contention.

Isambard Kingdom Brunel. Again in *Notes and Queries*,[38d] Alfred John Dunkin, of Dartford, claimed that I. K. Brunel, whom he described as 'the projector of the Hungerford Suspension Bridge', had personally told him that he was the first to convey the news of Waterloo to the Government in the person of Lord Harrowby, the President of the Council. According to Mr Dunkin, Brunel's story was so suspect that 'he was immediately placed under surveillance'. Brunel, who did in fact construct the Hungerford Suspension Bridge between 1841 and 1845, was nine years old at the time of Waterloo. Apart from the possibility that Mr Dunkin confused him with his father Sir Marc, for which there is no evidence, the Brunel attribution can be rejected.

Cook. 'I remember perfectly well,' said 'L.B.L.', once more in *Notes and Queries*,[38b] that the name of the gentleman who brought the news of Waterloo from Ghent was Cook.' 'L.B.L.' had remarkable hearing. He was living near Canterbury and 'heard the firing all day on Sunday'. He went to a cricket match on the Tuesday evening, 'where there was a mysterious feeling pervading the whole company that a great battle had been fought and won'. I think we may leave him in the hands of his aurist.

L'Oracle. There is yet another story as to how NM got early information about the result of the battle, cited by Lucien Wolf[9] and repeated, perhaps from a different source, by Elizabeth Longford.[43] Throughout 18th June, when the battle was raging, 'Gazettes Extraordinaires' are said to have been published by the authorities in Brussels. They are also said to have contained bulletins on the progress of the battle, signed by the Secretary of State, Baron de Capellen, and published in a fly-sheet called *L'Oracle* (of which I have not been able to find a copy). The final victory was, apparently, announced in a special issue just before midnight on 18th June. NM's agent obtained a copy and went straight to Dunkirk with it, arriving at about 10 a.m. on Monday, 19th June. From there Captain Hunt Cullen carried the fly-sheet to Deal and thence to NM at New Court, very late on that night. It was taken the next morning to Lord Liverpool. This story does not, of course, attempt to identify the bearer of the good news; but it may indicate its original source.

John Roworth. I have left to the last the least improbable of all the candidates for the prize of having been first with the news of Waterloo. It is none other than John Roworth, the author of that significant letter to NM already quoted: 'I am informed by Commissary White you have done well by the early information which you had of the Victory gaind [sic] at Waterloo.' According to 'ELLCEE', again in *Notes and Queries*,[38e] Roworth told him that he had spent the night before Waterloo on the battlefield, 'under some slight shelter'. As soon as Napoleon's defeat 'was assured', at about 7.00 p.m. on Sunday, 18th June, Roworth went as fast as possible to the coast 'and crossed the Channel in an open boat', despite a fierce storm. This story has some plausibility. It would, however, be more consistent with Roworth's letter to NM if, instead of 'you have done well by the early information which you had of the Victory', Roworth had written, 'you have done well by the early information which you had *from me* of the Victory'. Roworth could have set off for England on the evening of 18th June, no doubt helped by the earlier activities of NM's brother-in-law, Moses Montefiore, whom NM had persuaded to set up a special news agency at Dunkirk. [9] Conceivably he could have arrived in London late on the night of Monday, 19th June, thus enabling NM to take the news of Waterloo to the Prime Minister on the morning of Tuesday, 20th June. But NM's altruism, it seems, was in vain. Lord Liverpool did not believe NM, because the daunting news of Ligny and Quatre Bras reached him at about the same time.

If NM's courier was indeed among all those I have named, the evidence points to Roworth as being the most probable.

Here I must quote another version of NM's arrival at Downing Street: first, because it bears the stamp of family legend handed down from generation to generation; secondly, because it mentions not only NM's early possession of the news from Waterloo, but also the use to which he is said to have put it. The tale is contained in a letter published in *The Daily Telegraph* on 9th November 1962 by Lady Colyer-Fergusson: a grand-daughter of Benjamin Cohen (to whom NM left £10,000 in his Will), the brother of NM's wife Hannah:

> Mr. Frederic Morton's recent and interesting book 'The Rothschilds' brought to my mind the following story in connection with my own family.
>
> My grandfather Benjamin Cohen, went with Nathan Rothschild to see Lord Castlereagh, who was then Prime Minister, to tell him that the Battle of Waterloo had been won. When they arrived the butler refused to admit them and all remonstrances were met with the same answer: 'His Lordship is sleeping and is not to be disturbed.'
>
> I may add as a further item of interest to the story that immediately after having visited Lord Castlereagh Nathan Rothschild bought up all the shares that were then very low, thereby founding the vast fortune.

Lord Castlereagh was not, of course, Prime Minister in 1815, but Foreign Secretary. The letter is nevertheless illuminating, both of NM's public spirit in trying to see the Prime Minister and of his subsequent Stock Exchange operations. These we shall now examine.

A Million out of Waterloo?

Although it is virtually part of English history that NM made 'a million' or 'millions' out of his early information about the Battle of Waterloo, the evidence is slender: little more, in fact, than Roworth's letter to NM – 'you have done well' – bolstered by a persistent legend. In the absence of contemporary records at New Court, it is impossible to estimate the size of his gain. But knowing the structure of the market in 1815, we can at least discover the maximum sum he could have made. The British Government securities most frequently mentioned in this context are Consols 3%.[44] Their movement during 1815, according to Van Sommer's Tables, published in 1848, are shown at Annex 4.[45] The sharp fall, from just above 59, to just below 53, occurred well before the Battle of Waterloo as did the recovery on about 9th June. This sharp fall is not recorded in the daily prices published in *The Morning Chronicle* (Table 3).

Consols were quoted only from 1st to 3rd June inclusive during the whole of that month. It was, however, possible to buy them 'for Account', which was equivalent to buying 'on margin' (but without paying anything), which in fact is not permitted in the gilt edged market nowadays. NM could have bought 3% Consols 'for Account' on Tuesday, 20th June 1815 at 56½ and sold them at 60½ on Wednesday, 28th June, without having had to pay for them, even if they had remained at 56½, because 28th June was before settlement day, 18th July. The previous settlement day was 26th May. To have made £1 million by this operation, NM would have had to 'risk' £14.125 million, though the risk was negligible. But a purchase of this magnitude would not have been possible. An expenditure of £20,000 by each of five agents would have been the maximum, which implies a profit of £7,080.

The position was different with Omnium, a kind of Government investment trust containing only Government securities.

TABLE 3

CONSOLS FOR ACCOUNT

Extracted from The Morning Chronicle Stock Market Report

Date	Transaction prices					
Wed. 21 June 1815	$56\frac{1}{2}$	$56\frac{5}{8}$	$56\frac{1}{8}$	$56\frac{3}{8}$	$56\frac{1}{8}$	$56\frac{1}{2}$
Thur. 22 June 1815	$56\frac{7}{8}$	57	$56\frac{3}{4}$	$57\frac{1}{4}$	$57\frac{1}{8}$	
Frid. 23 June 1815	$58\frac{3}{4}$	59	$57\frac{1}{2}$	$58\frac{1}{8}$		
Sat. 24 June 1815						
Mon. 26 June 1815						
Tues. 27 June 1815	60	$59\frac{7}{8}$	$60\frac{3}{8}$	$60\frac{1}{4}$		
Wed. 28 June 1815	$60\frac{3}{4}$	61	$60\frac{3}{8}$	$60\frac{5}{8}$		
Thur. 29 June 1815	$60\frac{3}{4}$	61	$60\frac{3}{8}$			

On Tuesday, 20th June, NM could have bought these at a premium of $4\frac{1}{2}$ and sold them on Wednesday, 28th June at a premium of $12\frac{1}{2}$. And he would not have had to pay £104½ for them, perhaps only just over £20, because they could be bought in partly paid form. But as with Consols, there would have been no possibility of NM buying enough partly paid Omnium stock to make a profit of £1 million. The market was not big enough.

We must conclude, therefore, that however much NM made out of Waterloo, it must have been very considerably less than a million pounds, let alone 'millions'.

Creation of the Alliance

The Alliance[47] started business on 23rd March 1824 under the name 'The Alliance British and Foreign Life and Fire Assurance Company'. An article in *The Times* of 18th March 1824 said correctly that the company had been planned and initiated by

NM and his brother-in-law, Moses Montefiore. The enterprise thus linked two of the most notable Anglo-Jewish families. Sir Moses Montefiore (1784–1885), stockbroker, merchant and philanthropist, married Judith Cohen, a sister of NM's wife, Hannah. He devoted much of his life to the amelioration throughout the world of Jewish communities less fortunate than his own. Created a baronet in 1846 (a distinction which NM declined) he lived to celebrate his centenary in the private synagogue in his Ramsgate house.

Shortly after the inauguration of the Alliance, the board persuaded Thomas Fowell Buxton, one of its auditors and a Member of Parliament (see page 106), to introduce a Bill into the House of Commons lifting the monopoly of marine insurance business, at that time confined to Lloyd's, the London Assurance and the Royal Exchange. In April 1824, NM wrote to his old associate J. C. Herries enlisting support for the bill:[48]

> My dear Sir,
>
> I beg leave to enclose a note which I have just received from an eminent banker at Amsterdam, informing me of a Company about to be instituted under the charter and special protection of the King of the Netherlands.
>
> The object of this Society is to promote all kinds of national industry, by affording facilities in the advancement of Capital, and to protect Commercial men and society in general by granting insurancies on shipping and every species of property exposed to risks.
>
> There are other ends, equally salutory, towards which the views of the Company will be directed, all tending to give an impetus to manufactures, and to attract and retain in their ports every branch of foreign commerce.
>
> This is not merely the policy of the Netherlands, but it is that of the whole European Continent at the present moment: everywhere, efforts are making to introduce a spirit of commercial enterprise, to revive trade where it has languished, and to discover new channels in which it may be directed.
>
> Of these facts I have many proofs in my possession, if any were wanting, where [sic] my assistance and advice are sought.

I avail myself, therefore, of the present opportunity to request you will bring this subject before the consideration of my Lord Liverpool, who will no doubt perceive in these facts additional grounds for persevering in that liberal principle, upon which His Majesty's Government has acted, by removing every obstacle in the way of an open, free, and unrestricted trade.

In referring to the two [sic] companies which possess in this country the exclusive privilege of effecting insurancies on shipping, I do not mean in the most remote sense to impugn their respectability or good faith, but I do venture to assert that there is wanting in both of them that energy and those liberal extended views which are necessary, at the present day, to retain the advantages which they have hitherto monopolised, and I am sure I shall be borne out in the assertion that if insurancies are to be tied up by their old fashioned modes of thinking and acting, Establishments of a similar nature will arise in every part of the Continent, and will eventually wrest from their hands the business which they now conduct exclusively.

I remain,

My dear Sir

Your obed. and faithful Servant

N. M. Rothschild

The Bill received the Royal Assent on 24th June. The Alliance intended to transact marine business from 1st September of that year, but one of its shareholders, who was also an underwriter at Lloyd's, obtained an injunction to prevent their doing so. As a result, it was decided to incorporate a new company, the Alliance Marine Assurance Company, which was able to transact marine business without further problems.

Bailing out the Bank of England

Towards the end of 1825 a financial crisis of unparalleled severity afflicted the country. Between 1825 and 1826 some 145 banks went bankrupt. On 23rd November 1825 *The Times* reported that holders of commercial bills were experiencing difficulty in having them discounted by the Bank of England. The Bank, 'apprehensive of fresh exportation of gold', was being accused of excessive caution by contracting the bank note issue. The scarcity of money was particularly acute at a time when 'the wonderful enlargement of operations of every description calls for a great extension of discounts'.

The Directors of the Bank of England insisted that the Government should reduce its debt to the Bank so that the latter would have sufficient funds to carry out its discount function. *The Times*, however, ascribed the crisis to the Bank's earlier reckless policies rather than to its more recent caution, and accused the Bank of having put too much money into circulation and of having created too much credit. The discounting of bills should, *The Times* argued on 23rd November, be reduced still further 'to reduce the number of those wild and desperate – those hollow, fraudulent and destructive enterprises, at once a disgrace to the country in which they have grown up – a snare for industry and ingenuity which they have seduced from their lawful objects, and a gulf in which property, principle and reputation have frequently and lamentably perished'. As far as the impending disaster was concerned, *The Times* expressed the view that 'the sooner it arrives, the less terrible will be the ruin'.

On 24th November the Governor and the Deputy Governor of the Bank of England met the Chancellor and said that when Exchequer bills were called in for payment, they would not be able to meet the expected demand for cash.

Between 2nd and 15th December there was financial chaos, Sir W. Elford's bank, that of Messrs. Wentford Chaloner & Company and that of Messrs. Pole, Thornton & Company failing, though the last of these was rescued, at any rate once, by NM.[49] According to *The Times* of 13th December 'an indescribable gloom was diffused through the City'.

An interesting account of the crisis is to be found in the diary entries for 17th and 20th December of Mrs Arbuthnot, the Duke of Wellington's confidante:[50]

> 17th – I was interrupted when I had written so far by the arrival of the Duke, and yesterday morning Mr. A. received a letter from Mr. Herries describing the state of

affairs in London as so alarming as to require the presence
of all those interested in the Gov^t. We came to London
immediately & saw Mr. Herries, who came up to the
Duke's house. He told the Duke the Cabinet was sitting, &
he immediately set off to it. Mr. Herries told us that such
had been the extraordinary demand for gold to supply the
country bankers & to meet the general run upon them that
the Bank of England was completely drained of its specie
& was reduced to 100,000 sovereigns, with which it w^d
have to open today & meet demands of probably four
times that amount. The Bank expects to be obliged to
suspend cash payments tomorrow, and they want the
Government to step forward to their assistance & order
the suspension. Lord Liverpool is unwilling to do this &
wishes the Bank to do it upon their own responsibility. By
Mr. Herries's account there seems to be considerable irrita-
tion between the Gov^t & the Governors of the bank. They
trace all these money difficulties to the encouragement
given by members of the Government to the foreign loans
& speculations, which all go out of the country in gold,
and to Mr. Huskisson's commercial liberality which
drains the country of gold in another way. Such is the
detestation in which he is held in the City that L^d L[iver-
pool] & Mr. Canning did not think it prudent to summon
him to London till all the Cabinet were sent for &, in the
discussions with the Bank, he is kept out of sight. He repays
them with equal hatred & told Lord Liverpool that, if
they stopped payment, it w^d be a good opportunity of
taking their Charter from them, although he knows their
circulation is but 18 million & we owe them 30 million.
Ld Liverpool is so afraid of Mr. Huskisson that he entered
into this scandalous scheme & was for letting the Bank
break, tho' the consequences w^d be ruin both at home &
abroad, rather than take any responsibility upon the
Gov^t. Mr. Herries remonstrated with Lord Liverpool &
asked him how he meant to pay the Dividends & the
Army & Navy? This a little stopped him, & he was
frightened again by Mr. Baring who told him all the Bank
distresses were caused by the Gov^t and read him a lecture
upon it.

Mr. Huskisson has done all he can also to ruin Rothschild by spreading reports that their house was in danger, & he made Mr. Canning write to Paris to enquire into the affairs of that brother. Ld Granville sent his private secretary to pump Rothschild. R[othschild] found out what he was at & instantly shewed him his accounts & proved to him that he was worth 2½ millions. Rothschild has made most gigantic efforts to assist the Bank & he told Mr. Herries that, if he had been applied to sooner, he w^d have prevented all the difficulty. As it is, if they can hold out till Monday or Tuesday, he will have enormous sums over in sovereigns from Paris, & the pressure will be entirely relieved. Mr. Herries, I see, expects that the Bank will suspend their payments tomorrow. They have but 100,000 sovereigns left, tho' they have a large quantity of uncoined bullion in the Mint. Mr. Herries said that the City merchants appeared to have the utmost contempt for Mr. Robinson, who was wholly without plan or expedients & who did not appear to have the least idea what to do.

What will happen in the country I don't know. The banks are breaking in every direction &, as the circulation is entirely in local notes, there is now in fact no circulation for gold cannot be supplied & every thing is at a stand [sic]. In the manufacturing districts they do not know how to pay the wages & serious riots are expected.

We remained at the Duke's till he returned from the Cabinet, which was not till 2 o'clock in the morning. He had taken just the line I expected he w^d take. He told Lord Liverpool while there was life there was hope; that there was a chance of the Bank standing &, while that chance remained, he w^d not despair; that the Government were bound to support them to the very utmost of their power & that, if they were forced to suspend their payments, it must be done in the manner most beneficial to the Bank, for that their interests were those of the country & their difficulties caused by no imprudence on their part but by the fault of the Gov^t in encouraging foreign speculations & allowing the country banks to inundate every district with one & two pound notes. Lord Liverpool professed to the Duke great desire to serve the Bank.

147

20th. – Two or three more anxious days have passed. The Bank have been able to continue cash payments, tho' at one moment they had but 60,000 sovereigns left, & yesterday when they closed they had not much more. Rothschild was to receive 200,000 this morning and, as he sent 25 couriers off last week to buy sovereigns wherever they could be got, I hope they will now begin to pour in. The state of the country at this moment is most extraordinary; there is no circulating medium, no means of getting money or of paying for any thing. Sir Chas Knightley, a gentleman of large property near Daventry, came to London two days ago & was obliged to ride part of the way & to borrow a few sovereigns, which his little girl had hoarded, to be able to pay for his journey, and told us that at this moment he had not the means of getting a shilling. The bank he deals with have suspended their payments and, tho' he feels sure they are perfectly solvent, yet the momentary embarrassment is as great as if they were bankrupts.

The Duke's coming up did great good; the Bank's Directors & all those who are not under the influence of the Canning part of the Cabinet look up to him as a protector & one who will not be afraid of responsibility & vigorous measures. The Bank & the Treasury were delighted when they heard he was arrived, & said that now at least the country w^d not be ruined by cowardice. He told me he is quite sure that he is a most inconvenient person in the Cabinet, that they are all afraid of him, that in his presence they dare not name even any of their shabby wishes to shirk responsibility, that they know he will always come out with his fair & honest opinion, & the consequence is that they sit & look at each other & say nothing. This applies to Messrs. Canning, Huskisson & Robinson. There has not been a word uttered since he came to town about taking the Charter from the Bank, which the Duke said, whether right or wrong under ordinary circumstances, w^d be scandalous in a moment of difficulty caused by our own false policy.

Apart from Mrs Arbuthnot's testimony, there is no doubt

that NM was the principal saviour of the Bank of England. As
A. G. Stapleton remarked when reviewing *The Greville Journals*
in 1875:[51]

> It was on that memorable Friday night [16th Decem-
> ber], when the Cabinet sat till two in the morning (as I
> well remember), and had the courage to refuse its sanction
> to a suspension of cash payments, that the Rothschilds
> poured into the Bank £300,000 coin. The Bank had up-
> wards of a million of bullion in their coffers, and although
> coining went on unceasingly, yet at that period the Mint
> could not coin more than £200,000 a week. In the course of
> the Saturday, coin came in from all quarters, so that the
> stoppage was averted.

NM himself said in his evidence to the 'Committee of Security
on the Bank of England Charter; With the Minutes of Evidence',
printed by order of the House of Commons on 11th August 1832
(p. 385):[52]

> 4838. In the winter of 1825, was the supply of gold that
> was required for this country, supplied in great measure by
> the Bank of France? – No; there was a good deal supplied
> from the whole world; I imported it, and it was imported
> almost from every country; we got it from Russia, from
> Turkey, from Austria, from almost every quarter in the
> world.
> 4839. Did not a considerable portion of that supply
> arrive in sovereigns? – No; in the beginning we imported
> about 400,000 or 500,000 sovereigns which had been sent
> over to France when such an enormous quantity of goods
> came to this country in 1824, in consequence of Mr. Hus-
> kisson's measure at that time.*

In addition in 1839, the Duke of Wellington said:[53]

---

* The witness who immediately preceded NM was my wife's great great uncle
George Grote. He was a reforming member of parliament, one of the four
founders of London University (*via* University College), a philosopher and
author. His *History of Greece* is still famous. In addition, he was a full partner in
his family bank, Grote Prescott & Co., which later, after numerous changes,
became part of the National Westminster Bank. He married an eccentric wife
who, Sydney Smith affected to believe, was the origin of the word 'grotesque'.

For my part, I was in the Cabinet in 1826 and I well remember that had it not been for most extraordinary exertions – above all on the part of old Rothschild – the Bank must have stopped payment.

Even in the autumn of 1826 J. C. Herries could write to Lord Liverpool:[54]

> I have seen Rothschild on the subject of the gold exported . . . He continues to be delivering gold to the Bank and I understand his engagement to be to the extent of ten Millions. He has, I believe, delivered seven Millions.

In the light of NM's readiness to rescue the Bank of England in its hour of distress, another of those Rothschild anecdotes with which City men entertain each other appears particularly preposterous.

It is that when NM presented a bill for a large sum which he had received from one of his brothers, the Bank of England refused to pay, claiming that it cashed only its own notes, not those of private persons. 'So, private persons!' NM is said to have exclaimed, 'I will show them what kind of private persons the Rothschilds are.' Here is one version of the revenge he is alleged to have taken:[24c]

> The best weapon in the hand of a Rothschild is money, and he ordered his agents to secure as many Bank of England notes as they possibly could. For three weeks they continued to collect them, then, when the Bank opened one morning, Nathan Rothschild stood at the counter. He took a five-pound note from his swollen purse, and asked the chief cashier with freezing politeness, to give him gold for it. It was given with equal politeness, the cashier restraining his astonishment that the great financier should waste his time in such trifles. Nathan Rothschild carefully examined each sovereign and put it in a leather sack. Then he calmly produced a second five-pound note, and repeated his action a second, third, fourth, fifth, and tenth time, in every detail. He continued to change notes until the hour of closing, and in a single day had lessened the gold-reserve of the Bank by £210,000. While Nathan himself 'operated'

at the chief counter, nine of his clerks were busy changing paper into gold at the other counters.

Everybody now understood the manoeuvre, and laughed at the original means that Rothschild had adopted to punish the Bank; they saw that he was in a position to restrict the circulation of gold, and the great institution was quite powerless to resist him. The whole city – except the directors of the Bank – was amused. If the directors were at first disposed to laugh, they soon changed their mind, for Nathan Rothschild was at his post again the next morning, with his band of clerks, ready to continue changing notes. The manager hurriedly went to him and asked why he was annoying the Bank in this way. He smiled grimly, and said –

> "You said that you were not prepared to change my bills. It seems that you have no confidence in them. Well, if you entertain a doubt about me, I am free to entertain one about you. I am determined to demand gold for every one of your notes. I began yesterday, and I give you notice that I shall keep your cashier busy changing notes for at least two months."

Two months! If Rothschild persisted in his work for that length of time, he would take at least eleven million pounds out of the Bank's gold-reserve. That would not do at all. A meeting of the directors was called at once, and it was decided to send an apology to Nathan Rothschild, together with an assurance that the Bank of England would always be pleased to cash his bills, whatever kind they were.

This latter-day version of David and Goliath, like much else told of NM, may strain credulity. No such doubt, however, attaches to this wise and compassionate letter,[55] written by NM to the Prime Minister, Lord Liverpool. It is dated 21st August 1826, 20 years before the worst of those recurrent famines which plagued 19th-century Ireland and left the bitterest of legacies:

> It has occurred to me, that in the present State of Ireland, supposing the accounts we read from that Quarter are true, even making allowance for some exaggeration

of the distress some easy and direct mode of relief is at the disposal of Government but the benefit of which might be lost by delay.

I beg to suggest the Purchase of American and East India Rice before speculators come into the market the price of which is at present low and the Stock large and which in case of a deficiency of the Potato Crop, would supply the numerous Poor of that Country with a wholesome food during the Winter. I venture to address this suggestion to Your Lordship, which in my humble opinion if acted upon might prove beneficial to a suffering Community and prevent those mischiefs which a threatened famine might otherwise produce.

If the Prime Minister sent a reply, it has not survived. And the rest, as so often, is silence.

The Death of NM

In June 1836, NM travelled to Frankfurt for the marriage of his son Lionel to his cousin Charlotte, the daughter of Carl. On the 11th, four days before the ceremony, the bridegroom wrote to his brother Nathaniel in London:[56] 'Papa has not yet left his bed, his boil has not come to a head and gives him a great deal of pain . . . he has declared the Wedding shall not be postponed.' Although in intense discomfort, NM attended the ceremony. It required, wrote Lionel, 'but a little resolution of which you know Papa has enough'.[57]

Thereafter his condition fluctuated, as he more than once submitted to the knife of a 'Professor from Heidelberg',[58, 59] perhaps called Professor Chelius. The eminent British surgeon, Benjamin Travers, was also summoned, but by then the patient was beyond help. The 'boil' to which Lionel referred was in fact a large ischio-rectal abscess which would not heal, causing NM to die of septicaemia. Normally, even before antibiotics, such abscesses eventually healed after adequate drainage, a treatment with which the Professor from Heidelberg was familiar. When such infections fail to respond to the body's defence mechanisms, there must be a suspicion that they have been caused by a more fundamental disease, such as diabetes or a carcinoma.

NM died on 28th July 1836, in his sixtieth year. It may be presumed that the intelligence service of *The Times* was less nimble than that established by NM, for it was not until six days later that the newspaper printed the following account:

> The intelligence of Mr. Rothschild's death, which arrived this morning, has occupied attention here to the exclusion of all other topics. The event was indeed firmly believed yesterday to have taken place, and it appears now that the communication was made from Boulogne yesterday morning by pigeon, and that it reached the City in the course of the afternoon. It was made in three words only – 'Il est mort,' the simplicity of the announcement being not inappropriate to the importance of the individual. Government securities of all descriptions, but more particularly those of the foreign market, have been falling in value during the week, in anticipation of this event, but its confirmation has had a contrary effect, probably on account of the understanding there is that his business, under the management of his sons, will go on as usual. The original apprehension was, in fact, a very absurd one, as it was not to be expected in any case that a family so wealthy would bring the various securities they held upon the market in such a manner as to produce any inconvenience.

On an earlier occasion NM had the same illness which this time caused his death,[60] something of which he had a premonition, and therefore made his first Will. It was signed and witnessed on 27th July, the day before he died. He entrusted it to Jonas Rothschild of Frankfurt, with instructions for it to be delivered to his brother Salomon or, in his absence, to another of his brothers. It was proved at the Prerogative Court of Canterbury in the following month at a little over one million pounds; but there are some reasons for thinking that in those days what was included in a Will represented only part of a testator's fortune. An NM mourning scarf bears the statement that he died 'leaving property to the amount of £5,000,000 Sterling'. In the currency of 1982, that is equivalent to £175 million.

25

'YOU HAVE IT, MADAM'

Introduction

THE *dramatis personae* in this episode, a short strand in the skein of Britain's history in the nineteenth century, were Disraeli; my great grandfather Baron Lionel de Rothschild; the Suez Canal (though not a *persona*); and the Khedive of Egypt Ismā'īl Pasha. So much has been written about Disraeli, starting with Monypenny and Buckle[61a] and ending, nearly, with Lord Blake,[62] as to make it superfluous to say anything specifically about him in this essay; though from time to time some facets of that complex personality may be apparent. The three others, however, merit brief attention.

Lionel de Rothschild

Someone said that no young man can bear a heavier burden than a distinguished and eminent father. Whether the aphorism is true or not – and examples for and against it can be adduced – Lionel certainly had such a father, the formidable N. M. Rothschild, founder of the English branch of my family.

It could not have been easy to become head of N. M. Rothschild & Sons at the age of twenty-eight, succeeding the man who, among other things, had financed the Battle of Waterloo. But NM, as he was usually called, had paid great attention to his eldest son's education. He was first sent to a boarding school and then, if his brothers' education is a guide, had a tutor. Later he went to the University of Göttingen and, after that, spent two years in London under NM's watchful eye. In 1830 he was sent to de Rothschild Frères in Paris, working under NM's powerful and influential brother James. After that, before his return to London in 1836 when he became the head of N. M. Rothschild & Sons, NM put him in charge of the firm's affairs in Madrid.

Lionel did not have his father's virtuosity and genius for business – who did? The two might be compared to Hobbs and Sutcliffe, the one with all the strokes, the other, impregnable but

FIGURE 10
Baron Lionel de Rothschild

more limited. But he was shrewd, cautious and successful from the time when he took over the bank. As is well known, under his leadership N. M. Rothschild & Sons were involved, more often than not as principals, in no less than forty government loans.[63] One of Lionel's most important financial operations, apart from that which is the subject of this essay, occurred at the end of the Franco-German war in 1871. As head of a group of financiers he guaranteed the maintenance of the foreign exchanges, which made possible the payment of the French indemnity, amounting to £239 million, to Germany.

One of the most famous incidents in Lionel's life concerned his repeated efforts to take his seat in the House of Commons without having to swear allegiance to the Crown 'upon the true faith of a Christian'. He was first elected as one of the Whig members for the City of London in 1847. Re-elected in 1849, 1852 and 1857 (twice), it was only in 1858, through the perseverance of Lord John Russell, that Lionel was allowed to take his seat. Until 1874, when he lost it, Lionel never spoke in the House, which prompts me to believe that he had no political ambitions but was motivated to become an MP by a desire to advance the cause of British Jews.

Lionel was quiet, reserved, cultivated and serious, with a sardonic sense of humour. Sidonia, in Disraeli's novel Coningsby,[64] has often been said to have been modelled on him. This is what Disraeli had to say about Sidonia. He had:

> a penetrative intellect that, matured by long meditation, and assisted by that absolute freedom from prejudice, which was the compensatory possession of a man without a country, permitted Sidonia to fathom, as it were by intuition, the depth of questions apparently the most difficult and profound. He possessed the rare faculty of communicating with precision ideas the most abstruse, and in general a power of expression which arrests and satisfies attention.

*　　*　　*

> To a man in his position there might yet seem one unfailing source of felicity and joy; independent of creed, independent of country, independent even of character.

155

He might have discovered that perpetual spring of happiness in the sensibility of the heart. But this was a sealed fountain to Sidonia. In his organisation there was a peculiarity, perhaps a great deficiency. He was a man without affections. It would be harsh to say he had no heart, for he was susceptible of deep emotions, but not for individuals. He was capable of rebuilding a town that was burned down; of restoring a colony that had been destroyed by some awful visitation of Nature; of redeeming to liberty a horde of captives; and of doing these great acts in secret; for, void of all self-love, public approbation was worthless to him; but the individual never touched him. Woman was to him a toy, man a machine.

Women may have been toys to Sidonia, but this is how Lionel wrote from Paris to his fiancée (and first cousin) Charlotte on January 7, 1835:[65]

> Dearest beloved Charlotte,
>   This morning at the house I had but a few minutes to employ in the agreeable occupation of writing to you and am now alone at the hotel, quite free from every interruption and as happy in passing my time in the present manner as I possibly can to be away from you Dearest Charlotte: if you could but see me, you would be better able to answer the question you so often made to me, than I ever was able. Now that I am separated, I only know the meaning of the word and am only able to judge of my love, of my entirely devoted love for you Dear Charlotte, & wish I were able to express it in words. But I cannot, even in endeavouring to do so my pen has fallen from my hand and more than an hour has passed thinking of you, without taking it up – you will laugh at me, perhaps not understanding, if so have only compassion and believe me I am as sincere as a man can be and only pray that you will think me so . . .

This letter, and many others written after his marriage to Charlotte, refute the idea that, like Sidonia, Lionel was incapable of a normal, loving, human relationship.

I turn now to another facet of Lionel's character, as portrayed by the following events. The reader may wonder in due course how it came about that Lionel's eldest son Nathaniel (usually called Natty) became a baronet during the lifetime of his father, who had no English title though he was allowed by 'Royal License' to use and retain the 'style and dignity' of an Austrian Baron. In fact, Lionel was offered a baronetcy in October or November 1846. His brother Anthony wrote to him saying:[66]

> I am glad Her Majesty wishes to make you Sir Lionel – follow my advice and take it and if you don't like it for yourself, accept it for one of us; these things are always better to have when one can.

Lionel's mother Hannah, the widow of NM, thought the same, in spite of Lionel's doubts:[67]

> I do not think it good taste to refuse it.

and, on November 24, 1846, his cousin Anselm wrote from Frankfurt to say:[68]

> I had the pleasure of receiving your private line of the 20th and hasten to answer that you ought to accept without the least hesitation the title of a Baronet which the Government proposes to confer on you. It is always a great distinction and it does not matter at all that others, not so worthy of it, were favoured in the same way before you. As an Englishman it becomes you much better to be an English Baronet than a foreign baron and therefore I advise you to accept the title you have been offered.

The 'others' to whom Anselm referred were Sir Isaac Goldsmid, who was made a baronet in 1841 by Lord Melbourne's outgoing ministry, and Sir Moses Montefiore who was knighted in 1837 and made a baronet on 23rd July 1846. Clearly, Lionel's refusal was at any rate in part caused by pique at not being the first Jew to be made a baronet. But he took his brother Anthony's hint, quoted above, and somehow arranged for him to be made a baronet, on the 12th January 1847. Not only did he arrange this, but also that Anthony's baronetcy should, surprisingly and exceptionally, have a special remainder such that if he had no male heirs or successors, it would devolve on Lionel's three sons, Nathaniel, Alfred and Leopold, in that order and with the 'failed male heirs' proviso in each case.

In the event, Anthony had no son, so when he died in 1876, Lionel's eldest son became Sir Nathaniel de Rothschild, Lionel retaining 'the style and dignity' of an Austrian Baron. He died three years after his brother Anthony, in 1879.

The Suez Canal

The importance of the Suez Canal for world sea traffic is made vividly clear by the following table in which the distances in nautical miles between certain ports are given *via* the Cape of Good Hope and *via* the Canal.[69]

Port	Cape	Canal	Reduction, %
London to:			
Bombay	10,800	6,300	42
Kuwait	11,300	6,500	42
Calcutta	11,700	7,900	32
Singapore	11,800	8,300	30
Marseille to:			
Bombay	10,400	4,600	56
Melbourne	11,900	9,400	21
New York to:			
Bombay	11,800	8,200	31
Singapore	12,500	10,200	18
Ras Tannūrah (Saudi Arabia)	11,900	8,300	30

The first canal in this part of Egypt was dug in the xxth Century B.C. by Iesostus and was extended as far as the Red Sea by the Ptolemys. The object then was not to make a passage between the Mediterranean and the Indian Ocean but to facilitate trade from the Nile delta to the Red Sea: and the Romans had the same object when they extended the Canal and called it after the Emperor Trajan. It was not until the 15th century, by when 'Trajan's Canal' had been filled in, that the idea of a direct link between the

Mediterranean and the Red Sea was mooted, by the Venetians. This idea, and subsequent similar proposals, were unacceptable to the Ottomans until November 1854 when the Khedive (or Viceroy) of Egypt, Muhammad Sa'īd, granted an Act of Concession to build the Suez Canal to a brilliant, resourceful and unscrupulous Frenchman, Ferdinand de Lesseps. The British Government was wholly opposed to the scheme. The Prime Minister, Lord Palmerston, who believed de Lesseps was either a lunatic or a swindler, personally told him that the Canal was not a commercial proposition. He feared it would prejudice Great Britain's commercial and maritime advantages, which in turn would damage Great Britain's friendly relationships with France. The Foreign Secretary, Lord Clarendon, said the same, also to de Lesseps. A little over a year later, in January 1856, an International Commission was set up to make what would now be called a feasibility study. The Commission, which included three British engineers in a private capacity, the British Government having refused to nominate any members though invited to do so, pronounced favourably on the scheme and expressed the incredibly optimistic view that the Canal would not cost more than £6 million. In the event, it cost about £16 million. In spite of the Commission's Report, which made the Canal a business proposition, the British Government continued, obstinately and myopically, to oppose its construction. As Lucien Wolf said:[70]

> In nothing has British statesmanship blundered so badly as in its early attitude towards the Canal.

The Chancellor of the Exchequer, Disraeli, believed it impossible to construct the Canal and averred that:[71]

> the operation of nature would in a short time defeat the ingenuity of man.

Some twenty years later, Disraeli, wiser as Prime Minister, fearful that the dispute then going on with de Lesseps might lead to the closure of the Canal, or with new imperial objectives in mind, executed a total *volte face* which is, of course, the subject of this essay. The Canal was formally opened in November 1869, the Empress Eugénie being present. Given the character and idiosyncrasies of the Khedive, Ismā'īl Pasha, the opening was inevitably executed with an unparalleled degree of ostentation and vulgarity.

Ismāʿīl Pasha, Khedive of Egypt

In 1875 Egypt was part of the Ottoman Empire which at one time also included Algeria, Tunisia, Libya, Palestine, Syria, Iraq, Hungary, the Crimea and most of south-eastern Europe. Egypt itself was ruled by a Khedive or Viceroy, who was appointed and could, of course, be dismissed, by the Sultan.

Ismāʿīl Pasha succeeded his uncle Saʿīd as Khedive in 1863. Born in 1830, he had been sent to Paris and educated at the Ecole d'Etat Major. He returned to Egypt on the death of his brother to become heir to Saʿīd who despatched him as his envoy, first to the Pope, then to the Sultan and, after that, to Napoleon III. In 1861 he was sent to put down a rebellion in the Sudan which he successfully did.[72]

When Saʿīd died, Ismāʿīl found himself ruling a country that had been temporarily enriched by the rise in the price of Egyptian long-staple cotton because of the American Civil War. Egypt's annual revenue had increased five-fold to about £25 million. Ismāʿīl had inherited his grandfather's enthusiasm for modernisation, as well as his extravagance and love of luxury. Those who met Ismāʿīl were persuaded of his many talents and his awe-inspiring personality. He was a short, squat, ugly man with one defective eye and tufts of red hair sprouting from his face. He wore a tarboosh and a frock-coat with an oriental cut, and blinked noticeably at his visitors. Someone who knew Ismāʿīl well said: 'People used to say that he heard with one eye and spoke with the other. When, many years afterwards, I reported this to him, he said, "Yes, and I think with both"';[73a] but in spite of this he gave the impression of considerable grandeur. Beneath his French education and manners he remained an oriental potentate in his extravagance and arbitrary behaviour. He was mean about small matters and lavish about large ones; luxurious and ambitious but, so far as large projects were concerned, the sky was the limit and his own glorification was never far from his mind.

On becoming Khedive, Ismāʿīl at once began a vast programme of public expenditure, treating the Egyptian Treasury as if it was his private property. By the time peace in America had brought the price of cotton down, work had already begun in Egypt on a railway, improvements to the streets and buildings of Cairo and Alexandria, a sugar-refining industry to process the cane from his own estate, and schemes for irrigation and land reclamation.

When Ismā'īl ran out of money, he transferred his debts to the State and began to borrow on a vast scale. He believed that his own standing and security depended on the social condition and development of Egypt which, whatever the cost, were to be comparable with those of a European country.

In 1873 he bribed the Sultan to grant a firman (or edict) which made him almost, but not quite, independent of the authority of the Sultan and the Turkish Government.

His extravagance increased and, as it did, financiers descended on Egypt to arrange even larger loans at more ruinous rates of interest. With the help of this borrowed money he remodelled the customs, the post office, and the educational system, stimulated trade, maintained a theatre and an opera house and built more palaces. His entertainment was lavish and extravagant. A French guest left a banquet saying 'J'ai mangé le patrimoine de trois fellahs',[73b] and these miserable peasants were the people who, by paying exorbitant taxes, supported the Khedive's expenditure. All European visitors were treated like princes, especially if they were potential lenders of money or businessmen. It was not that Ismā'īl was duped or taken in by such people: he just had no idea how to control his expenditure.

The land produced most of Egypt's wealth but it needed constant irrigation. The Khedive, the largest landowner in Egypt with an estate of 450,000 feddans (= acres), was responsible for the improvement of a great deal of land. But his fault was to establish industries before the estates were ready to supply them with the products, such as sugar, that they needed, and to place them so far from the estates that the expense of transportation and the difficulty of supervision nullified the advantages of the improvements. Again, in the case of the railway system, lack of good management and adequate accounting meant that the revenues were one fifth of what they should have been.

The Khedive's obligation to supply labour and land to the

Suez Canal Company was brought about by the negotiating skill of Ferdinand de Lesseps, both with Sa'īd and with Ismā'īl. The agreements he forced on them irreparably damaged the finances of Egypt and eventually the power of the Khedive. The only people who benefited were the owners and users of the Canal and, by the time he was dismissed by the Sultan in 1879, Ismā'īl had managed to increase the Egyptian national debt from £7 million, when he became Khedive, to almost £100 million, a factor of 14.

Since his youth, Sa'īd had been friendly with Ferdinand de Lesseps whose father had been French Consul-General in Egypt. When Sa'īd became Khedive, de Lesseps returned to Egypt and persuaded Sa'īd to grant him a concession to construct a canal from the Red Sea to the Mediterranean. After failing to get political and financial support from England, de Lesseps formed his own Compagnie Universelle du Canal Maritime de Suez and altered the original concession. The Company now had rights over a strip of land between the Nile and the original site which had been granted before, where a fresh water canal could be constructed. The Company also obtained freedom from taxation and the right of cultivation over this strip. In return, the Egyptian Government received preference shares the interest on which accounted for 15% of the net profits. A further 96,517 ordinary shares were taken up by the Egyptian Government when the subscription list was opened (24·13% of the total issue of 400,000 ordinary shares), and this would have secured the Egyptians 33% of the net profits; but Sa'īd had agreed, in a secret annex to the second concession, to supply free all the forced labour the Company needed for the completion of the Canal.

When the subscription list closed, Great Britain, Russia and the U.S.A. had not taken up the 85,506 shares allotted to them. Work could not begin until they were sold and de Lesseps announced that Sa'īd himself had decided to take them up. Sa'īd contradicted this in a letter to all his foreign Consulates and warned de Lesseps that he should not begin work until the Sultan had agreed to the concession. De Lesseps enlisted French support to sway the Sultan, but at this stage the British, and especially their Ambassador to the Sublime Porte in Constantinople, Sir Henry Elliot, were still against the scheme and halted the construction by protesting about the use of forced labour. In addition,

Sir Henry pressed the Sultan to refuse to ratify the concession. The subject of forced labour was argued with great vehemence: there was no benefit for the fellaheen as there had been in the case of the irrigation canals, which were only constructed at times when there was little work on the land. Such forced labour, Sir Henry said, was tantamount to slavery.

Until Sa'īd died, little work was done, but Ismā'īl, anxious to obtain prestige for his country and himself, and to stay friendly with both France and Britain, agreed to the construction of the Canal, saying that he would alter the terms of the concession. Although he was under no obligation to do so, he took up the 85,506 shares that Sa'īd, persuaded by de Lesseps, had agreed to buy, in spite of de Lesseps having defied him and the Sultan by beginning work on the Canal without their consent. A French tribunal, set up to change the terms of the concession, made Ismā'īl pay the Company £1,520,000 for failing to supply labour, and another £1,840,000 for the return of his rights over the land reserved for the fresh water canal.

In 1865, the Sultan issued a firman permitting the construction work to proceed and, once all political obstacles had been overcome, the engineering work was rapidly done and the Canal was finished in four years. In spite of the kudos attached to this achievement, Ismā'īl's true position was less satisfactory. He had lost much of his independence to the French as the Canal Company depended on its French shareholders. Moreover, he had incurred vast debts in his efforts to raise money for the Canal's completion and his other projects by borrowing, at exorbitant rates of interest, from European banking houses such as Oppenheim Alberti & Co. and the Anglo-Egyptian Bank. Other enterprising financiers, such as M. Edouard Dervieu of Paris, joined his brother André in Cairo to take advantage of the Khedive's need for money and willingness to borrow. By 1875, the Egyptian Treasury had paid £16,075,119 for the construction of the Canal and had borrowed £35,437,474 at rates of interest between 12·36% p.a. (1873 State Loan) and 26·9% p.a. (Railways Loan of 1866). As security the Khedive had pledged virtually everything eligible for such purposes in Egypt. By 1875, the only income left to him was his share in the Suez Canal Company.

The £3,976,583 that came from the sale, described later, of

this share did little to restore the balance. The Sultan had gone bankrupt in October 1875 and the Khedive could obtain no further loans from anywhere. He asked for a party of British Treasury officials to be sent out to supervise Egypt's finances and, in December 1875, Mr Stephen Cave was despatched from England to prepare a report, which was published in April, 1876.[74] He recommended that foreign powers should intervene to restore Egyptian credit. Subsequently a Caisse de la Dette Publique was established. In October, an Anglo-French commission under Mr G. J. (later Lord) Goschen and M. Hentsch Joubert took control and finally, the commission of Major Evelyn Baring (later Lord Cromer) conducted an enquiry that resulted in Ismāʿīl making over his estate to the nation and becoming a constitutional monarch. Nubar Pasha, who, as Ismāʿīl's Foreign Minister, had negotiated the sale of the Suez Canal shares, became Premier, Mr (later Sir Charles) Rivers Wilson, Finance Minister, and a M. de Blignieres, Minister of Public Works. Ismāʿīl was satisfied: 'Egypt is no longer in Africa; it is part of Europe.'[72] But after six months, he dismissed his Ministers and when Germany and Austria seemed inclined to use force to get him to pay his still outstanding debts, England and France told him to abdicate. A few days later, in June 1879, when he had still not stepped down, two telegrams arrived from the Sultan, one addressed to ex-Khedive Ismāʿīl and one to Khedive Tawfīq (his son). Ismāʿīl obeyed the telegram and resigned, leaving his son to govern Egypt.[73c] On the 30th June he left Egypt in the royal yacht *Mahroussa* (with £3 million and all the jewels he could lay his hands on) and retired to his palace at Emirghian on the Bosphorus. He remained there a prisoner of state until he died on 2nd March 1895.

Ismāʿīl's talents might have greatly benefited Egypt if his subjects had been liberated and not bound by feudal restrictions, his bureaucracy less corrupt and cowardly, his foreign investors less keen to pocket whatever profits might be extracted from Egypt; and if he had been more moderate in his schemes and improvements. But these factors, together with his personal failings and the nature of Egyptian society, were responsible for his deposition and later, the occupation of Egypt by the British.

The Suez Canal, although profitable only to the French and

British investors in it, was Ismā'īl's single work of permanent utility. By agreeing to the concessions and allowing de Lesseps to continue, he also ensured a European presence in Egypt that lasted for eighty years.

'You have it, Madam'

The news that the Khedive was trying to raise money on the security of his shares in the Suez Canal Company, or sell them, reached the Prime Minister, Disraeli, and the Foreign Secretary, Lord Derby (from Frederick Greenwood), on the 15th November 1875. Ten days later, on the 25th November, Ismā'īl Sadek, the Khedive's Finance Minister, and General Edward Stanton, our Consul-General in Cairo, had signed a document transferring 176,602 out of the total, 400,000, of ordinary shares in the Suez Canal Company to Her Majesty's Government, for £4,000,000 (£27½m in 1979 money).

Although the purchase was hailed, both in England and in many other countries, as a major political and diplomatic coup, the sale of the shares, the rapidity with which the money was raised, and Disraeli's reasons for making the acquisition were questioned at the time, even by members of the Cabinet who had been persuaded to agree to the purchase even on the first occasion, the 17th November, that the Cabinet discussed the matter, without any detailed knowledge of the situation. The conduct of Baron Lionel, who had advanced the money at, it is said, a day's notice and charged a commission of 2½% and interest at 5% per year for a few months, was also criticised, these charges being conveniently annualised by his critics to make them seem higher than they actually were.

The Khedive was virtually ruined. He had loans amounting to more than £30 million outstanding with various European banking houses and he had pledged almost all the dues, taxes, revenues and wealth of Egypt for their repayment, having raised new loans to pay off old debts. The Sultan, whose Viceroy he was, had gone bankrupt the previous October. The Khedive's shares in the Suez Canal Company were the only possession on which he could hope to raise money and even on these, he had borrowed money on the security of the coupons until 1894, so that the British Government received no dividends on their shares until that date. By the 30th November 1875 he was bound to raise between three and four million pounds.

At first he decided to mortgage the shares and approached the Parisian financier Edouard Dervieu who, as already mentioned, had arranged several loans for the Khedive. Dervieu went to two banks, the Société Générale and the Anglo-Egyptian Bank (which had strong French connections); as a result the Khedive gave them an option on his shares. Henry Oppenheim, whose uncle controlled the Oppenheim Syndicate which had invested heavily, and at high rates of interest, in various Egyptian loans, and whose willingness to give credit caused much of the Khedive's trouble, heard of the offer of the two French banks. Oppenheim claimed, for motives that are far from clear, to be unable, as a proprietor of the *Daily News*, to give the information to the British Government,[70] and therefore told Baron Lionel and Frederick Greenwood, the editor of the *Pall Mall Gazette*. Neither of these made any attempt to take personal advantage of the news, but communicated it at once to the British Government. Greenwood told Lord Derby[75a] and Baron Lionel, it is supposed, informed Disraeli.

Lord Derby's first reaction was that the deal must be stopped and he telegraphed to General Stanton in Cairo requesting him to investigate the rumour. His second reaction, to Lord Lyons, our ambassador in Paris, on hearing that Disraeli wanted to persuade the Khedive to sell his shares to the British Government, was to say: 'The acquisition would be a bad one financially and the affair might involve us in disagreeable correspondence both with France and the Porte.' (i.e. the Sultan and his Government).[76a]

When Lord Derby received a telegram from General Stanton saying that the Khedive would prefer to transfer his shares to England rather than elsewhere, he and Disraeli brought the matter before the Cabinet, on the 17th November, and then again on the 18th, 19th, 22nd, 23rd and 24th. The Cabinet was conducting its usual Autumn meetings, Parliament being in recess.

Disraeli reported these meetings to the Queen as follows:[77a]

Confidential
> 2, Whitehall Gardens,
> S.W.
>
> Nov. 18: 75

Mr. Disraeli with his humble duty to Yr. Majesty

The Khedive, on the eve of bankruptcy, appears desirous of parting with his shares in the Suez Canal, & has communicated, confidentially, with General Stanton. There is a French company in negotiation with His Highness, but they purpose only to make an advance with complicated stipulations.

'Tis an affair of millions; about four, at least, but wo^d. give the possessor an immense, not to say preponderating, influence in the management of the Canal.

It is vital to Her Majesty's authority & power at this critical moment, that the Canal should belong to England, & I was so decided & absolute with Lord Derby on this head, that he ultimately adopted my views & brought the matter before the Cabinet yesterday. The Cabinet was unanimous in their decision, that the interest of the Khedive sh^d., if possible, be obtained, & we telegraphed accordingly.

Last night, there was another telegram from Genl. Stanton, (not in reply) which indicated some new difficulties, but the Cabinet meets again today (at two o'clock) & we shall consider them.

The Khedive now says, that it is absolutely necessary that he should have between three & four millions sterling by the 30th. of this month!

Scarcely breathing time! But the thing must be done.

Mr. Disraeli perceives, that, in his hurry, he has not expressed himself according to etiquette. Your Majesty will be graciously pleased to pardon him! There is no time to re-write it. The messenger for Balmoral is waiting. He thought Yr Majesty sh^d. know all this, & could not write last night, as fresh intelligence was hourly expected.

Lord Derby telegraphed to General Stanton a request that the Khedive should suspend negotiations with the French companies; he wanted more information about the deal. The Khedive, it then appeared, would not sell his shares but would give the British Government an option to buy them if they should choose to do so. The Cabinet met and debated the news which General Stanton had sent after talking to the Khedive. Disraeli reported to the Queen on November 19:[77b]

> 2, Whitehall Gardens,
> S.W.
>
> Nov 19   :75
>
> Mr. Disraeli with his humble duty to Y^r Majesty.
>
> The Cabinet considered the affairs of the Khedive for one hour & $\frac{1}{2}$, & had, before them, Lord Tenterden & Colonel Stokes, who has been engaged by Yr Majesty's government on the affairs of the Suez Canal.
>
> The pecuniary embarassments of the Khedive appear to be very serious, & it is doubtful, whether a financial catastrophe can be avoided. The business is difficult, but it is as important, as difficult, & must not be relinquished – We received telegrams from General Stanton, who had personally seen the Khedive, & we also returned telegrams.
>
> The Khedive voluntarily pledged himself, that, whatever happened, Yr Majesty's Government sh^d. have the refusal of his interest in the Canal. All that can be done, now, is to keep the business well in hand.

The Cabinet was won round (once again) and as Disraeli told the Queen the following day, the 20th November, 'carte blanche' had been given 'to Mr. Disraeli to carry it into effect',[77c] though the carte was not so blanche as to make it unnecessary for Disraeli to refer the matter again to the Cabinet, on the 22nd, 23rd and 24th November.

Baron Lionel, the head of N. M. Rothschild & Sons, had been a close friend of Disraeli's for many years. They dined together on Sundays and discussed many matters with the wide variety of guests that Baron Lionel invited. As already mentioned, Disraeli is believed to have based the character of Sidonia on his friend; but such was the affinity between Disraeli and Lionel that

Sidonia was sometimes taken, according to Lord Palmerston, also to be a self-portrait of Disraeli.

Baron Lionel was a Liberal, but on many matters, particularly those concerning the Jews in England, Disraeli, in spite of being a Conservative, agreed with his friend and often voted in opposition to his own party. When, in 1874, the conduct of de Lesseps had threatened the future of the Canal, inasmuch as he had raised the dues in defiance of an International Commission set up specifically to investigate them, Disraeli approached Baron Lionel for help to gratify his ambition to have the Suez Canal administered by an International Commission, so that no Government, or the Company itself, could close it to shipping. Baron Lionel's eldest son Natty, M.P. for Aylesbury, was also sent secretly to Paris to ask de Lesseps if he would sell the Company to the British Government, but the mission was a failure: the sale was not on.[70]

Disraeli, still faced with covert if not overt opposition from some members of his Cabinet such as Lord Derby, decided again to proceed by stealth and use his friendship with Baron Lionel to acquire for the Government the Khedive's Suez Canal shares. Disraeli had a plan to secure the money at very short notice. Montagu Corry, his private secretary, was stationed outside the door to the Cabinet room while, on the 24th November, the Cabinet debated the purchase. As soon as they had agreed to buy the shares, Disraeli opened the door and said 'Yes', upon which Corry set off to New Court, where he was taken to Baron Lionel. Corry asked for a loan, and the following dialogue is said to have ensued, if Corry and subsequent embellishers are to be believed:

How much?
Four million pounds.
When?
Tomorrow.
What is your security?
The British Government.
You shall have it.

At the risk of being thought a spoil sport, I must mention that as Lord Blake[62] hints, this dialogue, and Baron Lionel's alleged antics with muscatel grapes, eating them and spitting out the pips during the discussion, are most unlikely to have occurred, at any rate in the form handed down to posterity. Disraeli and Baron Lionel had almost certainly talked about the deal before the Cabinet meetings to discuss it took place. The value of the Khedive's shares was known and it would not have been difficult to make a rough estimate of what he would accept for them, given his acute pecuniary embarrassments. 'Tomorrow' may have been shorthand for 'As from tomorrow' though, even then, 'tomorrow' was out of the question unless the whole operation had been settled by Disraeli and Baron Lionel before Corry's visit to the latter (which does not seem credible). In the event, the first request Rothschilds had for payment, from the Khedive's Finance Minister Ismaïl Seddik (his spelling), was dated the 30th November 1875. Baron Lionel had telegraphed to Ismaïl Seddik on the 29th November saying that he would hold £2 million at the disposition of the Egyptian Government as from the 1st December, £1 million as from the 15th December, and the last tranche, a further £1 million, as from the beginning of January.

The last nail in the coffin, before the story is buried, is to be found in Sir Stafford Northcote's letter to Disraeli of the 24th November in which he said: 'I find Smith and Welby a good deal startled by the largeness of Rothschild's commission.'[78a] Clearly, therefore, the details of the deal were known on the 24th November and there was no point in Corry visiting Baron Lionel after the Cabinet meeting to discuss them. That Northcote heard these details *at* the Cabinet meeting on the 24th November and not in private from Disraeli is confirmed by the entry for that day in Lord Derby's diary (unpublished): 'we agreed to accept: subject, that is, to the consent of parliament. Rothschild undertakes to find the money, and takes the risk of parliament refusing the bargain, which is not likely to happen: there was no difference of opinion among us, Northcote being as ready as any. I telegraphed accordingly.'

Disraeli may just possibly have sent Corry to see Baron Lionel after the Cabinet meeting on the 19th November, during which it will be remembered that Disraeli, according to himself in a letter dated the 20th November to Queen Victoria, had been given '*carte blanche*' to complete the purchase, without reference to the Cabinet. But why, then, was it necessary to have three further

Cabinet meetings to discuss the matter, at the second of which, on the 23rd November, there was 'No definite conclusion' according to the entry in Lord Derby's diary (also unpublished) for that day?

After the Cabinet meeting at which the final decision to buy was taken Disraeli wrote a triumphant letter to the Queen:[78b]

Nov 24   2 Whitehall Gardens,
                                                    S.W.

Mr. Disraeli with his humble duty to Yr Majesty.

It is just settled: you have it, Madam. The French Government has been outgeneraled. They tried too much, offering loans at an usurious rate, & with conditions wh: would have virtually given them the government of Egypt.

The Khedive, in despair & disgust, offered Yr Majesty's Government to purchase his shares outright – he never would listen to such a proposition before.

Four millions sterling! and almost immediately. There was only one firm that cd do it – Rothschilds. They behaved admirably; advanced the money at a low rate, and the entire interest of the Khedive is now yours, Madam.

Yesterday the Cabinet sate four hours & more on this & Mr. Disraeli has not had one moments rest today; therefore this despatch must be pardoned, as his head is rather weak. He will tell the whole wondrous tale tomorrow.

He was in Cabinet today, when Yr Majesty's second tel: arrived, wh. must be his excuse for his brief & stupid answer – but it was the crisis.

The Gov^t. and Rothschilds agreed to keep it secret, but there is little doubt that it will be known tomorrow from <u>Kairo.</u>

Although this letter may be held to reveal Disraeli's well-known powers of hyperbole its contents were not so wide of the mark as some might think. The French Government was certainly aware, as we shall see later, of the efforts being made by the Société Générale and the Anglo-Egyptian Bank to acquire the Khedive's shares and, though fearful of offending England, wanted the Société Générale to be successful. Disraeli was not, however, correct in saying that the Khedive offered his shares to

England 'in despair & disgust', although he hoped for less onerous terms from the British than from the French. About the statement that Rothschilds advanced the money at 'a low rate', Mr Gladstone had a different view. He considered the commission and interest received by Rothschilds, when annualized to make the figures look worse, implied that British credit-worthiness was at the same level as that of Bolivia or Ecuador – not to mention Egypt under the Khedive himself. Disraeli was also not strictly correct in saying that the Khedive's interest now belonged entirely to the Queen, because he had pawned his share coupons until 1894. In any case, much of the Khedive's interest did not reside in the ownership of the shares but in his rule over Egypt.

In his letter to Lady Bradford on the following day, November 25, Disraeli's powers of imagination did tend to conflict with reality. He did not have 'all the gamblers, capitalists, financiers of the world, organized and platooned in bands of plunderers, arrayed against us, and secret emissaries in every corner'.[79a] Disraeli's prophecy, in the same letter, that the French, if they had owned the Canal, 'might have shut it up!' is also questionable. The ownership of a large tranche of the ordinary shares would neither have provided the right nor the power to shut or open the Canal, as can be seen by studying the company statutes.[80]

The Prince of Wales, who had been in India when the shares were bought and who had paid a state visit to Cairo in October at the start of his Eastern journey, was told of the purchase in a letter from Disraeli on December 11. Disraeli declared that:[78a]

> For some time it was rumoured, that Yr. Rl. Hss had been mainly instrumental in this result, & I have never denied it, & certainly the visit of Yr. Rl. Hss to Cairo, & the investiture of the then apparent with the Grand Cross, gave a colour & a graceful one, to this impression.

This, Disraelian flattery as it was, may have had an element of truth in it. The Prince of Wales' visit, and the Order conferred on the Khedive, may have been partly responsible for his willingness to suspend negotiations with the French banks and await the decision of Her Majesty's Government.

The Prince of Wales had been friendly with Baron Lionel's sons during his year at Cambridge and he remained friendly with them for the rest of his life. Disraeli says more to him about the role of N. M. Rothschild & Sons in the affair than to any other correspondent:[78a]

> Our friends, the Rothschilds, distinguished themselves. They alone cd. have accomplished what we wanted, & they had only 4 & 20 hours to make up their minds, whether they wd, or could, incur an immediate liability of 4 millions. One of their difficulties was, that they cd. not appeal to their strongest ally, their own family in Paris, for Alphonse is si francese that he wd. have betrayed the whole scheme instantly. Weguelin, a liberal, & a Bank Director, & a man of considerable abilities, told Mr. Corry yesterday, that it was a positive fact, that the Rothschilds had not made the slightest use of the intelligence, as they considered themselves standing in the position of the Government. The world, of course, gives them credit for having made at least $\frac{1}{4}$ of a million.

The Rothschilds, unlike many other banking houses, had not made significant investments in the earlier Egyptian loans. In 1864 Baron Nathaniel wrote to his brother Lionel from Paris:[81]

> I do not think that with money at 8% in London and loans wanted by almost every Government in Europe that there is any particular advantage in lending one's money to the Pasha of Egypt – in times like the present one ought first to look at home and make oneself comfortable: husband one's resources . . .

The Khedive, who had 'a reverence for the name Rothschild and for the authority of the House' (according to a letter from E. Landau & Co. Alexandria, apparently to H. Landau of Turin),[82] was anxious to obtain their backing against the depredations incurred by other, less scrupulous, firms. All this in spite of Nathaniel having advised Lionel not to lend £4,000,000 to the Khedive in 1864 and having refused to lend money to de Lesseps at the inception of the Suez scheme, which in turn contributed to the foundation of the Compagnie Universelle du Canal Maritime de Suez.

But in the present case the money was to be advanced to the British Government though, in fact, Rothschilds made payments directly to the Khedive's creditors. The Government, which paid Baron Lionel's commission of $2\frac{1}{2}\%$, £100,000, stipulated that the Khedive should pay interest at 5% a year on the advance. As mentioned earlier, there were those who said that, given that the advance was backed by the British Government, Rothschilds were not justified in charging a commission of $2\frac{1}{2}$ per cent. Montagu Corry, Disraeli's secretary and also a friend of the Rothschilds, interviewed Baron Lionel on the 19th February, 1876, a few days after the first Parliamentary debate on the subject, to clarify the situation before the second debate on February 21. Corry sent this letter to Disraeli:[83a]

Baron Rothschild points out that his contract was to find four millions sterling <u>during the month of December.</u> That contract was signed on the 27th(?) of Nov^r.

As a fact, <u>two</u> millions <u>were</u> provided by him, at the disposal of the Khedive, on the 1st of December. The second payment (of <u>one</u> million) was demanded of, and made by him, on Dec. 16th. And the last payment (of <u>one</u> million) was made on January 5th.

The Khedive might have demanded that each of these payments should be made in sovereigns, and at earlier dates than, actually, the amounts were paid.

Had the Khedive ordered – say – the first payment (of two millions) to be made in gold, the withdrawal of such a sum, in sovereigns, would have infallibly damaged seriously the money market, and have rendered it impossible for the Firm to meet the subsequent demands upon the comparatively advantageous terms on which (as the Baron admits) they were able to meet them.

Beyond this, unforeseen events might have occurred, between the dates of the contract and the payments, which would have, perhaps largely, increased the price of money.

These contingent considerations had great weight with the Baron in determining the amount of commission which he should ask.

He points out, in addition, that the withdrawal of four millions from the reserves of a Firm, for a period (already considerable) entails a large derangement of the routine of its business and disturbance of its financial arrangements. For instance, a Foreign Government, accustomed to do business with the Rothschilds might have called upon that Firm to undertake a transaction involving large ready money payments, and, finding the Firm unable to meet the demand, have transferred the business to other hands. But, even if no such contingency should arise, the 'standing out' of so large a sum must be taken to cripple the resources and opportunities of a house of business accustomed to make rapid and great profits.

It is for the above reasons that the House of Rothschild fixed their commission so high as 2½ per cent.

Baron Rothschild denies that the risk of Parliament declining to vote the four millions was an element in his consideration of the matter, and leaves it to the Government to determine whether so impossible an eventuality should be alleged as having influenced their view of the proper commission.

He declares that the transaction is entirely without precedent, and that the Government have never before called upon a Firm to advance a sum of money. The case of the payment of the Alabama indemnity is not at all analogous. In that instance payments were made in London to the Firm of Morton Rose & Co. 'à mésure' that they paid sums to the American Government, and as a fact, they received part of the money here, before they made their first payment in New York.

As to the question whether the Government should not have applied to the Bank of England, Baron Rothschild – giving no opinion as to the Bank's power – says that he understands the authorities to be about equally divided (even now) on the point of their <u>willingness</u> to have acted as the agents of the Government in this transaction. It is a point, moreover, which could only have been determined by the full Board, at the obvious sacrifice of dispatch and secrecy. Mr. Hubbard, for one, is clear that the Bank could not, and would not, have acted,* while Mr. Gibbs and Mr. Thomson Hankey take the other view.

* Mr Hubbard tells me that he is prepared to say this in Parliament. M.C.

Baron Rothschild imagines that the Government might, possibly, have <u>compelled</u> the Bank to find the four millions.* But this would have been a violent act, before the commission of which, he maintains, they were bound to use every endeavour to obtain the money from independent Firms. He declares, too, without hesitation, that the Bank of England could not have found the required sum without grave disturbance of the money market.

It is upon the entire absence of such disturbance, under his operations, that he, from a public point of view, rests his vindication of the commission charged, and is content that the matter should be judged by the result.

He reminded me – as a proof that this result is considerable – of the trepidation which filled the mind of the Chancellor of the Exchequer and the City when the payment of the Alabama indemnity was impending, though, in that case, long previous notice had enabled all concerned to discount the effect of the operation, and the amount to be paid was less.

M.C.

* And at a lower rate of commission.   Feb. 19 1876

Many of Rothschilds' customers would have benefited from advance notice of the deal, but Baron Lionel ensured that the Government had time to act before anyone else was informed through rumour or the Press.

The original agreement under which the purchase had been made was a verbal one. Rothschilds then wrote to the Chancellor of the Exchequer, Sir Stafford Northcote, confirming it (see below).

A Treasury Minute of November 25th, 1875 states that Rothschilds had agreed to act as agents for Her Majesty's Government and would 'undertake to hold 1,000,000*l* sterling at the disposal of the Egyptian Government',[84a] once the shares had been handed over to Her Majesty's Consul-General in Egypt, General Stanton. The rest of the money was to be provided in December and January. It was understood that 177,642 shares were to be bought. W. H. Smith, Secretary to the Treasury, sent this information to Rothschilds who replied:[84b]

'You have it, Madam'

New Court, November 25th 1875

Sir,

We have the honour to acknowledge receipt of a letter from the Secretary of the Treasury, in which are stated the conditions upon which we are willing to undertake the operations to which the said letter refers, and in answer to which we beg to state that the said conditions are in accordance with our verbal agreement, namely:

As soon as we receive the orders from the Lords Commissioners of Her Majesty's Treasury, we shall be prepared to hold at the disposal of the Egyptian Government the sum of 4,000,000*l*., (four millions sterling); 1,000,000*l*. (one million sterling) to be at the disposal of the Egyptian Government on the 1st December and the remaining 3,000,000*l*. (three millions sterling) during the months of December and January, in such manner as may be arranged between the Egyptian Government and ourselves.

It is also understood that we are to charge Her Majesty's Government a commission of 2½ (two and one half per cent upon the 4,000,000*l*. (four millions sterling) and 5 per cent (five per cent. per annum) interest until the date of repayment.

This advance is also made on the distinct understanding that Her Majesty's Government will, as soon as practicable, apply to Parliament for a grant of money to enable Her Majesty's Government to repay the said advance.

> We have the honour to remain,
> Sir,
> Your obedient servants,
> N. M. Rothschild & Sons.

The agreement was that £4,000,000 would be advanced to Her Majesty's Government and put at the Khedive's disposal. The shares would be delivered to Stanton in Cairo, thus passing directly into the hands of the British Government. At no time did they belong to Rothschilds.

Subsequent arguments about the nature of the deal came from misunderstanding and misinformation about the documents in which the agreement was set out. Rothschilds had no responsibility for the shares themselves; they were the concern of General Stanton.

Disraeli's report to the Prince of Wales that Baron Lionel could not approach his French cousins was correct. There are no letters between the Houses about the shares before 23rd November 1875, but in an undated letter (obviously after November 25, 1875) from Paris, Alphonse referred to the deal, and expressed gratitude for the chance of participation:[85]

> My dear Cousins,
> We have had the pleasure of receiving your good letters in which you have told us of the operation you have concluded with the English Government. We accept with great pleasure your offer of participation and will keep the money ready at the times you indicate. The news of the acquisition of a part of the Suez Canal shares by England has produced a very strong reaction here . . .

In this instance the Rothschilds did not act in their usual way with intimate and high speed cooperation between the different Houses. As usual, however, unity of family feeling overcame any unfavourable reaction that Alphonse, the French patriot, might have had towards this English deal. There was no query from Paris about the security of the advance, even though it would not be known until February whether or not Parliament would vote the money. Disraeli knew how the family behaved:[83b]

> The prosperity of the Rothschilds was as much owing to the unity of feeling whc: alike pervaded all branches of that numerous family as on their capital and ability. They were like an Arabian tribe . . .

General Stanton told Lord Derby that the Khedive, instead of being able to sell the previously mentioned 177,642 shares, had overestimated the number and had only 176,602.[84c] This reduced the value of the shares to £3,976,582:2:6. The Egyptian Government was pledged to pay 5% a year interest on the money until the share coupons were liberated, which meant that the Khedive would have to draw about £100,000 every six months from the revenues of the Egyptian Government.

The shares were sealed in seven large boxes and deposited at the Consulate under General Stanton's control.

Although Baron Lionel had no responsibility for the shares themselves, he continued to advise the Government, at the request of the Chancellor, Sir Stafford Northcote, about their collection and supervision. This was his advice:[77d]

New Court
26th Nov 1873 [in error for 1875]

Dear Sir Stafford Northcote,

I return your telegram with thanks.

In answer to your enquiry what ought to be done before the shares are sent here, I should recommend you to telegraph to General Stanton to let a Public Notary make a list of the shares with their numbers and all particulars. These particulars he would enter in his own books and give General Stanton two certified copies of these particulars, one copy to be provided to you with the shares and the other copy to be sent to you by another messenger on opportunity.

Please let me know if you require any further information, which I shall be most happy to give you if in my power.

Believe me,
Lionel de Rothschild

This advice was telegraphed to General Stanton, who did as requested. As a result two shares were found to be missing and two more duplicated, a minor matter which was easily rectified.

Rothschilds were to negotiate with the Khedive about whom he wanted the money delivered to and, as reported by Corry following his interview with Baron Lionel, not one but two million pounds were demanded to be paid on 1st December, the rest to follow on the 16th December and 5th January.

Further advice that the Treasury received from Baron Lionel was:[77d]

that it might be well to instruct Her Majesty's Ambassador in Paris to give notice to the Suez Canal Co. at Paris of the purchase by this country of the Khedive's shares, and of the time and mode in which they are to be brought to England.

He also suggested that the Company should be given a list of the shares.

The reason for all this solicited advice must have been that the Government and the Treasury were unused to dealing in shares (despite the taunt made by Lowe, Chancellor of the Exchequer in Gladstone's Government, that this was a 'stock-jobbing Ministry').[79b] Baron Lionel and the Firm were acting in the place of the Bank of England and gave all the advice, and took all the action, that the Bank would have done, with the advantage that their experience in international finance, as Disraeli knew well, was unparalleled. 'There was only one firm that cd do it – Rothschilds.'[78b]

The first payment was made on 1st December, as directed in a telegram from General Stanton which was passed on to Rothschilds by Lord Tenterden:[77d]

Cairo, 30 Nov.

To Lord Derby

In conformity with the desire expressed by Messrs. N. Rothschild to the Egyptian Govt. I am requested to acquaint those gentlemen through Yr. Lordship that the Finance Minister will request them by telegraph to pay on the 1st December to the London & Westminster Bank to the account of Messieurs Aide & Co. the sum of one hundred and sixty thousand pounds sterling; – further that he will telegraph about the 8th December asking them to pay on the 10th three hundred and twenty one thousand pounds sterling to the Anglo Egyptian Bank. For the remainder of the payments to be made the Minister will have time to correspond with Messieurs Rothschild by letter.

The firms mentioned in the telegram were those from whom the Khedive had previously borrowed money and who were pressing for the repayment of their loans. The Khedive's own financial organization was in chaos. He had already requested Lord Derby to send out two Treasury officials to report on and re-organize the finances of Egypt, and Stephen Cave was completing his report on the subject at this time. It was a great advantage to the Khedive to be able to call upon Rothschilds to handle the repayment of his debts, as he respected them highly (see p. 173) and had never been able to enlist their services before.

Rothschild replied to Tenterden himself:[77d]

New Court 1st Dec. 1875

Dear Lord Tenterden,

I am much obliged for the copy of the telegram you were so good as to send me last night.

We have made the payment for account of the Egypt. Govt. everything having been in perfect order.

Believe me,

Yrs most truly,

Lionel de Rothschild

Lionel did not, apparently, think it necessary to tell Lord Tenterden that for at least six days, and possibly longer, he had been in direct telegraphic communication with Ismā'īl's finance minister, Ismā'īl Sadek, about precisely those matters itemized by General Stanton to the Foreign Office. The telegrams are in the New Court Archives.

More instructions arrived the following day by telegram from Cairo:[77d]

To Earl of Derby   Cairo 2nd December

I am requested to acquaint Messrs Rothschild through your Lordship that assignments of the following amounts payable the 10th instant have been made on them by the Egyptian Government viz. Two hundred and forty nine thousand one hundred and twenty two pounds seven shillings and two pence to Anglo Egyptian Banking Company, forty three thousand nine hundred and ninety four pounds four pence to Bank of Alexandria and twenty eight thousand and eight pounds six shillings to the Anglo Austrian Bank.

Edwd. Stanton

When the final payment had been made to the Khedive, the shares themselves, in their seven zinc boxes, were put on board *HMS Malabar*, on the 16th December, and arrived at Portsmouth on the last day of the year. They were then taken to the Bank of England where they were again checked. Rothschilds were not concerned with this part of the business. They were, however, concerned about Parliament voting them the money that was now in the Khedive's hands. An undated and cryptic note from Baron Lionel to his son Leo at Cambridge, presumably written at the end of December 1875, may reflect this concern:

> ... today we had a long talk about Egyptian matters, not such a pleasant way of passing one's time ... but we live in hopes on Dizzy's speech and refusal to publish the Cave report.[86, 87]

On 2nd February 1876 W. H. Smith sent this letter to Rothschilds about the vote in Parliament:[88]

In the reply to this Letter
the following Number should
    be quoted.
    1.908.76   TREASURY CHAMBERS,
                                          2nd February, 1876

Gentlemen,
    I am directed by the Lords Commissioners of Her Majesty's Treasury to inform you that they will, as soon as practicable after the opening of Parliament, ask the House of Commons to vote the money required to make good to you the advances which you have made to the Egyptian Government, on account of the Shares in the Suez Canal purchased by H.M. Government, and also to pay you the Commission agreed upon between yourselves and this Board.
    The vote will form part of the arrangements of the current financial year, and will therefore come in course of payment on or before the 31st March next.
    Assuming for the moment that the House will grant the money, I am to say that My Lords would be anxious to regulate their payment so as to suit, as far as may be, your convenience, and with that object They would ask you to inform Them at what dates and in what instalments during the month of March you will wish to receive the money.
    My Lords might perhaps suggest a payment of three instalments, the first being fixed for the 10th, the second

for the 20th, and the third for the 31st of that month, but other arrangements would probably suit Them equally well.

I am further to ask that you will notify to Them the dates and amounts of the several advances which you have made to the Egyptian Government under your agreement with this Board.

I am,

Gentlemen,

Your obedient Servant,

W. H. Smith

Messrs, N. M. de Rothschild & Son.

Rothschilds replied two days later:[77e]

New Court E.C.

4th February 1876

Sir,

We have the honour to acknowledge the receipt of your letter of the 2nd inst. No. 1908.76 in which you inform us that the vote required to repay to us our advances made to the Egyptian Government for the Suez Canal Shares will be submitted to Parliament very shortly and that you have been desired by Her Majesty's Treasury to ask us if the dates mentioned in your letter for payment of the same will be convenient to us.

We have only to say that this arrangement will suit us if convenient to Their Lordships.

We beg also that you will be so good as to inform the Right Honourable the Lords Commissioners of the Treasury that we placed at the disposal of the Egyptian Government

£2,000,000	on the 1st December 1875
1,000,000	,, ,, 16th ,, 1875
976,582.2/6	,, ,, 5th January 1876

£3,976,582.2/6 (Say three millions nine hundred and seventy six thousand five hundred and eighty

two pounds 2/6) which said amount has been paid
by us.

We have the honour to remain,

Sir,

Your most obedient servants,

N. M. Rothschild & Sons

W. H. Smith Esq. M.P.

Secretary to the Treasury

Treasury Chambers

This was confirmed in a telegram to General Stanton and a draft was prepared for presentation to Parliament.

The debate on the purchase of the Khedive's shares did not begin in the House of Commons on February the 14th, 1876. Opinions had been expressed publicly and privately almost as soon as the prospect of the sale became known and, to begin with, some of Disraeli's most important opponents came from within his own party and, even, his own Cabinet. The more one looks at the opinions of those around Disraeli, the clearer it becomes that the purchase of the shares and the voting of the money were personal victories for him, not so much against 'all the gamblers, capitalists, financiers of the world, organized and platooned in bands of plunderers' but against Sir Stafford Northcote (who later changed his mind and agreed with Disraeli), Lord Derby and the Opposition.

The classic account of the Suez Canal operation (in English) was that of Lucien Wolf, in *The Times*, on the 26th December 1905.[70] His account of the myopic, reactionary and almost imbecile attitude of earlier British Governments, and Lord Palmerston in particular, towards the Suez Canal is as instructive today as it was damaging then. Wolf says that Rothschilds had spent most of the summer of 1875, after Natty's abortive visit to Paris, approaching de Lesseps to try and secure as many shares in the Suez Canal Company as possible for the Government. But de Lesseps, who was hostile to England because of her refusal to participate in the early days, was not interested in these offers and continued to cause difficulties to British shipping passing through the Canal by raising the dues, contrary to the terms of the Company's Constitution. If, as is probable, Wolf is right, the victory must be seen as one for Baron Lionel as well as for Disraeli who was willing enough to give credit to his friend (when he was not ascribing the *coup* to the Prince of Wales) and was excited at the chance of adventuring into international finance with one of the two Sidonias.

When Frederick Greenwood told Lord Derby that the shares were for sale (see p. 165) and should be bought by England, the latter refused to do anything until Disraeli, had persuaded him that 'the thing must be done'.[77a] Although he gave his assent in Cabinet, he continued to doubt the propriety of the purchase. In the absence of the French Ambassador, the Chargé d'Affaires, M. Gavard, called on Lord Derby on the 20th November, to find out if the British Government would object to the Khedive's shares being sold to the Société Générale or the Anglo-Egyptian Bank. Lord Derby saw no reason to mention to M. Gavard either that he had already got this information from Frederick Greenwood on the 15th November, or that three days earlier, on the 17th November (and seven days before the Cabinet finally reached agreement on the issue), a telegram was sent to General Stanton in which the latter was instructed 'to inform the Egyptian Government that Her Majesty's Government are disposed to purchase His Highness' shares if satisfactory terms can be arranged'.[84d] On the contrary, Lord Derby told M. Gavard that although the Canal 'had been originated by a Frenchman, executed by French engineers, and carried out principally by means of French capital', nearly four-fifths of the traffic through it was British. He was, therefore, opposed to the Khedive parting with his shares[84d] (see also Annexes 5 and 6). Lord Derby's own scheme, which he had propounded in the House of Lords, was that the Canal should be managed by an International Commission so that no single Government should control it. The only possible interpretation of Lord Derby's Janus-like behaviour must be that the telegram to General Stanton, referred to above, was forced unwillingly on him by Disraeli.

In a later speech made on the 18th December, 1875, in Edinburgh,[89] his argument was the same as that he had used to the French Chargé d'Affaires. All Britain had done was to secure 'free and uninterrupted passage through Egypt to India' and to prevent the great highway, three quarters of whose traffic was

British, from being 'exclusively in the hands of the foreign share-holders of a foreign company'. In such circumstances it was expedient to buy the shares. The meeting at Edinburgh at which Lord Derby spoke was enthusiastic when he first mentioned the purchase but lost interest when he came to this conclusion. Queen Victoria wrote to Disraeli about the speech on December 3rd:[61b]

> Lord Derby tried to pour as much cold water as he could on the great success of the affair of the Suez Canal, though he seemed pleased at the feeling shown everywhere about it.

Two other opponents of the deal, at any rate to begin with, were Sir Stafford Northcote and W. H. Smith. The former, as Chancellor, had to defend the purchase in the Commons and was at first unwilling for it to go through. He spoke against it in Manchester on 7th December, having written beforehand to Disraeli on the 26th November:[90a]

> Our policy, or our proceedings, with regard to the Canal, has not been such as to gain us much credit for magnanimity. We opposed it in its origin; we refused to help Lesseps in his difficulties; we have used it when it has succeeded: we have fought the battle of our shipowners very stiffly; and now we avail ourselves of our influence with Egypt to get a quiet slice of what promises to be a good thing.
> Suspicion will be excited that we mean quietly to buy ourselves into a preponderating position, and then turn the whole thing into an English property.
> I don't like it.

Even before this, on the 23rd November, Northcote had written to Disraeli saying that he would back a French mortgage against an English purchase:[90b]

> What would best suit us would be an International arrangement by which the Canal could be placed under the guardianship of all the Powers interested in maintaining the communication . . .
> I am more inclined to seek my leverage in the accept-

ance of this mortgage by the Societe Generale [sic] than in any attempt to get it for ourselves, which I fear may set other countries against us. We ought boldly to avow our legitimate interest in the question, and make a frank proposal.

Northcote's ambivalent views about the purchase of the Suez Canal shares are well exemplified by the fact that on the 3rd December he wrote to Lord Carnarvon saying that he and others 'are decidedly against purchasing',[90b] whereas four days later, in Manchester, obviously briefed by Disraeli, he said:[90c]

If we have become the possessors of a considerable interest in that important highway of maritime communication, and if we have become the possessors of that interest with a view to the maintainance of our own communication with our Eastern empire, we have not done so in a spirit of exclusive selfishness, but in the entirely opposite spirit, of desiring to extend to all nations that freedom of communication that we desire to secure for ourselves. We honour and respect and admire the energy and genius of those who have planned, and who, against, great difficulties, carried through that great enterprise. We desire in no degree to rob them of their fair share of the honour, or in any way to mar the great work that they contemplated. We fully believe that which they always said, that they undertook that work not in the interest of individuals, or in the interest of a single nation, but in the spirit of those who wish to make a name for themselves in the proud role of the world's benefactors; and if we associate ourselves with that enterprise now, we do so, not in order to thwart, but to forward that enterprise: it is with the hope that the Canal, which will always remain the monument of the energy and of the perseverance of M. de Lesseps, and of the great nation which has borne so large a part in the work, may be maintained as a highroad for nations, and not exclusively for the benefit of any one.

Sir Stafford's vacillations were finally revealed in a letter he wrote to Disraeli on the 26th January, 1876. In it, he said:[76b]

So far as the purchase of the Suez Canal shares is in question, I think our case is perfect.

W. H. Smith, though agreeing in general with the Chancellor, had reservations about the wisdom of appointing an International Commission to govern the Canal. Britain, with perhaps 75% of the burden, would have to allow the other maritime nations to spend her money 'until we quarrelled with them.'[91] He was in favour of buying the Canal outright; but this would not have solved the problem of the Khedive's control over the land through which it passed.

Mr Gladstone, a 'disembodied spirit' as he described himself in a letter dated November the 22nd, 1875 to Lord Granville (formerly Foreign Secretary),[76b] believed the purchase, if done 'in concert with the other Powers', to be 'an act of folly, fraught with future embarrassment'; if done without such concert, 'an act of folly fraught with personal danger'. This was on the 22nd November 1875 and he predicted that the Cabinet would go to 'some finance agent' for the money. Lord Granville believed there was a plot by de Lesseps and the Rothschilds to dupe the Government into taking up the shares, 'by threatening them with a purchase of French capitalists'.[76c] Mr Gladstone continued to work against the scheme: he believed that Lord Derby's view was 'only *relatively* the right one' and that those of the Government were 'more and more dangerously wrong'.[76c] Mr Gladstone, Lord Granville and Henry Reeve prepared their attack on the Government by studying the constitution of the Suez Canal Company, as they believed that the Government had acted hastily and in ignorance.

Disraeli, shortly before the opening of Parliament, predicted to Lady Bradford that:[79b]

> there is to be a war to the knife when the Houses meet; at least the Flea [a Mr Fleming] told me so whom I met yesterday morn. Gladstone is to rush into the arena; but Lowe is to be awful – crushing, overwhelming: a great invective against a stockjobbing Ministry.

Though several of his colleagues disliked or seemed to dislike the operation, Disraeli's venture was received with acclamation

abroad and with rapture by the country, the Press and the Royal
Family. The reaction in the country was no doubt influenced by
the various newspaper articles that praised Disraeli. Rightly or
wrongly, it was assumed, as was later mentioned in Parliament,
that the ownership of the shares gave England considerable influence over the management of the Canal. It was the supposed
political victory that was praised rather than the actual financial
coup. The Press had the same details as Disraeli sent in his Cabinet
minutes to the Queen, and most people were delighted by the
outsmarting of the foreign governments and financiers. The
Queen told Disraeli, so he repeated in a letter to Lady Bradford,
that what she liked most was that it was 'a blow to Bismarck',
'referring, I apprehend, to his insolent declarations that England
had ceased to be a political power.'[79c] In the same letter Disraeli
said: 'I believe the whole country will be with me. The Faery
[Queen Victoria] thinks so.' The City, industry and commerce
were unanimous in praising his action. Congratulations were sent
from every European country except Russia. Bismarck did not
admit to having been dealt a blow and told Lord Odo Russell, the
British Ambassador in Berlin, how pleased he was; other countries
expressed their approval and even France, which might have been
offended by the deal, became reconciled to it. De Lesseps wrote a
letter to his shareholders welcoming the operation. The British
Government, which in the past had put as many difficulties as
possible in the Company's way, was now able to cease its hostility
towards the original shareholders by taking up the shares that
had been reserved to her from the outset. The French Press did
not miss the political significance of the action. It seemed to
'Opinione' that Britain had acted wisely in view of Russian expan-
sion to the north of her Indian territories and that to take up an
interest in the Canal, after years of Palmerstonian hostility, could
only help her in securing her Empire. The purchase of the shares
only entitled the Government to ten votes at a general meeting of
shareholders and three seats on the Board of Directors, points to
which the Opposition drew attention in Parliament. In fact,
seven more English directors, to represent British shipping, were
invited to join the Board, making ten British Directors in all
(until 1956 when Nasser nationalized the Canal). The Government was therefore now able, for the first time, to negotiate the

settlement of dues, tonnage and surtax, matters that had previously bedevilled relations between the Suez Canal Company
and Britain.

A conference was held at Ismaïlia on the 3rd February, 1876
'to put an end to the differences between the Maritime Powers
and the Universal Company of the Suez Maritime Canal',[92a] on
the initiative of de Lesseps. Colonel John Stokes, the representative
of the British Government, who had already prepared a survey of
the Suez Canal, was the only person apart from de Lesseps
present and he persuaded the latter to revert to the original
terms of the Porte's regulations on dues, tonnage and surtax.
Further, that the Company should 'execute extraordinary works
of construction' in addition to ordinary repairs – up to a cost of
one million francs a year for 30 years.[92b]

This removed the previous disagreements with the Canal
Company that Disraeli and the Rothschilds had been trying to
eliminate; and it is doubtful, to put it mildly, whether de Lesseps
would have been prepared to be so helpful unless Britain had
bought the shares and acquired an interest in the Company commensurate with its position as the maritime nation with the
greatest use of the Canal.

So far as popular opinion, foreign affairs and England's relations with the Company were concerned, the operation was highly
successful. Disraeli had no opponents outside the Houses of
Parliament. But it was from the Commons that he had to obtain a
vote of money to repay Rothschilds: and the Opposition were
sharpening their knives.

The attack in the House of Commons

Because the debate was to determine whether or not Parliament
would vote £4,080,000 to Rothschilds, the attention of Parliament
in Committee was already on the Firm and a number of Opposition Members had investigated the nature of the deal between
Rothschilds and the Government, basing their attack on the
propriety of borrowing money from a private firm. Unfortunately,
Disraeli made a mistake in his first speech at the Opening of
Parliament when he reported saying to Rothschilds:[93]

"Will you purchase these shares on our engagement

that we will ask the House of Commons to take them off
your hands." They did so. That was a great risk.

Actually, Rothschilds did not buy the shares but advanced
the money for their purchase. The shares never passed through
their hands. Disraeli's remark also directed attention to the risk
run by the Firm, which determined the size of the commission.
The Government, expecting adverse comment on this point, had
asked Baron Lionel, through Montagu Corry, to explain his
reasons for setting the commission at $2\frac{1}{2}\%$ and the interest at 5%
per year. As we have seen, Baron Lionel had no difficulty in
countering this criticism.

The attacks made by the Opposition, and especially Mr
Gladstone, on Rothschilds were these: the Firm had charged the
Government what amounted to 15% per year on a loan of £4
million, when their risk had been negligible. The Government
had not applied to the Bank of England for the money and had
taken the unprecedented step of going to a private firm. There
had been no guarantee that Rothschilds would refrain from
giving advance warning to those who might benefit from knowledge of the sale before the news was published. Only £1 million
need have been provided overnight, the remaining £3 million
being raised later by the Government. Finally, misleading information had been passed to the Press.

The question of the commission and interest was somewhat
confused. The vote of £4,080,000 was to repay the advance and
pay the commission and incidental expenses. Although the
Government intended the Khedive to pay the 5% a year interest,
as indicated in their letter to Rothschilds, the latter, when confirming the agreement, wrote that the Government would pay
the interest which, as it was to the Government that the money
had been advanced, was correct. The Khedive would pay the
Government his 5% a year until the share coupons came out of
hock. The Government paid Rothschilds their interest, but the
money was not included in Parliament's vote.

The risk that Rothschilds ran is hard to estimate. Baron
Lionel calculated it in terms of the Firm being unable to conduct
its normal business with so much money being suddenly taken
away and of the problem of procuring a huge amount of gold if

the Khedive demanded it. He did not include the risk that the money would not be repaid which, as Mr Gladstone said, was negligible. Mr Gladstone was not trying to prevent the repayment of the advance, but to chastise Disraeli for taking unconstitutional liberties, running risks that he had not calculated, and buying shares that, according to Mr Gladstone, would give him inadequate control over the Company.

This led to the question of the propriety of going to a private firm at all. Could the money not have been got from the Bank of England, or voted by a rapidly called Parliament? The answer lay in the speed of the whole transaction. It was essential that the money should be available immediately and that absolute secrecy be maintained. If the Government had been turned down by the Bank – and there was no reason why they should not be – they would have lost the chance of bidding for the shares. To recall Parliament would have been to risk losing the bargain in the same way. It had been an authoritarian stroke of Disraeli's, a risk that other members of the Cabinet would not have taken without his initiative and persuasion; but it had succeeded and was popularly and internationally applauded. The only thing he could do was to go to a banker whom he knew and could trust to be discreet and responsible. Baron Lionel had been a close friend for many years and his bank had the highest reputation. The answer was obvious.

The Press had not been officially told about the deal. The over-enthusiastic leading article in *The Times* on November 26 had been greeted by Disraeli with this remark to Lady Bradford on 26th November: '*The Times* has only got half the news and very inaccurate, but it is evidently staggered.'[79d] This does not suggest that the Press had been deliberately given misleading information. Lord Derby corrected the obvious errors in his Edinburgh speech, which also showed that some members of the Cabinet were concerned that the truth should be known. Disraeli was, as on other occasions, the source of a good deal of hyperbole about the political triumph he had scored. He saw no reason to discourage enthusiasm about the operation, even if the enthusiasts were misinformed about some of the facts.

The only attack on Disraeli concerned his technical mistake in suggesting that Rothschilds had *bought* the shares for the Government. He was, however, vigorously defended by Sir H.

Drummond Wolff, who had also misunderstood some aspects of the deal. Given his reputation and friendship with Disraeli, Wolff's intervention may have been positively harmful.

The final criticism, that the operation was unprecedented, was well answered by Sir Stafford Northcote who had changed his mind about the whole matter. It was, he admitted, unprecedented, 'but so is the Suez Canal itself'.[90d]

These were the answers to the questions that concerned the part played by Rothschilds. The House of Commons was satisfied with the explanations of Sir Stafford and Disraeli about the conduct of the affair and voted the money. After the 'carping and captious attacks'[61c] of Lowe and Mr Gladstone, which dwelt on the less important matters to do with the size of the commission and the dates on which the money should have been borrowed, Disraeli's summing up of the debate was as magnanimous as Sir Stafford could have wished. The central question was whether to obtain some control of this vital passage to India by force, in time of emergency, or by diplomatic and financial methods, the methods of peace:[61d]

> If the government of the world was a mere alternation between abstract right and overwhelming force, I agree there is a good deal in that observation; but that is not the way in which the world is governed. The world is governed by conciliation, compromise, influence, varied interests, the recognition of the rights of others, coupled with an assertion of one's own; and in addition, a general conviction, resulting from explanation and good understanding, .that it is for the interest of all parties that matters should be conducted in a satisfactory and peaceful manner.

The purpose underlying the purchase of the shares was conciliation between the Government and the Company, compromise between French and English interests, and cooperation that would allow traffic to pass easily between the two seas joined by the Canal. But leaving aside the purpose, the purchase showed the power Disraeli had over the Cabinet and Queen Victoria, and the global power of Rothschilds in the world of finance. The resultant peaceable settlement was welcomed by all, with the possible exception of Russia.

AFTER THE ATTACK

On the 25th February 1876, after the money had been voted, W. H. Smith wrote to Baron Lionel suggesting a method of repaying the advance:[77e]

> Treasury
> Feb. 25 76
>
> Dear Sir,
>
> We propose to repay you for the advances which you made for the Canal Shares on the 10th, 20th and 31st March, as already agreed, and we should propose also that the instalments repaid shall be £1,500,000 on the 10th, £1,500,000 on the 20th and the balance on the 31st. Would you let me know if this arrangement would suit Messrs. Rothschilds' convenience or if they would prefer any other division of the amount due.
>
> Yours very truly,
> W. H. Smith
>
> We will write officially as soon as we get your answer.

Rothschilds agreed and, on 7th March 1876, a letter was sent from the Treasury to the Bank of England instructing them to open an account in the name of the Chief Cashier, to be called the 'Account of the Purchase money of the Shares of the British Government in the Suez Canal which formerly belonged to the Khedive of Egypt'. The Exchequer would from time to time fund this Account out of the £4,080,000 voted by the House of Commons.

Orders were given to pay N. M. Rothschild & Sons the following sums on three specified dates:[94]

10th March	£1,500,000
20th March	1,500,000
31st March	976,582 : 2 : 6
	£3,976,582 : 2 : 6
Commission	99,414 : 11 : 1
	£4,075,996 : 13 : 7

On 31st March Rothschilds sent their receipt for the total and notified W. H. Smith:[77e]

New Court
4 Apr 1876

Dear Sir,

We have the honour of addressing these few lines to confirm the letter we sent to the Bank of England in which we aknowledged the receipt of £4,075,996: 13: 7 being the amount paid by us to the Egyptian Government for the 176,602 Suez Canal Shares together with the commission due to us thereon and we now beg to enclose a statement showing the amount of interest due to us under the agreement with H.M. Government.

We have the honour to remain,
Dear Sir,
Your faithful servants,
N. M. Rothschild & Sons

Then there was a snag: Rothschilds had calculated the interest for the quarter, the Treasury for the number of days. In the latter case, as 1876 was a leap year, there was a discrepancy between the the two figures. The total came to £59,042: 11: 0 by Rothschilds' calculations, but £52,485: 3: 7 by the Treasury's. Rothschilds acknowledged their mistake and the money was paid by the Bank of England on 2nd June 1876. Rothschilds' receipt wound up the transaction:[77f]

To W. H. Smith New Court
2nd June

Sir,

We have the honour to acknowledge the receipt of your letter of this day informing us that the Bank of England has been instructed by the Lords Commissioners of Her Majesty's Treasury to pay us the sum of £52,485: 3: 7 (say Fifty two thousand four hundred eighty five pounds 3/7) being the interest due to us on the advances made by us for the purchase of the Suez Canal Shares.

The Bank of England has already placed the above mentioned sum to the credit of our account, thus balancing

the transaction which the Lords Commissioners of Her
Majesty's Treasury entrusted to our care.

We have the honour to remain
Sir, Your most obedient Servants
N. M. Rothschild

The financial success of the deal was rapidly apparent. Although the shares had been bought for £22 10s. 4d. per share
without coupons, whereas the market price with coupons was
£19, they rose in January 1876 to £34 12s. 6d., and the Khedive
was paying interest at 5% to compensate for the income lost
because the coupons had been pawned. The value of the shares
continued to rise steadily, until on the 31st March, 1935 they
were worth £93,199,777 or about £528 per share (probably the
maximum). For the year ended the 31st March, 1955, though
the market value of the shares had fallen greatly, the Government
received dividends worth £2,925,414, nearly three quarters of
the original purchase price. Even taking into account inflation
the investment was not, therefore, unrewarding.

An Exchequer Bonds Bill was passed on the 6th March 1876
to raise the money, this being effected by a 35-year loan of
£4,080,000 from the Post Office Savings Bank at 3½%. Sir
Stafford Northcote raised income tax by a penny to the penal
level of 4d. in the pound, for the first time in peace-time since
1842, to establish a Sinking Fund which must have been very
unwelcome to him. Such things as deficit financing and PSBR
were neither as commonplace nor as acceptable in 1876 as they
are today.

Rothschilds had made about £100,000 out of the deal, but
made no effort to speculate or cash in on the Stock Market
gyrations that immediately followed the purchase of the shares
in 1875. An account of these gyrations is given by D. A. Farnie,[75b]
where the vast profits made by speculators in Egyptian stock are
described. The 1873 loan rose from 54 on the 15th November
1875 to 72 on the 26th November when the official news of the
purchase came through. Farnie supposes that Henry Oppenheim, 'Rothschild in ordinary to the Khedive',[95] did use his
knowledge of the Khedive's offer and was the speculator who
made the most out of the deal.

Between the 23rd March and the 30th March, when the news of Disraeli's decision not to support the Khedive reached investors, Egyptian stock fell rapidly, the 1873 loan going down from 62 to 52. This, the Khedive's defeat in Abyssinia, the publication of the Cave Report and Jules Pastré's failure to float a loan, brought the Khedive to bankruptcy and an International Commission of the Public Debt took over the running of Egyptian finances.

Rothschilds' actual involvement in Egyptian investments is hard to estimate. Before and after the shares were bought, they only handled minor quantities of Egyptian stock and had, for example, a relatively small sum, £124,800, in the Loan of 1873. It was the Oppenheim syndicate that had the greatest interest in Egyptian Stock, which was why Henry Oppenheim was the first to know about the Khedive's plans.

There was only one accusation to be answered, that the Rothschilds had taken unfair advantage of their position and influence. This question was raised in the House of Commons on the 28th February 1876, by a Mr Biggar, who thought that as Natty was a Member of Parliament, the deal with his family's bank was a violation, on his part, of the Act on Privilege (22 Geo. 3, c. 45). Disraeli said that if the matter arose at all, it should come under the jurisdiction of the Courts of Law. Natty then made a personal statement in the House to the effect that he was not a Partner in the Firm, either in London or in Paris, and that his father would vouch for the fact.[96]

Baron Lionel was a Member of the House of Commons for many years, after he was allowed to take the oath on the Old Testament, as a Jew and not 'as a true Christian'. If he had retained his seat in 1875 he would have come under the jurisdiction of the Act on Privilege which forbade Members of Parliament to direct Government money to their own firms. But then, perhaps, he would have refused Monty Corry's request at New Court on the 24th November, 1875.

In the end, Rothschilds played its part in the affair of the Khedive's shares because of one thing: the friendship and admiration that existed between Baron Lionel and Disraeli. If it had not been for this relationship, Disraeli might not have learnt about the Khedive's plans in time, the money could not have been raised at once and Disraeli, lacking this financial support, would have been unable to make his offer before the Khedive had put his shares up for sale elsewhere.

The relationship between the two men continued throughout the transaction. Rothschild treated the Government as a favoured client and provided the services of information and immediate delivery of large sums of money, at the risk of losing business elsewhere. In an unprecedented way, Baron Lionel also put his friendship for Disraeli before that with the other branches of the family and did not, as was normal, pass any information to them before or at the time of the event. Paris was not consulted until the deal had gone through.

The Firm emerged with its reputation enhanced and Baron Lionel was praised almost as highly as Disraeli – it was even rumoured that he would get a Peerage for his services (as, later, Natty did) – and Disraeli, although he had been inaccurate and arbitrary at times, increased his power and influence at home and abroad.

The operation guaranteed Britain's interest in the Suez Canal. In addition, her relationship with the Company was greatly improved in comparison with the acrimonious squabbling, notably with de Lesseps, which previously had been the order of the day. The passage to India by the shortest route was more easily accessible to British shipping and the resultant increase in traffic, which raised the value of the shares and the yield on them so dramatically from then on, greatly benefited the Canal and England.

Epilogue

In 1979, the centenary of Baron Lionel's death, the Suez Canal shares of Her Majesty's Government were sold for some £22 million, a little over £3 million in terms of 1875 money, to be compared with the purchase price, £4 million, in 1875. N. M. Rothschild and Sons were not involved in the transaction.

FIGURE 11
Baron Edmond de Rothschild

26

THE FATHER OF THE YISHUV*

An Address at the Rothschild Prizes ceremony in Israel, 1981

AT PREVIOUS PRIZE-GIVING CEREMONIES I have sometimes used the occasion to give an account of Hanadiv's** current activities. On this occasion I thought it might be of interest, at any rate to the younger members of this audience, to say something about the history of the Rothschild family's association with Israel – and only a sentence or two about the future.

These Prizes had their origins 99 years ago when a tremendous innovation started in this country – tremendous both in concept and in practice. Apparently insuperable problems were overcome. Problems, albeit of a different nature, remain: but the concept is now a reality.

Baron Edmond de Rothschild began his work for Israel at Rishon-le-Zion in the year 1882 when, as a result of pogroms in eastern Europe, there was an influx of Jews to Palestine. He was determined to help them, but, from the very beginning, he did not believe in doing this by simply giving money to the victims of the pogroms. He had two objectives. The first was to bring the Jews back to the soil, thus transforming the traditional Jew of the ghetto into a free and independent farmer. The second objective was to establish, irreversibly, the fact of Jewish settlement in Palestine, 'in order', as he said, 'that one day, when we stand before the tribunal of nations, we can claim a homeland for the Jews', an echo of the Shivat Tzion of the Jews in Babylon as they wept, by its waters, 586 years before the birth of Christ. As St Gregory the First said about the Jews in the 6th Century, 'God having invested them with the seal of his mystery, they preferred their land.'

---

* =settlement.   ** See p. 201.

The first group of pioneers at Rishon-le-Zion soon discovered that they had neither the funds nor the expertise to make a success of farming. They appealed to Edmond. He responded, but not by sending them money. He commissioned a French agriculturalist to visit Rishon-le-Zion and guide the young farmers. He also provided the money to dig a well. That was how Edmond's involvement began. From then on, the number of applicants for help increased and so did Edmond's support, which became so intensive that a special administration had to be set up. That, needless to say, created its own problems. I daresay some of you have noticed, even in these enlightened days, that administration does not always proceed as smoothly as one might wish. We need administration; but it must not suffocate us with its own opinions and procedures to the exclusion of the outside world. To paraphrase Kissinger: 'Administrators are consumers and sometimes sterilizers of ideas – rarely creators of them.'

By 1957 about 45 settlements had been created or supported by Edmond and his son James.

Settlement in a land as barren and neglected as Palestine was an exceedingly complex series of operations. Edmond bought large tracts of land, mainly from their absentee landlords. These purchases were made in specific areas, in such a way that they were within one day's riding of each other. As a result, clusters of settlements came into being in Judea, Samaria and Galilee. By 1933 Edmond had acquired about 500,000 dunams (125,000 acres) of land, more than the Jewish authorities had at that time.

After the acquisition of land came the selection of farmers. Then water had to be found. A special water company, the Samaria Water Company, was created for this purpose, operating mainly in Lower Galilee. After that the soil had to be improved. The stones and rocks had to be removed, as they were a few years ago, after the Six Day War, near Latrun. Marshy land had to be drained and the Palestine Salt Company was set up for this purpose. The largest of these drainage operations was that of the Kabara marshes, 5,000 dunams. Then there was the planting of the large eucalyptus forest near Hadera, 1,200 dunams. Industries were set up to support the products of the land, such as wine manufacture and storage at Rishon-le-Zion and Zikhron Yaacov; a flour mill in Haifa; a glass factory in Tantura to produce wine bottles; a perfume factory at Benyamina to use the jasmine raised by Yemenite settlers; and a silk factory at Rosh Pina.

Later the Palestine Salt Company at Atlit, the Palestine Brewery at Rishon-le-Zion and, in partnership, the Fertilizers and Chemical plant at Haifa were created.

As agriculture and horticulture developed, Baron Edmond introduced many innovations such as special strains of vines, the grapefruit, Friesian cattle and the Leghorn chicken, not to mention the tractor. Edmond died in 1934. By that time the people of Israel knew him as:

Avi Hayishuv (the Father of the Yishuv)

Almost to the end of his life he retained a personal interest in all the developments in Palestine. In the hope of making the work he started more efficient, he set up in 1923 a company known as PICA and appointed his son James as its first President, an office he held until his death in 1957. From 1923 till 1957 James de Rothschild devoted much of his time and energy to consolidating and extending his father's pioneering work. After his death the activities of PICA ended and its land was handed over to Israel. About a quarter of a century ago, Jimmy, as everyone called him, stimulated me, in his idiosyncratic way, to become interested in Israel.

Twenty years after his death Baron Edmond and his wife returned to the land on which he had lavished so much love and care, to their last resting place at Ramat Hanadiv. Few of you in this audience will remember that extraordinary and moving moment in what I think it fair to call the history of Israel.

The second of Baron Edmond's aims was to create a base for the future claim of a Jewish homeland. Ben Gurion said that 'no single individual has contributed so much to the creation of the State as has Baron Edmond'. This aim was endorsed by my cousin James when, in his Will, he provided the money to build the Knesset. As he said in his letter to Ben Gurion, 'Let the Knesset be a symbol of the permanence of the State of Israel'.

After James's death, his widow Dorothy de Rothschild continued and continues PICA's work, but in a different way, through a foundation called Hanadiv. Its terms of reference are to support learning, science, art, religion and culture, words susceptible of a wide variety of interpretations. Many projects, several of a highly innovative character, have been started or supported by Hanadiv. Some of these are, or involve support of:

Instructional Television
The Centre for Educational Technology
Everyman's University
Hospitals and old-age homes
Aids for the blind, the deaf, the retarded and the
    handicapped
The Rothschild Prizes for virtually all academic studies
The Rothschild Prizes for innovation and export-
    orientated technology
The Centre for Advanced Studies at Jerusalem
Solar Ponds
Fellowships for young academics
The Animal Breeding Centre at the Weizmann
    Institute, *and* its endowment
The Golf Course at Caesarea
Biotechnology
Electric cars or vehicles
Removal of *some* of the television aerials in Jerusalem

In addition, Hanadiv has, among other things, given Israel oil paintings by such masters as Cézanne, Van Gogh and Gauguin. You can see them any time in Jerusalem.

I believe that Hanadiv has so far kept alive the flame of innovation lit in Israel by Baron Edmond. But from now on, our successes will depend more on new ideas and concepts from our friends in Israel, rather than from elsewhere.

The old, like me, have a tendency to look back at the achievements of the past rather than forward at the unknown and usually unpredictable events of the future. That tendency of the old *must* be resisted. I am the last to forget Moses, David, Isaiah and their more recent homonyms. But the past, and memories of it, are less vital than the future, troubled, uncertain and sombre as it so often seems. These Prizes, which I have the honour to give away today, are a symbol of Hanadiv's belief in the future and in the young men and women of Israel who will shape and guide it.

27

THE FILE IS NEVER
CLOSED

MANY PEOPLE, I suppose, suffer blows which seem devastating, crushing and beyond belief. I have had three such blows, the last nearly twenty years ago when I was told by 'the authorities' that a former close friend of mine, Anthony Blunt, had confessed to having been a Soviet agent for many years. I found it almost impossible to believe and childishly, felt like telephoning Blunt to ask him if this appalling news was true. But there *was* no doubt; and why should 'they' wish to play a cruel and meaningless practical joke on me? What might I be stimulated to confess in return? The short answer was: nothing. As 'they' knew, I was not a Soviet agent.

I think I first got to know Blunt about a year after I went to Cambridge as an undergraduate. Like many others, I was immediately impressed by his outstanding intellectual abilities, both artistic and mathematical, and by what, for want of a better phrase, I must call his high moral or ethical principles. I knew or suspected he was a homosexual, but I saw no reason why this characteristic should conflict with the others mentioned above.

When I refer to his high moral or ethical principles, I mean that he was one of those rare persons, like Leonard Woolf*, to whom I might have gone for advice when in doubt about some particular course of action.

Blunt seemed to me a somewhat cold and ascetic figure but with a sense of humour. He was an excellent conversationalist and a habitual party-goer. I don't ever remember having seen him the worse for drink though in later years I heard that he drank a great deal.

I was very ignorant about politics and ideologies in those days, being, so I thought, too busy with my scientific work, sport and

* I do not mention anyone alive. Otherwise some unwitting omission might cause offence.

social life to have much time for anything else. I remember, very vaguely, once thinking that an article about porcelain by Anthony Blunt in the *Spectator* or the *New Statesman* – I forget which – dragged in Marxism in a way I thought unnecessary and irrelevant.

I have never kept a diary so when I cast my mind back more than fifty years, little remains except isolated and somewhat trivial episodes. I remember Blunt asking me whether I would lend him £100. It seemed quite a lot of money in 1932 and indeed it was in comparison with £100 in 1981 (see Ch. 8). What did he want it for? To buy a painting by someone called Poussin, Blunt said. My father had told me – or my mother said my father believed – that if humanly possible, one should never lend people money as it almost invariably made them hate you. You should give them the money if you could, and if it could be done without embarrassment. So I gave Blunt £100. Perhaps I shall soon see the Poussin, for the first time, in the Fitzwilliam Museum at Cambridge.

Blunt joined the Security Service during World War II some time after me, and our paths rarely crossed because I was concerned with bombs whereas he, after a brief incubation period, became involved in highly secret work, so secret that 'the weeders' will see that it is not disclosed, even after thirty years.

Blunt inevitably came into contact with a close friend of mine at the top of the Security Service, G. M. Liddell, a brilliant, sensitive and delightful man whose image, I am sorry to say, has become somewhat tarnished, with no justification, by what are nowadays called investigative reporters. If I am sure that anyone was loyal to his or her country, it was Guy Liddell. As Aristippus said: εἰ γὰρ οἱ κύνες ψευδολογοῦντες ἐν τῷ ἰδίῳ κόπρῳ πνίγοιντο.

But of course the crushing blow about Blunt has destroyed my confidence. For whom would I put my hand in the fire? I can still name a few and among them would, undoubtedly, be Guy Liddell.

The 'authorities' knew, of course, that many years before, I had been a close friend of Blunt, though we drifted apart in about 1950; and they were therefore interested in anything, anything, I could tell them about him, his friends and acquaintances. So appalled was I by their news, as I am sure they expected, that I felt it essential to help them in every possible way: and this I did within the limits of an imperfect memory. Curiously, perhaps, this did not make me cast doubt on any of those for whom I was already prepared to put my hand in the fire.

You never get over a blow of this sort. What about John, Peter, Thomas and so forth, one asks oneself? The Intelligence Services ask the same questions and, of course, many more. In their world the file is never closed.

28

COMMONPLACE

FEW WORDS in the English language can have such antithetical connotations as does 'commonplace'. This is my commonplace book. Are its contents trite and platitudinous as one meaning of 'commonplace' suggests? Or is this chapter full of wise saws and modern instances? You will not, I think, find it difficult to decide. But there is another side to commonplace books. From time to time people say they shed some light on the character of their originator. Perhaps that will not be so easy to decide from the contents of this chapter.

'Abstain from needless innovation, particularly when dictated by logic.'
Winston Churchill

In 1841 Lord Melbourne, when Prime Minister, leaned over the banisters at 10 Downing Street and shouted to his Cabinet colleagues as they left a meeting on the Corn Laws: 'Stop a bit. What did we decide? Is it to lower the price of bread, or isn't it? It doesn't matter which, but we must all say the same thing.'

'When a man speaks the truth he teaches me nothing. But let me listen to enough of his falsehoods and I will show you the dark places of his soul.'
Grand Inquisitor, 16th century

'One who would peep and botanize
Upon his mother's grave.'
William Wordsworth (on scientists)

'There is nothing more difficult to take in hand, more perilous to conduct, or more uncertain in its success than the introduction of a new order of things, because the innovator has for enemies all those who have done well under the old conditions and lukewarm defenders in those who may do well under the new.'
Niccolo Machiavelli

'The chief danger to our philosophy, apart from laziness and woolliness, is "scholasticism", the essence of which is treating what is vague as if it were precise, and trying to fit it into an exact category.'

F. P. Ramsey

'Not all problems are capable of an economic solution.'

Lionel Robbins

'Do not climb down the ladder; I have taken it away.'

Samuel Beckett

'When I was a Minister I made a practice of having others do more work than myself. One must never allow oneself to be buried under paper work; instead, one should hire men who are good at that sort of thing.'

Duc de Choiseul

The most important human qualities a man should possess, according to Frederick Forsyth, are 'Strength without brutality, honesty without priggishness, courage without recklessness, humour without frivolity, humanity without sentimentality, intelligence without deviousness, scepticism without cynicism.'

'We are none of us infallible, even the youngest of us.'

William Hepworth Thompson

Clemenceau said that the USA was the only country that had passed from barbarism to decadence without the intervening stage of civilization.

'Local anaesthetic! I can afford one which isn't provincial.'

Jewish anecdote

'Artificial respiration! Why not the genuine article?'

Jewish anecdote

'What joy for the heavenly Father,' she said, 'that His people finally can show their true talents, which He gave them – and all this is in their own land, on their own soil, which was denied them for centuries.'

Mother Superior Basilea Schlink

'A set of lazy drunken sots, confounded logger heads, and illiterate whelps.'

Richard Bentley, Master of Trinity College, Cambridge, referring to its Fellows.

'Two wrongs don't make a right so we had better try three.'

President Nixon

'Invade Central Asia.'

Telegram from British Government to Government of India, in 1876.

'The optimist thinks this is the best of all possible worlds and the pessimist knows it.'

Robert Oppenheimer

'Physical particles are not trained in human common sense.'

William Feller

'A hypergeometric loan.'

R.

'I think we realize too little how often our arguments are of the form: A.: "I went to Grantchester this afternoon." B.: "No I didn't."'

F. P. Ramsey

'Let us confront this difficulty squarely, and pass on.'

Unknown preacher

'Heisenberg may have been here.'

Graffito

'On doit donner au problème une forme telle qu'il soit toujours possible de le résoudre.'

N. H. Abel

'There are things that annoy me, that nag at me. There are things I think I ought to understand and that I think other people understand, or things that people think they understand but I don't think they do, or things no one understands; and these things just worry me. I just *have* to get it straight in my mind and I go on, for month after month, very often not knowing what problem it is that I'm supposed to be working on; I just have the feeling that I don't understand this. And then finally I find the reason that I don't understand it is that there really is something that has to be done – something worth doing, something original; and then I do it.'

Steven Weinberg

'These people [like Dirac] take incredible magic leaps that you can't explain at all. For me it's been a process of unhappy worrying; if someone asks me what I'm working on I haven't been able to explain it – because I haven't been able to work out what is wrong with the present situation.'

Steven Weinberg

'For a fortnight I struggled to prove that no functions analogous to those I have since called Fuchsian functions could exist; I was then very ignorant. Every day I sat down at my work table where I spent an hour or two; I tried a great number of combinations and arrived at no result. One evening, contrary to my custom, I took black coffee; I could not go to sleep, ideas swarmed up in clouds; I sensed them clashing until, as it were, a pair would hook together to form a stable combination. By morning, I had established the existence of a class of Fuchsian functions . . .
I had only to write up the results, which took me a few hours.'

Henri Poincaré

'Test everything; hold fast what is good.'

Thessalonians i, v. 21

'We see death coming into our midst like black smoke, a plague which cuts off the young, a rootless phantom which has no mercy for fair countenance. Woe is me of the shilling in the arm-pit; it is seething, terrible, wherever it may come, a head that gives pain and causes a loud cry, a burden carried under the arms, a painful angry knob, a white lump. . . . They are like a shower of peas, the early ornaments of black death, cinders of the peelings of the cockle weed, a mixed multitude, a black plague like halfpence, like berries. It is a grievous thing that they should be on a fair skin.'

Ieuan Gethin

'Il y a quelque chose dans le malheur des autres qui ne nous déplait pas.'

Duc de la Rochefoucauld

'L'importance n'est pas d'être heureux mais que les autres ne ne soient pas.'

Jules Renard

'Il disait de mal de moi et pourtant je ne lui avais jamais fait du bien.'

Jules Renard

'O, he is as tedious
As a tired horse, a railing wife,
Worse than a smoky house: I had rather live
With cheese and garlic in a windmill, far,
Than feed on cates and have him talk to me
In any summer-house in Christendom.'

Hotspur about a Welsh Nationalist

'Some people can't take yes for an answer.'

Aubrey Eban

'He had a unique gift of compression. He knew how to compress the minimum amount of thought into the maximum number of words.'

Aubrey Eban

'He experienced a unique spasm of lucidity.'

Aubrey Eban

'He has many impressive qualities but these do not include a spectacular talent for reticence.'

Aubrey Eban

'So many problems, so few solutions.'

R.

'Ut nihil amplius desiderandum relictum sit' (that nothing further remains to be done).

Carl Friedrich Gauss

In 1793 Coffinhal, President of the French Revolutionary Tribunal, dismissed Lavoisier's appeal against the death sentence with the words 'La République n'a pas besoin de savants.'

'So then because thou art lukewarm, and neither cold nor hot, I will spue thee out of my mouth.'

Revelations III, 16

'So keen on parties that she would go to the opening of an envelope.'

(Unknown)

Commonplace

'When an elderly and distinguished scientist tells you that something is impossible, he is almost certainly wrong.'

A. C. Clarke

'Common sense is a deposit of prejudice laid down in the mind before the age of eighteen.'

Albert Einstein

'Conscience is a most fallacious guide, since it consists of vague reminiscences of precepts heeded in early youth, so that it is never wiser than its possessor's nurse or mother.'

Bertrand Russell

'I declare the products of Great Britain have terribly fallen off. You can never get a good thing nowadays. My dear Augusta, I feel it is nearly over with us. I think we are on the decline. It is money, money, money with us.'

General Gordon writing to his sister

'Men of age object too much, consult too long, adventure too little, repent too soon, and seldom drive business home to the full period, but content themselves with the mediocrity of success.

Young men, in the conduct and manage of actions, embrace more than they can hold; stir more than they can quiet; fly to the end, without consideration of the means and degrees; pursue some few principles which they have chanced upon absurdly; use extreme remedies at first; and, that which doubleth all errors, will not acknowledge or retract them; like an unready horse, that will neither stop nor turn.'

Francis Bacon

'The Science Research Council has become so confused and ineffective in its dealings with University research workers that in many respects it is now an undone fly-button; it neither protects merit nor restrains impropriety.'

Donald Michie

'The human mind is not capable of grasping the Universe. We are like a little child entering a huge library. The walls are covered to the ceilings with books in many different tongues. This child knows that someone must have written these books. It does not know who or how. It does not understand the languages in which they are written. But the child notes a definite plan in the arrangement of the books – a mysterious order which it does not comprehend, but only dimly suspects.'

Albert Einstein

'Brothers, I am sorry I have no Morrison's pill for curing the maladies of Society.'

Thomas Carlyle

'When society requires to be rebuilt, there is no use in attempting to rebuild it on the old plan.'

John Stuart Mill

'It concerns the man who made buggy whips in Illinois. It was generally accepted that his buggy whips were the finest in the State. He spent a great deal of time and energy, and perhaps money, on researching into how to make even better whips. What he omitted to notice was that a gentleman called Henry Ford had started manufacturing the kind of buggy which didn't need his kind of whip at all. The moral of the legend is that research has to be more fundamental than merely related to product quality or even manufacturing costs and that had he realized this he might have ended up as head of the Ethyl Corporation.'

Sir David Barran

The late Lord Macmillan said, about whisky and water, that whisky could never be made in private in England and water could never be made in public.

'Great nations are never impoverished by private, though they sometimes are by public prodigality and misconduct. It is the highest impertinence and presumption, therefore, in kings and ministers, to pretend to watch over the economy of private people. For kings and ministers are themselves always, and without exception, the greatest spendthrifts in the society.'

Adam Smith

'Mr Vidal parodies not only the rhetoric of eco-freaks, doom-watchers and the over-population lobby, but also (or do I imagine?) the ruthless conceit of all radicals and revolutionaries who wish to reconstruct the world in their own image.'

Auberon Waugh

'Old soldiers never die – they just write their memoirs.'

Art Buchwald

Commonplace

'Science is not the mere collection of facts, which are infinitely numerous and mostly uninteresting, but the attempt by the human mind to order those facts into satisfying patterns.'

C. N. Hinshelwood

'The virtuous ruler must be the first to feel forebodings of misfortune, the last to rejoice at successes.'

Chinese proverb

'The use of reason is to justify the obscure desires that move our conduct, to justify impulses, passions, prejudices and follies, and also our fears.'

Joseph Conrad

'Never before in history have the victors sued for peace while the vanquished demand unconditional surrender.'

Aubrey Eban (about Israel after the 6-day war)

'Never before in history have so few owed so little to so many.'

Aubrey Eban (about Israel after the 6-day war)

'Without a country you are the bastards of humanity.'

Giuseppe Mazzini

'He paints with his hands in my pockets.'

Edgar Degas (about Forain)

'Physical science is thus approaching the stage when it will be complete, and therefore uninteresting.'

Bertrand Russell

'Do not adjust your mind – there is a fault in reality.'

Graffito

'When I see the admirable work of the Eastern wind, so long to last beyond the custom of nature, I see, as in a crystal, the right figure of my folly, that ventured supernatural haps upon the point of frenetical imputation.'

Queen Elizabeth I

'I assure you the travaile of your creased words shall passe the boundes of too many landes with an imputation of such levytie, as when the true sonnshine of my sincere dealing and extraordinary care ever for your safety and honor shall overshade too far the dymme and mystic clowdes of false invectyves.'

Queen Elizabeth I

'Owing to lack of interest tomorrow has been cancelled.'

Graffito

'Committees are consumers and sometimes sterilizers of ideas, rarely creators of them.'

Henry Kissinger

'This Treasury paper, by its very length, defends itself against the risk of being read.'

Winston Churchill

'My dear Eddy,

Harcourt and Chamberlain have both been here this morning and at my chief about yesterday's Cabinet proceedings. They cannot agree about what occurred. There must have been some decision as Bright's resignation shows. My chief has told me to ask you what the devil was decided for he be damned if he knows. Will you ask Mr. G. in more conventional and less pungent terms.'

One Minister's private secretary to the
Prime Minister's private sectetary, 1881

'I hate and detest that animal called man; although I heartily love John, Peter, Thomas and so forth.'

Jonathan Swift

'No great improvements in the lot of mankind are possible until a great change takes place in the fundamental constitution of their modes of thought.'

John Stuart Mill

'Goodnight, then, sleep to gather strength for the morning, for the morning will come. Brightly will it shine on the brave and true, the kindly, on all who suffer for the cause, and gloriously upon the tombs of heroes. Thus will shine the dawn!'

Winston Churchill

'I am a friend not won with trifles, nor lost with the like.'

Queen Elizabeth I

'Read your compositions, and wherever you meet with a passage which you think is particularly fine, strike it out.'

Dr Johnson

Annex 1

BILLS OF EXCHANGE

A BILL OF EXCHANGE is defined in the Bills of Exchange Act 1882 as:

> A Bill of Exchange is an unconditional order in writing, addressed by one person to another, signed by the person giving it, and requiring the person to whom it is addressed to pay on demand or at a fixed or determinable future time, a sum certain in money to or to the order of a specified person or to bearer.

A cheque is a modern Bill of Exchange drawn on a bank and payable on demand, when endorsed by the payee.

Bills of Exchange were usually drawn on a bank and issued in triplicate. The three bills were normally given to the person who had locally produced the cash, who sent all three to London, by different routes, for payment. The bank on whom the bills were drawn would honour the first to arrive but not, of course, the other two if they were in fact ever presented.

During the Peninsular War, Wellington presumably drew Bills of Exchange on the Treasury or the Bank of England, to be paid 90 days after drawing. These Bills would then be sold locally, at a considerable discount, to pay for local supplies. There were ample opportunities for NM to buy these discounted bills through his local agents, ship them to London and encash them at a considerable profit, notwithstanding the delay involved.

At the time of the Peninsular War Spain and Portugal were under-developed whereas Britain was developing industrially with great rapidity. Even, therefore, if there had not been a war, there would have been a steady drain of gold and silver from the non-industrialized to the industrialized countries; so there would have been little specie available in exchange for bills. The Peninsular War exacerbated this process and no doubt explains why it was possible to ship specie profitably to the Peninsula during the war.

Annex 2

3 PER CENT CONSOLS 1817[45]

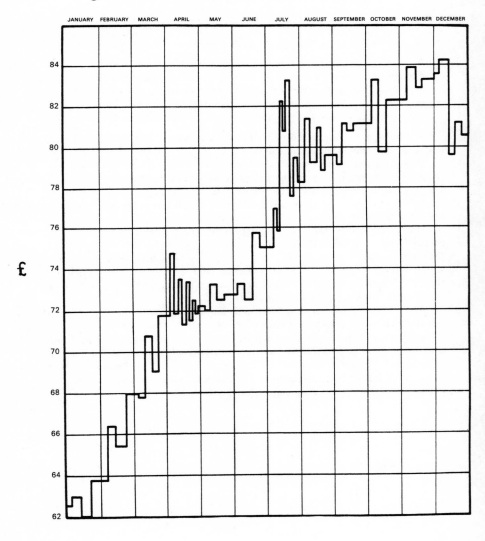

THE ROMANCE OF THE
ROTHSCHILDS BY IGNATIUS BALLA

THE HISTORIAN LUCIEN WOLF had this to say after the publication of Ignatius Balla's book *The Romance of the Rothschilds*,[24] much of which was copied from Reeves:[13]

> Unconsciously, Herr Balla's book has been well named. Except where it deals with the public activities of the Rothschilds, as recorded in reputable newspapers and other works of reference, it contains little else than "romance". It is really nothing more than an industrious collection of the aforesaid legends interwoven with a slipshod narrative of the more authentic facts. And yet, although it is dubbed romance, the whole is presented, and even vouched for, as sober and authentic history. It would be a tedious task to correct all its errors, and expose its "romances", but perhaps a couple of typical examples will suffice.
>
> None more characteristic of Herr Balla's inaccuracy could be given than his account of the origin of the Rothschild family. Here he had no need of any personal confidences. The municipal and Jewish archives of Frankfurt are rich in information concerning the Judengasse and its denizens, and they have been very diligently and fruitfully explored by the local antiquaries, more particularly Dr. Horovitz, Herr Ullman and Dr. Alexander Dietz, who has chiefly dealt with the Rothschilds. Of these labours, so important for his book, Herr Balla has apparently never heard. He knows of no ancestor earlier than Amschel Moses Rothschild, who died in 1755; and of him, he assures us, "history tells us nothing", and that he had no surname until he settled in Frankfurt "and put a red shield over the door of his house".

Several of the anecdotes recounted in this book were known long before the publication of Balla's book in 1913. Sir Thomas Fowell Buxton knew some of them. So, of course, did John Reeves in 1887, as did the anonymous contributor to *The Gentleman's Magazine* of November 1871.[19c] Reeves got a good deal of his information from *Das Haus Rothschild: Seine Geschichte und seine Geschäfte*, published in Prague in 1857.

3 PER CENT CONSOLS 1815[45]

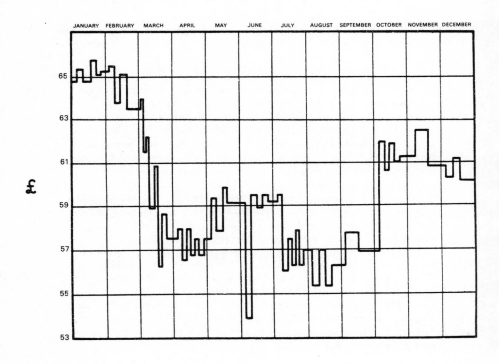

JANUARY FEBRUARY MARCH APRIL MAY JUNE JULY AUGUST SEPTEMBER OCTOBER NOVEMBER DECEMBER

£

Annex 5

CALENDAR OF EVENTS, 1875

November 14	Henry Oppenheim tells Frederick Greenwood and Baron Lionel about negotiations for transfer of Khedive's shares to French interests or to raise money on the security of the shares.
November 15	Disraeli and Lord Derby learn Oppenheim's news.
November 17	Lord Derby reports to Cabinet (on Disraeli's insistence) that the Khedive would prefer to sell his shares to England rather than elsewhere. Cabinet authorises telegram to General Stanton saying that the Khedive's shares should, if possible, be acquired.
November 18	Cabinet again discusses the Suez affair. Khedive wants loan on security of his shares, but will give HMG first refusal if he decides to sell.
November 19	Cabinet again discusses the Suez affair and, for the first time, gives Disraeli 'carte blanche' to proceed with the purchase of the shares.
November 20	French Chargé d'Affaires calls on Lord Derby to enquire if Her Majesty's Government would object to the Khedive's shares being sold to the Société Générale or the Anglo-Egyptian Bank. Lord Derby does object.
November 22	Cabinet agrees, for the second time, to Disraeli buying the shares if he gets the chance.
November 23	Cabinet again discusses the Suez affair. After it, telegram sent to Stanton telling him if possible to prevent sale of Khedive's shares to French companies.
November 24	Cabinet again discusses the Suez Canal affair and again agrees to purchase of the shares, after learning that de Lesseps had offered the Khedive £4m. for his shares. Baron Lionel asked to advance £4m. and agrees to do so (perhaps before the 24th November).
November 25	The Khedive's Finance Minister endorses sale of 176,602 shares of the Suez Canal Company to Her Majesty's Government.

Annex 6

CALENDAR OF EVENTS, 1875, THROUGH FRENCH EYES[97]

November 13	Edouard Dervieu starts discussions with Société Générale who want to buy the Khedive's shares.
November 13 or 14	Anglo-Egyptian Bank tries, through Ismā'īl Sadek, to muscle in with the Société Générale. Edouard Dervieu also approaches Crédit Foncier.
November 16	Edouard, *via* the Khedive's agent in Paris, Ferdinand Barrot, gets the Khedive to delay for 3 days granting any options on his shares.
November 17	Edouard receives telegram from Cairo saying that Stanton is discussing the Khedive's shares with Nubar Pasha and Sadek.
November 18	Derby tells Stanton that HMG will buy the Khedive's shares. Stanton informs the Khedive. André Dervieu signs a contract with the Khedive for an advance of 85 million francs on the security of his shares and the Canal revenues for 3 months at 18% p.a. The contract is only valid if endorsed by the 'Syndicate' in Paris and by Barrot, Ismā'īl's representative in Paris.
November 19	The duc Decazes, France's Foreign Minister, telegraphs to Gavard, his Chargé d'Affaires in London, instructing him to ask Lord Derby if Her Majesty's Government would object to a group of French capitalists buying the Khedive's shares.
November 20	Gavard gives Derby Decazes' message. Derby objects and Gavard tells Decazes the next day.

Annex 7

A HYDRODYNAMIC MODEL OF
GAMBLING IN GREAT BRITAIN

The diagram facing page 85 is intended to be a model of the five most important gambling systems in Great Britain. They are the football pools, gaming machines (amusements with prizes or jackpot machines), casinos (in which the principal games played are roulette, blackjack, craps, chemin-de-fer and punto banco, the first two accounting for about 75% of all money staked in casinos), licensed cash bingo and horse and dog racing.

It is assumed in the model that there is no interaction between the money flows within these five systems; that is to say that if a gambler wins, for example in a casino, he does not re-stake his winnings in gaming machines, horse and dog racing, etc., but only in a casino.

Money changes hands at different rates in each system because of the variations in the frequency at which bets are made. In the model, a sum of money is represented by a volume of fluid and the fluid velocity in each system is chosen so that the time taken for an element of fluid to go completely round a pipe corresponds to the typical time between making one bet and making another in that system. The fluid velocity is indicated by the lengths of the unbroken arrows in the pipes.

The rate at which a volume of fluid (or money) flows is thus proportional to the velocity for that system and to the cross-sectional area of the pipe at the region in question.

The total input of new money in the course of a year is denoted by the different amounts of fluid in the reservoirs at the top left-hand side of the model.

The diameters of the five concentric pipes are chosen so as just to accommodate the total annual throughput of new money at the circulation velocities described above. If, therefore, two types of gambling have the same circulation velocity, the ratio of the cross-sectional areas of the respective pipes is equal to the ratio of the total annual flow of money through the pipes. But if two types of gambling have the same annual *throughput* of money, but one has a faster velocity of circulation than the other, the former pipe will be narrower and contain longer arrows than the latter.

NOTES AND REFERENCES

1. Rothschild, Lord, 1977, *Meditations of a Broomstick*. Collins, London.
2. Reduction of average fern (bracken) sperm speed from 95 μm/sec. in white light to 50 μm/sec. in green light.
3. Rothschild, Lord, 1951, *Proc. Roy. Soc.* B, 138, 272–277.
4. Lord Bancroft G.C.B.
5. Of the French Customs and Excise.
6. See part of the Rothschild family tree at Annex 8 for Gutle and other members of the Rothschild family mentioned in this book. Gutle was also sometimes known as Gudula and Gitle.
7. Not Schnappe as in the D.N.B. 1917 xvii, p. 306.
8. Manchester to begin with.
9. Wolf, Lucien, 1934, *Essays in Jewish History*, edited by Cecil Roth, pp. 283–284. The Jewish Historical Society of England, London.
10. Buxton, Charles, 1872, *Memoirs of Sir Thomas Fowell Buxton, Bart.*, pp. 160–161. John Murray, London.
11. NM's Will, 27 July 1836. R.A.L.* RFamFP/16.
12. Louise to NM, September 1831. R.A.L. T22/59.
13a. Reeves, John, 1887, *The Rothschilds: the Financial Rulers of Nations*, p. 176. Sampson Low, Marston, Searle and Rivington, London.
13b. —— ——, p. 200.
13c. —— ——, pp. 169–175.
14. M. Davidson to NM, 24 June 1814. R.A.L. 38/81a/10.
15. Salomon to NM, 24 June 1814. R.A.L. T29/41 109/0 File 2.
16. Amschel to NM, 17 August 1814. R.A.L. T29/143 109/0 File 6.
17. Mayer Amschel to NM, 1805. R.A.L. 86/0 T27/23.
18. NM to Carl, 22 December 1814. R.A.L. T29(2)/114.
19a. The House of Rothschild, *The Gentleman's Magazine*, New Series VII, November 1871, p. 734. Grant, London.
19b. —— ——, p. 733.
19c. —— ——, pp. 732–733.
20. Herrick, Francis H. H., 1938, *Audubon the Naturalist: A History of his Life and Time*, pp. 206–207. D. Appleton-Century, New York and London.
21. Lionel to Nathaniel, 14 July 1836. R.A.L. RFamC/4/138.
22. Henry Abbott to NM, 20 June 1828. R.A.L. T6/87.
23. *The Letters of Thomas Babington Macaulay, VI, January 1856–December 1859*, edited by Thomas Pinney, pp. 227–228. Cambridge University Press, Cambridge.
24a. Balla, Ignatius, 1913, *The Romance of the Rothschilds*, p. 118. Eveleigh Nash, London.
24b. —— ——, pp. 114–116.
24c. —— ——, pp. 125–128.

* R.A.L., Rothschild Archives, London.

25. *Cambridge Modern History*, edited by Lord Acton, IX, p. 149. Cambridge University Press, Cambridge.

26a. Gurwood, Lieut. Colonel John, 1838, *The Dispatches of Field Marshall the Duke of Wellington*, XI, pp. 302–303. John Murray, London.

26b. —— ——, pp. 306–307.

26c. —— ——, p. 387.

26d. —— ——, p. 526.

27. 'pay of the Army in an acceptable form'. There is at New Court a blue velvet-lined case, apparently inscribed by NM to J. C. Herries with the date 'April–October 1815', containing examples of the gold and silver coins with which NM provided the Duke of Wellington (see Table 4). Why are they at New Court? Were they ever given to Herries? Were they offered and rejected? Were they bought later by N. M. Rothschild and Sons from the Herries family? No one is ever likely to know. Needless to say, there are no records at New Court which throw any light on the previous history of this mysterious and romantic collection of coins. The case itself is not the original one. It was probably made in about 1900 and perhaps was copied from an earlier version.

28. Chancellor of the Exchequer to J. C. Herries, 11 January 1814. R.A.L. T37/8 (Copy).

29. J. C. Herries to NM, 11 January 1814. R.A.L. T37/25.

30. NM to H.M. Treasury, 11 November 1817. R.A.L. TWJ/1.

31. Anonymous, 1846, *Première réponse officielle de M^r le Baron James Rothschild au pamphlet intitulé: Histoire édifante et curieuse de Rothschild Ier, roi des Juifs*, Seconde Édition. Bruxelles et Paris.

32. NM (London) to Carl (Amsterdam), 20 June 1815. R.A.L. T5/98.

33. Colby, Reginald, 1965, *The Waterloo Despatch*. H.M.S.O., London.

34. Roworth to NM, 27 July 1815. R.A.L. 112/51 T3/341.

35. R.A.L. 10/78, p. 236 (Account book entry for Burmarsh Farm).

36. Agie and Insinger to NM, 1 October 1824. R.A.L. 38/6A (18241001).

37. *A Portion of the Journal kept by Thomas Raikes, Esq. from 1831–1847*, 1857, III, p. 44. Longman, Brown, Green, Longmans & Roberts, London.

38a. *Notes and Queries*, 1868, 4th Series II, p. 375.

38b. ——, 1858, 2nd Series VI, 155, p. 502.

38c. ——, ——, 153, p. 434.

38d. ——, 1868, 4th Series II, p. 114.

38e. ——, ——, p. 283.

39. Wilson, P. W., 1927, *The Greville Diary*, I, p. 204. William Heinemann, London.

40. *The Croker Papers. The Correspondence and Diaries of the late Right Honourable John Wilson Croker, LL.D., F.R.S., Secretary to the Admiralty from 1809 to 1830*, 1885, edited by Louis J. Jennings, second edition revised, I, p. 60. John Murray, London.

41. *The Quarterly Review*, 1845, LXXVI, p. 223.

42. *The Courier*, 21 June 1815, p. 3.

43. Longford, Elizabeth, 1972, *Wellington Pillar of State*, p. 8. Weidenfeld & Nicolson, London.

44. For some reason which was not given *The Economist*[46] claimed in 1965 that NM bought 4% Consols.

TABLE 4 *An Account of Bullion & Specie furnished by Mr. N. M. Rothschi*

Date	Gold Ingots		Doubloons	Portugal Gold Coin	Bombay Mohurs
	No. of Ingots	Standard Weights			
		lbs oz dw gr	lbs oz dw gr	lbs oz dw gr	lbs gr dw gr
July 28	2	32 8 4 12			
	8	132 3 12 12			
	2	25 11 11 16			
	1	9 5 9 8			
			330 6 9 0		
				418 11 2 0	
Aug. 2					
8	31	378 11 18 4			
				25 0 0 0	
Sep 14					
Oct 20					
		20,607 0 5 5	698 1 3 0	709 2 16 12	91 7 18 0

Note: The columns do not add up to the column totals because the latter include previous pages of the account.

J. C. Herries Esqre. Commissary in Chief [1815]

Frederick's D'Ors	French Gold Coin	Dollars	French Crowns	Franc pieces	Price	Amount
lbs oz dw gr	lbs oz dw gr	lbs oz dw	lbs oz dw	lbs oz dw	per oz	£ s d
					89/5	1,753.11.5.
					89/7	7,111. 4.8.
					88/9	1,382.13.0.
					91/–	516. 5.5.
					86/–	17,055.14.8
					91/–	22,873. 6.1.
347 4 1 12					88/6	18,433.14.7.
		6,416 8 0			6/5	24,704. 3.4.
		250 0 0			6/4	950. 0.0.
		7,766 8 0			5/7	26,018. 6.8.
		1,732 0 0			5/7½	5,845.10.0.
		5,434 8 0			5/7	18,206. 2.8.
					91/–	20,692.19.7.
					91/–	1,365. 0.0.
		7,216 6 10			5/5½	23,634. 3.5.
		9,453 9 0			5/6	31,197. 7.6.
		83,781 10 10			5/7	280,669. 5.6.
		17,825 OR			4/8	57,633. 6.8.
		347,000 dollars			each	
47 4 1 12	55 8 10 0	220,183 10 0	38 2 15	65 1 5		£2,136,916.11.1.

225

45. Van Sommer, J., 1848, *Tables exhibiting the various fluctuations in Three Per Cent Consols.* Smith, Elder & Co., London.
46. *The Economist*, 1965, p. 1564, The Funds after Waterloo. The splendid myths of Nathan Mayer Rothschild.
47. Now the Sun Alliance & London Insurance Group.
48. NM to J. C. Herries, 6 April 1824. R.A.L. 218/3.
49. Forster, E. M., 1956, *Marianne Thornton 1797–1887. A Domestic Biography*, p. 122. Edward Arnold, London.
50. Bamford, F. and the Duke of Wellington, 1950, *The Journal of Mrs Arbuthnot 1820–1832*, I, pp. 426–429. Macmillan, London.
51. Stapleton, A. G., 1875, The Greville Journals, *Macmillan's Magazine*, XXXI, p. 157. Macmillan, London and Cambridge.
52. To consider the renewal of the Bank of England's Charter.
53. Philip Henry, 5th Earl Stanhope, 1888, *Notes of Conversations with the Duke of Wellington 1831–1851*, p. 159. John Murray, London.
54. J. C. Herries to Lord Liverpool, 27 September 1826. R.A.L. T37/158 (Copy).
55. NM to Lord Liverpool, 21 August 1826. R.A.L. 218/3.
56. Lionel to Nathaniel, 11 June 1836. R.A.L. RFamC/4/109.
57. Lionel to Anthony and Nathaniel, 15 June 1836. R.A.L. RFamC/4/114.
58. Lionel to Anthony and Nathaniel, 13 June 1836. R.A.L. RFamC/4/111.
59. Lionel to Anthony and Nathaniel, 30 June 1836. R.A.L. RFamC/4/123.
60. Lionel to Nathaniel, 13 June 1836. R.A.L. RFamC/4/113.
61a. Monypenny, W. F. and Buckle, G. E., 1929, *The Life of Benjamin Disraeli*, new and revised edition. John Murray, London.
61b. ——, ——, II, p. 792.
61c. ——, ——, II, p. 800.
61d. ——, ——, II, p. 801.
62. Blake, Robert, 1966, *Disraeli.* Eyre & Spottiswoode, London.
63. Ayer, J., 1905, *A Century of Finance. 1804–1904. The London House of Rothschild.* Wm. Neely, London.
64. Beaconsfield, Earl of, 1881, *Coningsby or the New Generation*, Hughenden Edition. Longmans, Green, London.
65. Lionel to Charlotte, 7 January 1835, R.A.L. RFamC/4(5.
66. Anthony to Lionel, R.A.L. T7/64, (109/58–1).
67. Hannah to Lionel, R.A.L. T7/36.
68. Anselm to Lionel, 24 November 1846, R.A.L. T7/86.
69. *Encyclopaedia Britannica*, 15th Edition, **17,** 768.
70. Wolf, Lucien, The Story of the Khedive's Shares, *The Times*, December 26, 1905, p. 7.
71. Marlowe, J., 1965, *Anglo-Egyptian Relations 1800–1956*, second edition, p. 65. Frank Cass.
72. *Encyclopaedia Britannica*, 11th Edition, **14,** 875.
73a. Anonymous, 1884, *Khedives and Pashas. By one who knows them well*, p. 6. Sampson Low, London.
73b. —— ——, p. 13.
73c. —— ——, p. 33.
74. Egypt. No. 7, 1876, *Report by Mr Cave on the Financial Condition of Egypt.* Presented to both Houses of Parliament by Command of Her Majesty,

[C.–1425]. Printed by Harrison and Sons, London, 1876.
75a. Farnie, D. A., 1969, *East and West of Suez*. Clarendon, Oxford.
75b. —— ——, pp. 229–256.
76a. Wilson, A. T., 1933, *The Suez Canal. Its Past, Present and Future*, p. 50. Oxford University Press, London.
76b. —— ——, p. 51.
76c. —— ——, p. 52.
77a. Public Record Office, CAB 41/6/33 (A 49 in the Royal Archives).
77b. ——, CAB 41/6/34 (A 50(1) in the Royal Archives).
77c. ——, CAB 41/6/35 (A 50(2) in the Royal Archives).
77d. ——, F.O. 78/38/2432.
77e. ——, T.1 7578A.
77f. ——, T.1 7578B/20779.
78a. Royal Archives, O 12.
78b. ——, A 50.
79a. Zetland, Marquis of, 1929, *The Letters of Disraeli to Lady Bradford and Lady Chesterfield*, I, p. 306. Ernest Benn, London.
79b. —— ——, II, p. 15. Disraeli to Lady Bradford, 28.1.1876.
79c. —— ——, I, p. 307.
79d. —— ——, I, pp. 307–308.
80. THE SUEZ CANAL *A Selection of Documents relating to the International Status of Suez Canal and the position of the Suez Canal Company November 30, 1854–July 26, 1956*, The Society of Comparative Legislation, London.
81. Nathaniel to Lionel, 28 August 1864, R.A.L. T9/36, (109/95).
82. E. Landau to H. Landau, R.A.L. T9/43.
83a. Hughenden Papers, B/XX/Co/114.
83b. ——, A/X/A/9.
84a. Egypt. No. 1, 1876, *Correspondence respecting the purchase by Her Majesty's Government of the Suez Canal Shares belonging to the Egyptian Government*. Presented to both Houses of Parliament by Command of Her Majesty, p. 5, [C.–1391]. Printed by Harrison and Sons, London, 1876.
84b. —— ——, p. 6.
84c. —— ——, pp. 25, 27.
84d. —— ——, pp. 2–3.
85. Alphonse to cousins, 23 November 1875, R.A.L. T12/16.
86. Lionel to Leo, R.A.L. T12/33.
87. The Cave Report was, of course, published. Why was Baron Lionel anxious that Cave's report should not be published? It contained nothing about the Rothschilds, favourable or detrimental. The answer could be that he feared further pressure from Disraeli to bail out the Khedive. Alternatively, the publication of the Cave report might have depressed the price of the Canal shares, in which case the price which the Government had paid for them might have been criticized – wrongly in the event.
88. W. H. Smith to Rothschilds, 2 February 1876, R.A.L. Suez Canal Papers 109/136.
89. *The Times*, 18.12.1875.
90a. Lang, A., 1890, *Life, Letters and Diaries of Sir Stafford Northcote, First Earl of Iddesleigh*, **2**, 84–85. Blackwood, Edinburgh and London.
90b. —— ——, **2**, p. 85.

90c. —— ——, **2,** pp. 82–83.

90d. —— ——, **2,** p. 86.

91. Maxwell, Sir Herbert, 1893, *Life and Times of the Right Honourable William Henry Smith, M.P.,* 1, 280. Blackwood, Edinburgh and London.

92a. Egypt. No. 2, 1876, *Further correspondence respecting the Suez Canal.* Presented to both Houses of Parliament by Command of Her Majesty, p. 21, [C.– 1525]. Printed by Harrison and Sons, London, 1876.

92b. —— ——, p. 25.

93. Hansard *Commons Debates,* February 8, 1876, 100.

94. Bank of England Records, CCO 493/1A.

95. Sidi Lokman el Hakim (John Ninet), 1873, *Les milles pertuis des finances du Khedive et les banques en Egypte,* p. 125. Agence Internationale, Vienne.

96. Hansard *Commons Debates,* February 28, 1876, 1019–1020.

97. Lesage, C., 1905, *L'Achat des actions de Suez,* La Revue de Paris, **6,** 325–369.

INDEX

Abbreviations used: NM = Nathan Meyer Rothschild
VR = Lord Rothschild (the author)

Abdul Aziz, Sultan of Turkey (1861–76)
  rival pressures on, over Suez Canal,
  162–3; permits construction (1865),
  163
  goes bankrupt (1875), 164
Abel, N. M., quoted, 208
Adrian, Lord, introduced to House of
  Lords by VR, 19
administrators, and ideas, 200
Agie and Insinger, Antwerp: on pigeon
  post (1824), 136
Agricultural Research Council, illness of
  Secretary of, 20
agriculture, in Palestine: Edmond de
  Rothschild and, 199, 200, 201
Aide and Co.: loans to Khedive from,
  repaid (1875), 180
Alabama Indemnity (1872), method of
  paying, 175, 176
Alliance British and Foreign Life and Fire
  Insurance Company, NM and
  establishment of (1824), 118, 142–4
Alliance Marine Assurance Company, 144
American Civil War, and price of
  Egyptian cotton, 160
Anglo-Austrian Bank: loans to Khedive
  from, repaid (1875), 181
Anglo-Egyptian Bank
  loans to Khedive from, 163; repaid
  (1875), 180, 181
  and Khedive's Suez Canal shares, 166,
  171, 185, 219
antibodies, 98–9
  monoclonal (produced by cell lines
  outside the body), 99
Arbuthnot, Mrs. confidante of Duke of
  Wellington: diary of, on bank crisis
  (1825), 145–8
Armstrong, Sir William, head of Civil
  Service (1974), 75
Audubon, J. J., tries to sell NM his
  Birds of America, 111–12

Bacon, Francis, quoted, 211
Balfour Committee of Enquiry into Royal
  Commissions (1910), 88, 90, 91
Balla, Ignatius, *The Romance of the
  Rothschilds* by (1913), 113–14, 131, 217

Bank of Alexandria: loans to Khedive
  from, repaid (1875), 181
Bank of England
  crisis in affairs of (1825), 144–8; NM to
  the rescue, 147, 148, 149–50; story of
  NM's quarrel with, 150–1
  should it have been employed in
  purchase of Khedive's Suez Canal
  shares? 175–6, 191, 192
  shares received and checked by, 181
Bank of England Charter, Committee of
  Security on (1832): NM's evidence to,
  149
Baring, Alexander (later Lord Ashburton),
  in Bank of England crisis, 146
Baring, Major Evelyn (later Lord
  Cromer), in Egypt, 164
Barran, Sir David, quoted, 212
Basnett, David, of GMWU, 79
Bathurst, Lord, Secretary of State for War
  Department, 135
  Wellington's letters to, 121–3
Beckett, Samuel, quoted, 207
Ben Gurion, D., on Edmond de
  Rothschild, 201
Benn, A. Wedgwood, and Think Tank, 75
Bentley, Richard, Master of Trinity,
  quoted, 208
Bexley, Lord, Chancellor of the
  Exchequer (1812–23), 117
  to Herries on NM. 124–6
Bible, quotations from, 16, 209
bibliosurgery, 52
Biffen, John, MP, 'No one has the right
  to expect a particular standard of
  living', 64
Biggar, J. G., MP for Cavan: raises
  question of Rothschild presence in
  House of Commons, and purchase of
  Suez Canal shares (1876), 197
Bills of Exchange, 215
  Wellington's, 126
biology, molecular: = biochemistry +
  molecular genetics, 98
biotechnology, 99
  child's guide to, 97–100
Bismarck, Otto von, and British purchase
  of Suez Canal shares, 189

Black Death, 209
Blackstone, Dr T., 75
Blake, Lord, *Disraeli* by (1966), 154, 169
Blignieres, M. de, Minister of Public
  Works, Egypt (1878), 164
Blunt, Anthony: VR and news of, as
  Soviet agent, 203–5
bomb fuses
  and delay mechanism, draughtsman
    able to illustrate, 59, 60
  first one taken to pieces by VR, 76
  given to VR on visit to instruct
    Americans on sabotage bombs (from
    bomb left by German submarine), 77
  screwdrivers for dismantling, 58
bombs, camouflaged: lecture to HM
  Customs and Excise on, 93
books, 18th-century: first editions of, as
  investments, 53–7
Boothby, Lord: political slogan of, 'Give
  the people a rest', 78
Boswell, James, first edition of *The Life of
  Samuel Johnson* by, 56
Bradford, Lady, letters from Disraeli to,
  172, 188, 189
Brenner, Dr Sydney, 97
British Government
  Rothschilds and loans of, 155
  represented on Board of Directors of
    Suez Canal, after purchase of
    Khedive's shares, 189
Brunel, Isambard Kingdom, 138–9
Brussels: *Gazettes extraordinaires* said to
  have been published in, at time of
  Waterloo, 139
Buchwald, Art, quoted, 21
Burmarsh Farm, near Hythe: bought by
  NM, as base for pigeon post? 135–6
Burney, Frances, first edition of *Evelina* by
  (1778), 56
Butler, Robin, in Think Tank, 81
Buxton, Sir Thomas Fowell, MP, 143, 217
  on NM, 106–8

Cabinet: meetings of, to discuss purchase
  of Suez Canal shares (1875), 166, 167,
  168, 171, 219
Canning, George, Foreign Secretary, in
  Bank of England crisis, 146, 147, 148
Capellen, Baron de, Secretary of State,
  Brussels (1815), 139
Carlyle, Thomas, quoted, 212
Carnarvon, Lord, Secretary of State for
  the Colonies (1874–8), letter from
  Northcote to, 187
Cartier, Bond Street jewellers, give VR
  screwdrivers for dismantling bombs, 58
casinos, profit from, 96
Castlereagh, Lord, Foreign Secretary
  (1815), 138, 140, 141

catalysts, 97
  enzymes as, 97–8
Cave, Stephen, sent to investigate Egyptian
  finances (1875), 164, 180
  Disraeli holds back report by, 182;
    report published, 197, 227
Caveat emptor, 22–52
Cecil, Lord Hugh, Provost of Eton,
  quoted, 96
cells, 97
  modifying gene structure of, 99
Central Asia, British Government's
  telegram to Government of India on
  (1876), 203
Central Limit Theorem, 93
Chamberlain, Joseph, President of Board
  of Trade (1881), 214
chemical reactions, 97
Chinese proverb, 213
Choiseul, Duc de, quoted, 207
chrysogene, carried by some Rothschilds,
  53
Churchill, Winston, quoted, 206, 214, 215
Civil Service, VR's experience in and of,
  93–4
Clarendon, Lord, Foreign Secretary
  (1854), and Suez Canal, 159
Clarke, A. C., quoted, 211
Clemenceau, G., quoted, 207
clubs, one-armed bandits in finances of, 95
Coffinhal, President of French
  Revolutionary Tribunal, quoted, 211
Cohen, Benjamin, brother of NM's wife
  Hannah, 140
Cohen, Judith, sister of NM's wife
  Hannah, wife of Moses Montefiore, 143
Cohen, Levi, father of NM's wife
  Hannah, 108
Coleridge, Samuel, first edition of *Lyrical
  Ballads* by Wordsworth and (1798), 57
collecting, by Rothschilds, 53
Colyer-Fergusson, Lady, grand-daughter
  of Benjamin Cohen, 140
commonplace, use of term, 206
Conrad, General B., in charge of Paris
  Communications Zone (1944), and
  VR's IQ, 63
Conrad, Joseph, quoted, 213
Consols, 3%, price of
  during 21–9 June, 1815, and possible
    gain from purchase and sale of, 141,
    142
  during 1815, 141, 218
  during 1817, 127, 216
Cooper, Duff, Ambassador in Paris (from
  1944), 16–17
Corry, Montagu, secretary to Disraeli,
  169, 174
  interview between Lionel de Rothschild
    and, 174–6

Index

cotton, Egyptian: American Civil War and price of, 160

cotton textiles, Manchester: purchased by NM, 106, 119

courier service of NM, 136–7

Crédit Foncier, approached about Khedive's Suez Canal shares, 220 .

cricket, first-class: VR's career in, playing for Northamptonshire, 77

Croker, J. W., Secretary to the Admiralty (1815), 137

Cullen, Captain Hunt, 109, 139

Customs and Excise, HM
percentage of stakes on horse and dog racing taken by, 94
speech at annual dinner of (1978), 92–6

cytochrome oxidase, in sperm cells of fern: inhibited by carbon monoxide in the dark, 62

Davidson, Myer, brother-in-law of NM: letter to NM from, 109–10

Davis, Inspector, of Cambridge police, 14–15

Decazes, Duc de, French Foreign Minister (1875), 220

Degas, Edgar, quoted, 213

Derby, Lord, Foreign Secretary (1875), 165, 180
hears of availability of Khedive's Suez Canal shares, 166, 167, 185, 219
at first against purchase of shares, 169, 185, but agrees to it with rest of Cabinet, 170, 171, 220, and admits expedience in speech in Edinburgh, 185–6, 192

Dervieux, André, and his brother Édouard, Paris financiers
Khedive borrows from, 163
and Khedive's Suez Canal shares, 166, 220

Dirac, P. A. M., 201
reported IQ of, 63

Disraeli, B., 154
close friend of Lionel de Rothschild, 168–9, 192, 197–8, on whom Sidonia in Coningsby is said to have been modelled, 155–6, (partly on himself also?) 168–9
as Chancellor of the Exchequer (1854), and construction of Suez Canal, 159
as Prime Minister (1875), hears of availability of Khedive's Suez Canal shares, 165, 166, 219; has preliminary talks with Lionel de Rothschild? 170; puts matter to Cabinet, 166, 167, 168, 171, 219; writes to Queen Victoria, 167, 168, 170, ('you have it, Madam') 171; and House of Commons debates on purchase of shares, 174, 188, 190–3; Corry to, on

his interview with Lionel de Rothschild after first day of debate, 174–6
on unity of Rothschild family, 178

DNA, carrying genetic information, 98
enzymes cutting, at specific places, 99

drugs, VR suspected of stealing, 15

East India Company, NM buys gold from, 106

Eban, Aubrey, quoted, 210, 213

Edward, Prince of Wales (later King Edward VII): Disraeli to, on his visit to Cairo, 172–3

Egyptian Government
shares of, in Suez Canal, 162
payments by, for canal construction, 163
changes in value of stocks of (1875–6), 196–7
International Commission for the Public Debt of, 197

Einstein, A., quoted, 66, 211, 212

Elizabeth I, Queen, quoted, 214, 215

Elliot, Sir Henry, Ambassador in Constantinople, 162–3

enzymes, 97–8
cutting DNA in specific places, 99

Eugénie, Empress, 159

exchange rates
NM and, 119
Rothschilds guarantee maintenance of, during payment of indemnity by France to Germany, 155

Exchequer Bonds Bill (1876), 196

Farnie, D. A., East and West of Suez by (1969), 196

Feller, William, quoted, 208

Fellner, Harold, book valuer, 54

fermentations, traditional forms of biotechnology based on, 99

Fielding, Henry
copy of first edition of Tom Jones by (1749), sold to VR, 22; discovered to be faked, 22–3; other copies of, from which pages could have been derived, 24–5
supplier sued over faked copy, 23; examination of VR in court, 26–34; cross-examination, 34–49, and re-examination, 49–50

Fish, Inspector, 60

Fish, junior, draughtsman, 59, 60, 61, 62

Fitzgerald, Rt Hon. Maurice, Knight of Kerry, 138

Flowers, Lord, Chairman of Computer Board, consultant to Think Tank, 82

form-filling, national disease, 74

France
colonies of, 120

231

NM and stocks of, 117–18
and sale of Khedive's Suez Canal shares
to Britain, 171
Franco-German War (1870–1),
Rothschilds guarantee maintenance of
foreign exchanges in connection with
indemnity paid to Germany after, 155
Frankfurt
estate of Gutle Rothschild, recorded in
archives of, 102–3
NM's brother Amschel in, 108
NM's death in, 152–3
Rothschild history in archives of, 217

gambling in UK
hydrodynamic model of five main
systems of, 221, opposite p. 85
Royal Commission on, with VR as
Chairman (1975–8), 85–7, 88, 91, 94,
96
Gaming Board
and probability theory, 94
and lotteries, 95
Gardiner, Gerald (later Lord Chancellor),
appears for VR in suit against Wells
(1942).
examination of VR by, 26–34
during cross-examination by Pearce, 38,
39, 44, 46–7
re-examination of VR by, 49–50
Gardiner, Professor Stanley, 14, 15
Gauss, Carl Friedrich, quoted, 210
Gavard, M., French Chargé d'Affaires in
London (1875), 185, 219, 220
genes, 98
splicing of DNA to produce new, 99
genetics, molecular, 98
Gentleman's Magazine, article on NM in,
131
Gethin, Ieuan, quoted, 209
Gibbon, Edward, third edition of *The
Decline and Fall of the Roman Empire* by
(1777), presented to Lord Sheffield, 55,
56, 57
Gibbs, H. H. (later Lord Aldenham),
Director of Bank of England (1875),
175
Gladstone, W. E.
and purchase of Suez Canal shares
(1875), 172, 188, 191, 192
question for, as Prime Minister (1881),
214
gold
bought by NM: from East India
Company, 106; to supply Wellington,
106, 124, 126; to rescue Bank of
England, 148
exported from Britain, preceding bank
crisis, 146, 150
Goldsmid, Isaac, made baronet (1841),
157

Gordon, General C. G., quoted, 211
Gordon, David (Polish), editor of *Magid*
(East Prussia), 128
Goschen, G. J. (later Lord Goschen), of
Anglo-French Commission in Egypt
(1876), 164
graffiti, quoted, 208, 214
Grand Inquisitor (16th century), quoted,
206
Granville, Lord (1st Earl), Ambassador at
Paris (1825), 147
Granville, Lord (2nd Earl), former
Foreign Minister, attacks Government
on purchase of Suez Canal shares, 188
Gray, Professor Sir James, 14
Greenwood, Frederick, editor of *Pall Mall
Gazette*: hears of availability of
Khedive's Suez Canal shares, and
informs Lord Derby, 165, 166, 185, 219
Gregory the Great, St, quoted, 199
Greville, Charles, diarist, on NM, 136,
149
Grote, George, MP, witness to
Committee on Bank of England charter,
149 footnote
gynandromorph orange tip butterfly, 13
and plate opposite 13

Hanadiv Foundation, Israel, 201
some achievements of, 202
Hankey, Thomas, Director of Bank of
England (1875), 175
Harcourt, Sir William, Home Secretary
(1881), 214
Hayward, John, author and bibliographer,
examines Jerome Kern copy of *Tom
Jones*, 22–3, 31–2
Heath, Edward, Prime Minister, and
Think Tank, 75–6
Heine, H., on Gutle Rothschild, 101–2
Herbert, A. P., quoted (on Royal
Commissions), 87, 89
Herries, J. C., Government Commissary
in Chief
entrusts financing of Wellington's army
to NM (1813), 124; NM's accounts
with, 126, 225
views of, on bank crisis (1825), 145,
146, 147, 150
box of sample gold and silver coins
apparently intended for (in
possession of Rothschilds), 224
Hesse Cassel, Prince of, entrusts his
fortune to Rothschilds, 108
Himsworth, Sir Harold, Secretary of
Medical Research Council, 20
Hinshelwood, C. N., quoted, 213
Home, Sir Alec, Foreign Secretary (1974),
and Think Tank, 74
Home, D. D., spiritualist medium, 74
Home Office, inquiry into gambling by

Research Unit of, 86–7
Hoover, J. Edgar, 77
House of Commons
  admission of Lionel de Rothschild to,
    155, 197
  debates in, on purchase of Suez Canal
    shares, 174, 184, 188, 190–3
  Select Committee of, on the Tote, 86
Hubbard, J. G. (later Lord Addington),
  Director of Bank of England (1875), 175
Huskisson, W., President of Board of
  Trade (1825), 146, 147, 148, 149
Huxley, Aldous, quoted, 20

industries: establishment of, in Palestine,
  200–1
insulin, biotechnical production of, 99
intelligence quotients (IQs), of VR and
  others, 63
interferon, biotechnical production of, 99
investments
  18th-century first editions and
    manuscripts as, 53–7
  Suez Canal shares as, 106
Ireland, NM on famine relief for, 151–2
Ismaïl Pasha, Khedive of Egypt
  (1863–79), 154, 160–2
  and Suez Canal, 159, 163
  debts of, 163–4; asks for Treasury
    officials to reorganise finances (1875),
    164, 180
  tries to raise money on, or sell, his Suez
    Canal shares, 164–5; tells Stanton he
    would prefer to transfer his shares to
    England, 160, 219; sale of shares
    agreed, 171
  his respect for Rothschilds, 173, 181
  price of shares transferred direct to his
    creditors, 174, 180, 181; to pay 5%
    on price of shares until share coupons
    liberated, 178, 191, 196
  defeated in Abyssinia, 197
  made to abdicate, 164
Ismaïl Sadek, Finance Minister of Egypt
  (1875), 170, 219, 220
  NM in communication with, 181
Ismailia, conference on Suez Canal at
  (1876), 190

Jennings, L. J., editor of Croker's papers,
  137
Jewish anecdotes, 207
Johnson, Dr Samuel, quoted, 215
Jones, Jack, of TGWU, 79
Joubert, Hentsch, of Anglo-French
  Commission in Egypt (1876), 164
Jupp, V. W. C., Captain of Northampton-
  shire cricket team, 77

Kern, Jerome
  sale of books of, 22; catalogue (Exhibit

1 in suit), 27, 51, 52
  copy of first edition of *Tom Jones* from
    sale, 27; lack of twelve pages from,
    not noticed, 52; second copy of,
    could have been used to complete
    first copy, 52
Kerry, Knight of, 138
Khedive, *see* Ismaïl Pasha
Kissinger, H. A., in charge of office of the
  President, USA (1974), 69
  quoted, 200, 214
Knightley, Sir Charles, Devon landowner,
  in bank crisis (1825), 148

Landau and Co., Alexandria, on
  Khedive's respect for Rothschilds, 173
Larwood, H., VR bats against, 77
Lavoisier, A. L., death of, 211
law, is very complicated, 23
lending money, Rothschild advice on, 204
lepidopterology, ruling passion in
  Rothschild family, 13
Lesseps, Ferdinand de, 159
  obtains land and labour for Suez Canal,
    162; begins work before receiving
    consent of Sultan or Khedive, 163
  raises Canal dues against British
    shipping, 169, 184
  Rothschilds try to buy Canal shares
    from (1875), 184
  offers to buy Khedive's shares, 219
  welcomes British purchase of shares,
    189, 190
Liddell, G. M., head of Security Service,
  204
List of the Great and Good (for public
  appointments), 74
Liverpool, Lord, Prime Minister (1812–27)
  and financing of Wellington's army, 124
  and news of Waterloo, 137, 138, 140
  in bank crisis (1825), 146, 147
  NM to, on Ireland, 151–2
London Airport (1980), for non-VIPs,
  67–8
Longford, Lady, 139
Lord Mayor of London, NM achieves
  ambition of dining with, 106
lotteries, deficiencies of recent legislation
  on, 95
Loudon, John, Chief Executive of Royal
  Dutch-Shell Group, 69
Louis XVIII of France, in accounts of
  transmission of news of Waterloo, 137
Lowe, Robert (later Lord Sherbrooke),
  Chancellor of the Exchequer (1868–75),
  and purchase of Suez Canal shares, 180,
  188
Lucas, stockbroker: said to have
  forestalled a purchase of stock by NM,
  by intruding on a conference and falling
  apparently unconscious, 114–15

Lyons, Lord, Ambassador in Paris
(1867–87), 166

Macaulay, T. B., on Lionel de
Rothschild's wine, 113
Maccabees, Festival of, 101–2
Machiavelli, Niccolo, quoted, 206
Macmillan, Lord, quoted, 212
Magee, Bryan, MP, refers to IQ of
Bernard Williams, 63
Maitland, Sir Donald, Chief Press
Officer at No. 10 Downing Street
(1974), 73, 82
Malabar, HMS, brings Khedive's Suez
Canal shares to Portsmouth (1875), 181
Malcolm, Admiral Sir Pulteney, in
account of transmission of news of
Waterloo, 138
Manchester, NM in, 106
manuscripts, 18th-century, as investments,
53–7
marine insurance: monopoly of Lloyds,
London Assurance, and Royal
Exchange, until 1824 Act, 143–4
Mathieu-Dairnvaell, G. M. ('Satan')
originator (1846) of malicious myth
about NM at Waterloo. 128, 129
Maudling, R., Home Secretary (1974),
and Think Tank, 74
Mayne, John, Civil Servant, in Think
Tank, 81
Mayor, Robin, philosopher and
educationalist, 21
Mazzini, Giuseppe, quoted, 213
Meir, Golda, Prime Minister of Israel, 101
Melbourne, Lord, quoted, 206
Michie, Donald, quoted, 212
Mill, John Stuart, quoted, 212, 215
Montefiore, Moses, brother-in-law of
NM's wife Hannah
news agency at Dunkirk under, 140
and Alliance Insurance Co., 143
made knight (1837) and baron (1846),
157
Morpho, butterfly, 13, and frontispiece
Mortimer, K., 75
Monypenny, W. F., and G. E. Buckle,
The Life of Benjamin Disraeli by, 154
Morton, Rose, and Co., and payment of
Alabama Indemnity, 175

Naples
NM's brother Carl in, 108
Rothschilds and stocks of, 117
Napoleon, NM in financing of war
against, 120–7
New Court, St Swithin's Lane, London,
office of Rothschilds at, 105
catalogue of NM's library at, 112
visitors to NM at, 111–15
Nixon, President, quoted, 208

Northcote, Sir Stafford (later Lord
Iddesleigh), Chancellor of the
Exchequer (1874–80), 170
at first against purchase of Suez Canal
shares, 184, 186, 187; to Disraeli,
against purchase, 187–8
in House of Commons, says purchase is
unprecedented, 'but so is Suez
Canal', 193
Lionel de Rothschild to, on transfer of
shares, 179
raises income tax by a penny in the
pound (to fourpence), to establish
Sinking Fund for purchase, 196
Nubar Pasha, Foreign Minister, later
Prime Minister, Egypt, 164

Omnium, Government investment trust:
prices of (20–28 June, 1815), and
possible gain from purchase and sale of,
141–2
one-armed bandits (fruit or jackpot
machines), Royal Commission on
Gambling, 94–5
Oppenheim, Henry, proprietor of *Daily
News*
tells Lionel de Rothschild and
Greenwood about availability of
Khedive's Suez Canal shares, 166,
219
speculates in connection with Canal
shares deal? 196
Oppenheim Alberti and Co., Khedive
borrows from, 163, 166, 197
Oppenheimer, Robert, quoted, 208
Ornithoptera paradisea, butterfly, 13, and
plate opposite 13

Palestine, work for
by Edmond de Rothschild, 199–201
by James and Dorothy de Rothschild,
201–2
Palestine Salt Company, 200
Palmerston, Lord, Prime Minister
(1855–8), and Suez Canal, 159, 184
Pastré, Jules, fails to float loan for Egypt
(1876), 197
Paris
NM's brother James in, 108
Préfet of (1945), 16
patronage, a precious and delicate
commodity, 74
Pearce, Holroyd (later Lord Pearce),
appears for defendant in suit brought
by VR against Wells
during examination of VR by
Gardiner, 27, 28, 29, 31, 32–3
cross-examination of VR by, 34–49
Percy, Major the Hon. Henry, brings
Wellington's despatches from Waterloo
to Lord Bathurst, 135, 137

PICA, company set up by Edmond de
Rothschild to further his work in
Palestine, 201
pigeon post, Rothschilds' use of, 135–6,
news of NM's death brought by, 136,
153
Poincaré, Henri, quoted, 209
Pope, Alexander
first edition of *Miscellanies in Prose and
Verse*, by Swift and, 56
part of MS of *Essay on Man* by, 22, 23
29
Portugal
NM and transfer of money to
Wellington in, 107
NM and stocks of, 118
Post Office Savings Bank, lends to
Exchequer to cover purchase of Suez
Canal shares, 196
Press Club, address to (1977), 73–9
proteins, genes specifying structure of, 98
public expenditure, Schultz on possibility
of reducing, 70
Public Sector Borrowing Requirement:
money staked on gambling annually in
UK as percentage of, 86, 94
Puckler-Muskau, Prince, visits NM at
New Court, 111

Raikes, Thomas: Paris diary of (1836),
reports birds of prey kept to intercept
pigeon post, 136
Ramsey, F. P., quoted, 207, 208
Reeve, Henry, writer in *The Times* on
foreign policy, against purchase of
Suez Canal shares, 188
Reeves, John, expands (1868) malicious
myth about NM at Waterloo, 218,
130–1
copied by Balla, 217
Renard, Jules, quoted, 210
Richardson, Samuel, first edition of
Pamela by (1741), 55, 56
Rishon-le-Zion, settlement established in
Palestine by Edmond de Rothschild
(1882), 199, 200
Robbins, Lionel, quoted, 207
Robinson, F. J. (later Lord Goderich),
Chancellor of the Exchequer (1823–7),
in bank crisis, 147, 148
Robinson, William H., Ltd, booksellers,
Pall Mall, 26
Kern copy of *Tom Jones* in shop of, 31,
41, 45, 47–8, 49
Kern copy of *Tom Jones* sent to, for
examination, 34
Rochefoucauld, Duc de, quoted, 210
Roscoe, Field: letter from, referred to in
suit by VR against Wells, 33
Rosenbach, Dr A. S., American bookseller
buys copy of first edition of *Tom Jones*

at Kern sale, and sells it to Young, 22
mentioned in suit over *Tom Jones* copy,
23, 44
second copy of first edition of *Tom Jones*
bought at same sale by, could have
been used to supply twelve pages
missing from first copy, 52
Ross, Dick, economist, in Think Tank, 81
Rothschild. Alfred, 158
Rothschild, Alphonse de, 173, 178
Rothschild, Amschel, in Frankfurt, 108
letter to NM from, 111
Rothschild, Anselm, Frankfurt: letter to
his cousin Lionel from, 157
Rothschild, Anthony
letter to Lionel from, 155
made baronet (1847), with remainder
to Lionel's sons, 157–8
Rothschild, Carl, in Naples, 108
Rothschild, Charlotte, 152
letters from Lionel to, 156
Rothschild, Dorothy de, wife of James, 73,
201–2
Rothschild, Baron Edmond de (1845–
1934)
portrait, opposite p. 199
work of, in Palestine, 199–201
final burial of, in Israel, 201
Rothschild, Gutle (1753–1849), of 148
Judengasse, Frankfurt, 101–3
portrait of, opposite p. 101
Rothschild, Baron Guy de, *Contre Bonne
Fortune* by (1983), 11
Rothschild, Hannah, wife of NM, 108,
157
Rothschild, Jacob, banker, 73, 96
Rothschild, James, in Paris, 108, 120, 126
refuses to be blackmailed, 128
his nephew Lionel works under, 154
Rothschild, James de
continues his father's work in Palestine,
201–2
leaves money to build Knesset, 201
Rothschild, Mrs James de, see Rothschild,
Dorothy de
Rothschild, Jonas, Frankfurt, 153
Rothschild, Leopold de, 158
Rothschild, Baron Lionel de (1800–79),
marriage of, at Frankfurt (1836), 152
early career of, 154–5
portrait of, opposite p. 154
Macaulay praises wine of, 113
admission of, to House of Commons,
155, 197
refuses baronetcy, 158
close friendship between Disraeli and,
168–9, 192, 197–8
hears of availability of Khedive's Suez
Canal shares; informs Disraeli, 166,
219; and purchase of shares, 165,
169–70, 191–2, 219; in

communication with Khedive's
finance minister, 181
Rothschild, Louise, 108
Rothschild, Miriam, *Dear Lord Rothschild*
by (1983), 11
Rothschild, Mayer Amschel, Frankfurt, 101
to his son NM, 111
Rothschild, Nathan (Nathaniel, Natty) de
(1840–1915), 169
sent to Paris to ask de Lesseps if he
would sell Suez Canal shares to
Britain (1875), 165
not a partner in London or Paris houses
(declared on objection to
Rothschilds' handling of Canal
shares deal because of his position as
MP), 197
inherits baronetcy from his uncle
Anthony (1876), 158
made baron (1886), 198
Rothschild, Nathan Meyer (1771–1836)
comes to England (1798), 104, 105
his secretive nature, and marvellous
memory, 105
early career of, related to T. F. Buxton,
106–8
relations of, with his brothers, 108–11
his wife, 118
stories of visits to: by Spohr, 110; by
Prince Puckler-Muskau, 111; by
Audubon, 111–12; by strange
bankers, 113; by (unconscious)
stockbroker, 114–15
finances war against Napoleon, 120–7,
215; transactions of, with Herries,
126, 225
had advance knowledge of result of
battle of Waterloo, 135; fiction of his
presence at Waterloo, 127–35, (his
alibi, 135), and of money made by
advance knowledge, 141–2; possible
means of conveyance of news to,
135–40, and his attempt to inform
Prime Minister, 140–1
and establishment of Alliance Insurance
Co., 118, 142–4
declines baronetcy, 143
in Bank of England crisis (1825), 147,
148, 149–51
suggestion by, for famine relief in
Ireland, 151–2
death of, in Frankfurt, 152–3; news of,
in England ('*il est mort*'), 136, 153
The Times obituary of, 115–20, 136, 153
will of, 153
Rothschild, N.M. and Sons
(Rothschilds)
and British Government loans, 155
and purchase of Suez Canal shares
('only one firm that could do it'),
171, 180; charge by, for transaction,

170, 171, 174–5, 177, 191; take no
advantage from advance knowledge
of transaction, 173, 176, 191; respect
of Khedive for, 173, 181; make
payments direct to Khedive's
creditors, 174, 180, 181; letters from
W. H. Smith to, respecting
repayment by Government, 182–3,
194, and replies, 183–4, 195–6;
repayments by Government, 194–5,
with hitch over calculation of
interest because 1876 was a leap year,
195
holdings of, in Egyptian shares, 197
Rothschild, Baron Nathaniel de, against
lending money to Egypt (1864), or to
de Lesseps, 173
Rothschild, Salomon (Salman), 108, 153
letter to NM from, 110–11
Rothschild family
Disraeli on unity of, 178
collecting by, 52
lepidopterology among, 13
Rothschild Prizes, Israel, speech at
presentation of (1981), 199–202
Roworth, John, Rothschild employee in
Paris (1815), 135
as courier with news of Waterloo?
139–40
Royal Commissions, address to British
Academy on (1978), 85–91
Royal Dutch shares: rise in value of, over
35 to 50 years, compared with that for
18th-century first editions and
manuscripts, 53–7
Royal Dutch-Shell Group, VR as
Research Director of, 69, 92
Russell, Bertrand
MS of broadcast on hydrogen bomb
by, 18–19
quoted, 19, 211, 213
Russell, Lord John, obtains admission of
Lionel de Rothschild to House of
Commons (1858), 155
Russell, Lord Odo, Ambassador in Berlin
(1875), 189

safe, in Department of Zoology,
Cambridge: VR suspected of stealing
drugs from, 15
Sa'īd, Muhammed, Khedive of Egypt,
grants concession for Suez Canal to de
Lesseps, 159, 162
Samaria Water Company, 200
Schacht, Dr, Hitler's Finance Minister,
IQ of, 63
Schlink, Mother Superior Basilea, quoted,
207
Schultz, Charlie, 69–70
scientists: eminence of, decreases with age,
66

screwdrivers: given to VR for dismantling
bombs, of sizes down to
marvellously small, 58
Shakespeare, *I Henry IV*, quoted, 210
Sheridan, Richard Brinsley, quoted, 120
Slater, Sir William, Secretary of
Agricultural Research Council, visits
Canada, 20
Smart, Christopher, first edition of *A Song
to David* by (1763), 56
Smith, Adam, quoted, 212–13
Smith, Sydney, quoted, 149
Smith, W. H., Secretary to Treasury
and transaction with Rothschilds
(1875), 170, 175, 177
to Rothschilds about repayment of loan,
182–3, 194; replies, 183–4, 195
Rothschilds to, acknowledging
repayment, 195–6
Société Générale, and Khedive's Suez
Canal shares, 166, 171, 185, 187, 219
Soviet press, 79
Spain
war between Britain and (from 1808),
120
Wellington cannot take troops of, into
France, until he can pay and feed
them, 122–3
NM refuses to deal in stocks of, 118
invades France (1823), 117
sperm cells, of fern
effect of carbon monoxide on, in green
and white light, 62
microscopic examination of, in known
gas mixture, 61
Spohr, Louis, composer, visits NM, 113
standard of living, examples of decline in
(1980), 64–5
Stanton, General Edward, Consul General
in Cairo (1875)
in negotiations for purchase of
Khedive's Suez Canal shares, 166,
167, 168, 185, 219, 220
signs transfer of shares, 165
Khedive's snares delivered to, 177, 179
on payments to be made by
Rothschilds, 180
Stapleton, A. G., editor of Greville's
journals, 149
Stein, Cyril, Cashcade lotteries of, 95
Stokes, Colonel John, sent to investigate
Suez Canal affairs, 168, 190
Suez Canal
history of previous canals, 158–9
building of, 163, and opening, 159–60
effect of, on distances from European to
Eastern ports, 158
traffic through, 75% British, 185, 190
International Commission to control,
proposed by Disraeli, 169, by Lord
Derby, 185, and by Stafford

Northcote, 186, opposed by W. H.
Smith, 188
nationalized (1956), 189
Suez Canal Company (Compagnie
Universelle du Canal Maritime de
Suez)
land and labour for, obtained by de
Lesseps, 162
shares in, 162; transfer of 44% of, from
Khedive to Britain (1875), 165;
dividends on transferred shares
mortgaged by Khedive until 1894,
172
value of shares in (1876–1935), 196, 198
sale of British shares in (1979), 198
surgical operation, preparation of patient
for (1980), 71–2
Swift, Jonathan
MS of *Directions to Servants* by (published
1745), 21
values of different copies of first edition
of *Gulliver's Travels* by (1726), 22
first serial printing of *Travels into
Several Remote Nations of the Earth* by
(1726), 56
first edition of *Miscellanies in Prose and
Verse*, by Pope and, 54, 56
MS of *Atlas* by, 56
MS of *To Charles Ford Esq. on his
birthday* by, 57
quoted, 214

Tawfiq, Khedive of Egypt (1879), 164
Tenterden, Lord, Under-Secretary,
Foreign Office, and purchase of Suez
Canal shares, 168, 180, 181
Think Tank (Central Policy Review Staff)
VR appointed head of (1974), takes 3
months' holiday, 69–70
VR asks Prime Minister and other
Ministers what they want from, 73–6
workings and interests of, 80–4
Thompson, W. H., Master of Trinity,
quoted, 207
Times, The
obituary of NM in, 115–20, 136, 153
on Alliance Insurance Co., 142–3
on Bank of England crisis, 165
on purchase of Suez Canal shares,
(1875), 192, (1905), 184
Trajan's Canal, Egypt, 158
Travers, Sir Benjamin, surgeon, called to
Frankfurt-in last illness of NM, 152
Treasury, The
NM to (1817), requesting
remuneration for services, 126–7
transaction with Rothschilds in records
of (1875), 176
Trend, Sir Burke (later Lord Trend),
Cabinet Secretary (1974), 75, 81, 82
Trevelyan, G. M., Master of Trinity, 21

Trinity College, Cambridge, gifts by VR
to library of collections of 18th-century
first editions and Swift MSS. 21
MS of Bertrand Russell's broadcast on
hydrogen bomb, 18–19

Vansittart, Nicholas, *see* Bexley, Lord
Victoria, Queen
Disraeli's letters to, on purchase of Suez
Canal shares, 167, 168, 170; 'you
have it, Madam', 171
on Lord Derby and Canal shares, 186
on purchase of Canal shares as 'a blow
to Bismarck', 189
Vienna, NM's brother Salomon in, 108
Vilmorin, Louise de, 16

Wade-Gery, Robert, in Think Tank, 81
Waterloo, battle of
how and when news of, reached
London, 105, 136–40
NM and, *see under* Rothschild, Nathan
Meyer
Waugh, Auberon, quoted, 213
Weinberg, Steven, quoted, 208–9
Welby, R. E. (later Lord Welby), of
Treasury (1875), 170
Wellington, Duke of
letters from, to Lord Bathurst, appealing
for money, 121–3
NM finances campaigns of, 120–7,
215
to Lord Bathurst, on money reaching
him, 123
in bank crisis (1825), 147, 148; on
NM's help, 149–50

Wells, Gabriel, American bookseller
sells VR copy of first edition of *Tom
Jones*, 22; refuses to buy it back on
discovery of faking of, 23
defendant in suit brought by VR, 26,
28, 32, 34–53 *passim*
correspondence with (Exhibit 2 in
suit), 33
Williams, Bernard, Provost of King's
College, IQ of, 63
Wilson, Charles Rivers, Finance Minister,
Egypt (1878), 164
Wilson, Harold, Prime Minister
and Think Tank, 76
minute from ('One that got away'), 80
wines, in Rothschild cellars, 113
Wolf, Lucien
on purchase of Suez Canal shares
(*The Times*, 1905), 159, 184
on Balla's *Romance of the Rothschilds*, 217
in *Essays in Jewish History* (1934), 139
Wolff, Sir H. Drummond, defends
Disraeli's purchase of Canal shares, 193
Woolf, Leonard, 203
Wordsworth, William
first edition of *Lyrical Ballads* by
Coleridge and (1798), 57
quoted, 206

yellow fever, in Portugal (1813), 123
Young, Owen D., American steel
magnate, buys Kern copy of first
edition of *Tom Jones*, 22, 30, 31, 40

Zuckerman, Lord, 75